Peter
Westenhanm

00/10/29

LEADERSHIP

LEADERSHIP

THE INNER SIDE OF GREATNESS

A PHILOSOPHY FOR LEADERS BY

PETER KOESTENBAUM

Jossey-Bass Publishers · San Francisco

Substantial discounts on bulk quantities of Jossey-Bass books are available to corporations, professional associations, and other organizations. For details and discount information, contact the special sales department at Jossey-Bass Inc., Publishers (415) 433-1740; Fax (800) 605-2665.

Jossey-Bass Web address: http://www.josseybass.com

Credits are on page 369.

JACKET DESIGN BY VARGAS/WILLIAMS/DESIGN

 Manufactured in the United States of America on Lyons Falls Turin Book. This paper is acid-free and 100 percent totally chlorine-free.

Library of Congress Cataloging-in-Publication Data

Koestenbaum, Peter. date.
　　Leadership : the inner side of greatness : a philosophy for leaders / Peter Koestenbaum. — 1st ed.
　　　　p.　cm. — (Jossey-Bass management series)
Includes bibliographical references and index.
ISBN 1-55542-218-7
1. Leadership.　I. Title.　II. Series.
HD57.7.K64　1991
303.3'4—dc20　　　　　　　　　　　　　　　　　　　　　　　90-50858

HB Printing　20 19 18 17 16 15 14 13 12 11

The Jossey-Bass
Management Series

Contents

Preface

The fundamental purpose of this book is to show that business can be an opportunity for both personal and organizational greatness—and that, in adopting this attitude, we not only ennoble human nature and strengthen our societies but also face squarely the critical success factor for meeting bottom-line business objectives in today's tough competitive environment.

To accomplish this goal, *Leadership: The Inner Side of Greatness* deals with the *personal* side of business leadership. This requires attention to depth, to feelings, and to inner struggles. A leader must wrestle with inward issues. He or she is expected to have great aspirations, confront great frustrations, achieve great self-control, suffer great betrayals, and manifest great compassion. Addressing the personal side of leadership also requires attention to vision and to scope, for the leader's mind must be all-encompassing. The executive is challenged always to keep his or her inner eye on the larger picture and to find ways of reacting quickly. This book asks how such a mind can be cultivated.

The personal side of leadership requires attention to such varied virtues as resourcefulness and trust, confidence and strength. It means learning the uses of power and developing a flexible imagination. The personal side of leadership challenges you to give meaning to your life through the quality of your work—how you manage your career or job, and how you invest your time and energy. The personal side of leadership also recognizes that deep thoughts and clever ideas are not enough. Executives must remind themselves that they are measured by cold effectiveness and hard results, for leadership success is tied to survival.

Leadership: The Inner Side of Greatness intends to support you in attaining a mindset capable of combining wisdom with profits, insight with survival, the soft with the hard. It intends to help you develop a leadership mind, which means that you will think and act the way a leader does. The humanities are an unused resource for touching the lost parts of the soul and thus can give rise to a strengthened leadership mind. This book challenges you to make the fundamental decision of refocusing your mind, thereby achieving a mental transformation — taking, as it were, an "oath of greatness." The leadership way of thinking and acting promoted here is in the spirit of a breakthrough — the conversion to a fresher way of being, and the resolve to renewed youthfulness and vigor.

Leadership is like health, happiness, love, or being strong. It is an intrinsic, not instrumental, value. You do not wonder how to make it work or how to apply it. You do not ask, "How do I apply health? How do I make happiness operational? What are the uses of love? How can I reap the practical benefits of being strong?" There is nothing more practical than a leadership mind. Human depth makes *business* sense. This book, its contents derived from everyday business struggles, is about personal maturity and its impact on the bottom line.

Leadership: The Inner Side of Greatness makes you a promise: to double your business leadership effectiveness on any measure you choose. Stretching your mind to reach, at all times and in all circumstances, the dimensions of what is called here the Leadership Diamond model will heighten your level of leadership awareness and show in everything you do.

Intended Audience

The audience that will find this book useful includes upper managers, middle managers, and students — the future leaders of the world. The Leadership Diamond material can easily be transferred to politics, the professions, the arts, journalism, religion, and the military: leadership is bigger than business.

It appears that the greater a person's managerial responsibilities, the greater also is that person's responsiveness to the
leadership challenge. As people get promoted to higher levels of
management, they also become more receptive to understanding the structure of leadership awareness. Recognizing the importance of leadership thinking and acting, and appreciating
the significance of leadership training, seem to be directly proportional to the amount of organizational responsibility with
which a manager is entrusted.

Leadership: The Inner Side of Greatness, therefore, addresses
upper managers—executives both burdened and privileged
with facing, in Shakespeare's words, "the storms of state." Their
inner struggles and proffered solutions are reported here. It is
also useful for middle and lower managers. This book addresses
and reports on their problems, with a degree of depth to which
managers seem unaccustomed. Frequent comments regarding
this material are "Why hasn't my boss been introduced to this?"
and "How can I make a thousand people aware of this?" For
ambitious young men and women who are interested in getting
ahead, the material in this book should probably be required
reading. The same, of course, applies to students. Having spent
most of my life in school and academic atmospheres, I am
sensitive to the needs of our students. Tomorrow they will be our
leaders. Studying the Leadership Diamond material early in
one's career and learning to apply it can make a marked difference in one's lifelong success.

The general principles of successful leadership, however,
apply to all people.

Overview of the Contents

Part One considers the need for greatness in business. *Greatness*
is a word with many meanings: excellence, standards, values,
ethics, achievement, worthiness, perfection, and so on. Greatness is one of civilization's noble ideals. Today there is a dual
need for greatness. On the organizational level, commitment to
greatness is necessary for business success. On the personal

level, commitment to greatness is required for personal health and longevity.

Part Two is the heart of this book, the detailed explication of the Leadership Diamond model. This model represents the structure of the leadership mind. It is what you must know and learn—indeed, what you must *be*—in order to become an effective leader. Here the details of your mental transformation are discussed, so that you will approach everything you do from now on with fresh effectiveness and richer results. The exposition of the Leadership Diamond model includes ancillary discussions—amplifications of the principal theme—on the nature of time, democracy, motivation, teamwork, salesmanship, and so forth. Part Two ends with practical steps to encourage the further development of your leadership mind.

Part Three implements the Leadership Diamond model. Using the model, this section analyzes a number of private and business leadership situations. Discussed here are sample Leadership Diamond diagnoses of marriage and money, human resources and the arts, cultures, the Third World, and other phenomena. You will also find in-depth diagnoses of individual executives. Part Three ends with a look at the Leadership Diamond as a guide for the next millennium.

The Resource at the end of the book includes material on the use of affirmations and on how to start a leadership day.

How to Use This Book

A good way to use this book is to start with a quick look at the core of the leadership material. Take a look at the Toolbox in Chapter Two, and then read Chapter Four, which is a good summary statement of the full theory. The pragmatic definition of greatness in Chapter Three will complete your introduction to this material. Chapter Ten gives examples of how Leadership Diamond theory works. The Resource at the end of the book helps you experience the practical use of this theoretical material.

Background of This Book

How did this book come about? It is the result of innumerable interviews, discussions, and dialogues with and observations of executives, managers, supervisors, and chief executive officers (CEOs) over a ten-year period. I have tried to learn from business leaders what their issues are, what kinds of attention they require, how the leaders struggle with them, and what solutions they come up with. This book is a record (as would be provided by a journalist) of learning experiences that have been systematized. But nothing really new is provided. You have here a teacher's manual — a way of presenting and remembering what everyone already knows about leadership but may have forgotten, may not have thought of, or may not have considered from this particular point of view. I have tried to deepen these dialogues with executives (many of them conducted in my Leadership Diamond seminars) through my own background in philosophy, which spilled over first into religion and theology and then into psychiatry and psychotherapy.

Presenting an approach to leadership enriched with philosophic depth can lead to difficulties in communication, sometimes bordering on culture shock. Some people respond to Leadership Diamond theory with enthusiasm and say, "We need more of this." Others seem to have trouble seeing its relevance. People occasionally respond with hostility. Successful executives often come equipped with what we might call engineering minds, finance minds, legal minds, scientific research minds — that is to say, essentially pragmatic and bottom-line minds. We have become accustomed to calling that *left-brain thinking*. Such explanations, however, are of limited value. We should all be open to exploring those regions of our minds that have been left dormant. (In my own case, I started my academic career with mathematics and theoretical physics and came only later to the psychological and business implications of philosophy explored in this book.)

Experience demonstrates repeatedly that — offered the opportunity — executives show a strong desire for depth: they want to explore the connections between daily routines and destiny questions, ordinary choices and creation myths, innovation and the mind of genius, making budget and striving for greatness.

Leadership: The Inner Side of Greatness meets a fundamental, largely unfilled need: exploration of depth in leadership. Effective leadership derives its credibility not from practices and techniques (important as they are) but from the person supporting them, the human being behind the leadership behaviors. This book addresses that issue squarely.

Acknowledgments

This book—and the work it represents—would not have been possible without the devoted help of many friends. Here are a few of them: David Belle-Isle, Gail Bidwell, Peter Block, Anders Byström, Jack Furrer, Kenn George, Dennis Green, Bill Hicks, Arne Johansson, J. C. Persson, Jean-Louis Servan-Schreiber, Al Solvay, Dan Werbin, and John Williamson (recently deceased). It is not fair that many more individuals deserving loyal thanks have been left out, but I trust they will understand and be forgiving.

Los Angeles, California   Peter Koestenbaum
March 1991

The Author

For the last ten years, Peter Koestenbaum has been a leadership consultant. His clients are both large and medium-size companies. He has consulted in Asia, Europe, North America, and Latin America.

For thirty-four years, Koestenbaum taught philosophy at San Jose State University and wrote books on the subject. Philosophy has been his lifelong passion. He sees the use of philosophy in leadership training as applied philosophy, a subject of increasing interest in the universities. The last third of Koestenbaum's teaching career was devoted to exploring the connections of philosophy (especially existentialism and phenomenology) with psychiatry and psychotherapy. His publications from 1971 to 1978 are all on the uses of philosophy in psychotherapy and include *The Vitality of Death, The New Image of the Person, Managing Anxiety, Existential Sexuality,* and *Is There an Answer to Death?*

Koestenbaum was born in Germany and grew up in Venezuela. He received his B.A. degree (1949) from Stanford University, his M.A. degree (1951) from Harvard University, and his Ph.D. degree (1958) from Boston University, all in philosophy. He has four adult children and is married to Patty Koestenbaum.

This book is dedicated to
I.S.K., E.N.K., W.E.K., and J.N.K.,
in testimony to the preciousness of life and love

LEADERSHIP

The Oath of Inner Greatness:
Nine Keys to Business Wisdom

One glance at today's news gives you an unmistakable message: worldwide, the need for leadership is unprecedented. Few appreciate how difficult it is to be an authentic leader. Just having money or authority does not make people into leaders. One feels gratitude toward real leaders, for they have the courage to serve others in circumstances that many individuals avoid or simply cannot handle.

It is difficult to run an organization well. It is difficult to be part of a management team. It is difficult to be accountable. Many executives work very hard and try to do their best. Frustrations are enormous and inevitable. Leaders can be targets of severe hostility—not that it is never deserved; sometimes it is. Nevertheless, the anger of others is difficult to bear.

Today's manager is expected to be a prophet, poet, philosopher, historian, genius, athlete—in short, a statesman. You need a simple "how to" answer to the toughest challenge you will ever face: what to do when you are required to be a leader.

What are today's key business issues? What must you really know to run a successful enterprise? What must you understand to be an effective leader? What kind of thinking will lead to promotions? How will you "grow the business"? How can you improve quality and productivity? What do you require to beat the competition? In short, what really matters?

Here are nine basic themes that can serve as answers.

1

None is new. Plato said that knowledge is recollection; the following is to remind you of what you already know.

What?

1. One job stands out above all: learning the meaning of *personal responsibility*, and knowing its rootedness in your *free will*. In some fundamental sense, it's all up to you. Freedom and responsibility — two faces of a single coin — are philosophical and theological, even political, concepts but not really scientific ones. And before you can use them, they must be clear to you. Civilization, let alone business, stands or falls on fully understanding and courageously implementing this one point. This insight, before you can fully utilize it and make it a tool, must be crystal clear to you.

Specifically, leading requires "ownership" of the meanings of personal responsibility and accountability. It means fully internalizing the human truth that, in your world, nothing happens unless you personally make it happen. You must understand that the consequences of your action and inaction are like your children — *you* create them, they are extensions of *you, you* are responsible for them, for you *are* they, but they live their own lives nevertheless. It is therefore a "fact" of the structure of human nature that you are responsible for your world. Dependency and paternalism are cruel illusions. The real world is made for the autonomous and self-reliant individual.

Leading also means achieving access to the will, the engine that propels you to action. Leading is to claim the power of your freedom, your essence as a self-starter. *Leading requires changing not only the way you think and the way you act but also the way you will.* Leading is taking charge of your will — the innermost core of your humanity.

The most important myth of our civilization, the Biblical story of creation, underscores this point: "In the beginning, God created the heavens and the earth." This is the ultimate symbol of initiative, of creativity, of being a self-starter, of freedom — in short, of free will. The very cosmos itself is supported by a metaphysical act of freedom. "God created man in his image, in his image created he him, male and female created he them." Not only is the Ground of Being a self-starter, *so are you!*

You are free. And we mean by this that you possess free will, not necessarily political freedom. Political freedom can be taken away from you, but your free will cannot. That freedom is a philosophic and theological "fact," not a scientific fact. But your freedom is constrained by two opposing facts. For one, you are not free to give up your freedom, that is, you are not free to "choose to choose." Only death can deprive you of that last sliver of free will. The second is that freedom is confronted with the fixed alternatives of the real world.

Happiness and success are directly proportional to how wide that spectrum of pure freedom is—between its two constraints of being born irrevocably free and living in a world governed by deterministic natural and social laws. The space of freedom you create for yourself between these two constraints is the source of your deepest fulfillment as a person and your most dramatic effectiveness as a leader.

2. Business is not about making money or even products, or offering services. Business, as commerce, is a vehicle to achieve *personal* and *organizational* greatness. It is for accomplishing something worthy and noble. Business is an institution that can enable you to make significant contributions to society. It is important that you connect your work with your personal depth. In fact, you must learn to value the pain of growing. And the significance of your job is not that it offers you security but that it demands from you personal growth.

But business is more than commerce. It is a conceptual framework and a way of thinking. It is the language of effectiveness, helping you to get things done.

The real world is governed by economic forces. Business, the heart and soul of the market economy, is therefore one of the strongest global forces. If today you want to participate in transforming the world we need tomorrow, then business is the right place for you. In business, money is critical, of course, but you will never get to where you want to go unless you remember one thing: for authentic leaders, profits and rewards are not the goals, but rather a way of keeping score.

3. Leadership has both a *strategic* and a *personal* side — one masculine, the other feminine; one left-brain, the other right-brain; one tough-minded, the other tender-minded. Strategic thinking deals with external alliances, product positioning, and organizational structure. Externally, the strategic side involves negotiating mergers and acquisitions, floating loans, and issuing shares. It concerns market penetration and corporate positioning, finance, engineering, law, research, and product definition. Internally, the strategic side of leadership involves product development, organizational structuring, reporting relationships, project management, self-managed work teams, assessment, compensation, benefits, and so forth. Strategies are the province of the natural, life, and behavioral sciences.

The personal side concerns motivation, character, maturity, will power, freedom, meaning, creativity, ethics and values, culture, responsibility and accountability, loyalty, commitment, self-sacrifice, love, courage, genius, and other qualities. These virtues are in the province of the humanities (such as philosophy, theology, literature, and the arts).

The strategic and the personal sides of leadership are sometimes called, respectively, *hard* and *soft*, but these are misnomers, for there is nothing harder than a resolute personal will — and nothing softer than a fresh commercial bakery product.

4. The sustained competitive advantage of any business is a *culture* that supports the company's short-term as well as long-term *business objectives*. The personal side must support the strategic side. Paradoxical as it may seem, the personal precedes the strategic; good strategy is created by a brilliant mind and implemented by a strong character, not the other way around. The relationship is transitive. It is a vector. So it is with high technology: computers do not make people, but people do make computers.

Too often, the fundamental relationship between the strategic and personal sides of leadership is not understood. Moreover, the personal side is all too commonly neglected — not taken seriously enough, not adequately cultivated, and not even managed professionally. The exquisite care and precision invested in research and finance are rarely replicated in the realms of managing feelings and coping with the will.

The strategic side may deal with leadership practices and behaviors, but the personal side deals with the free decisions that human beings make about values and how to treat one another and themselves. Leadership practices and behaviors may vary. Leadership personality types may differ, proliferating like the branches of a tree, but the freedom of the will is always one and the same, for it is the rooted trunk.

Project and matrix management, usual examples of internal strategy, should improve efficiency and quality but frequently fail to do so. The mistake lies in thinking that human beings improve if the system changes. This ignores the personal side, since *the deeper transformation required for productivity is an act of will: the free decision to be an adult and a mature human being* in the conflicting loyalties of the matrix organization. And that resoluteness comes from a different part of the soul—the heart, not the head; the personal side, not the strategic.

A manager may think that what is needed is more strategy when in fact the root problem is the manager's own depression, burnout, and lack of will—the unwillingness to generate internally the energy and enthusiasm required for remotivating the entire organization. What is needed are new health and fresh determination, not necessarily new data and new systems. This transformation occurs on the personal, not the strategic, side of leadership.

In sum, the personal side of leadership must always address the business objectives of your company. A business depends on its stock value to survive. It cannot be a charity, nor can we think of employees' welfare in isolation from business needs. At the same time, business is people. We often forget that, but even as we remember we still fail to manage people with authentic dignity.

The business objectives of a company are the four *p*'s: *profits, people* (or morale), *products* (or services), and *pride* (preeminence, prestige, or social significance). A company needs profits for survival. Making profits is the nature of business. A company must be an enriching place in which to work. Employees spend important years of their lives there, and working should produce fulfillment, not anxiety. A company's product or service, its raison d'être, must be of the highest quality, for quality is not only a business necessity but also a moral imperative. To give customers shoddy quality is to cheat them. Finally, a company has the additional ethical obligation to be a useful member of society, to contribute to a better world. If we integrate these four business objectives with the primacy of the personal side of leadership, we get the secret of gaining the competitive advantage: where people grow, profits grow.

5. Leadership requires teamwork. The leader has the special skill of combining aggressive personal ambition, independence of thought, and individual resourcefulness on the one hand with thinking always in terms of cooperation, communication, concern for others, doing things together, motivating people, interesting them in growth, and enlisting their help, on the other. This marriage of individualism with community is a consummate art form. It defines the mature leader.

How?

6. Leadership requires a change in how you act, preceded by a conversion-like *transformation* in how you think. Yesterday, confronting people was an overwhelming threat. Today, after transformation, you use confrontation continuously and forget what it was like to fear it. Yesterday, you were paralyzed under the weight of bureaucratic detail. Today, after transformation, you cannot even remember what it was like to worry. Yesterday, fixing your attention was impossible. Today, after transformation, nothing has the power to distract you. Yesterday, it embarrassed you to be different. Today, after transformation, being different makes you proud.

Leading requires a refocusing of the mind. Leadership is a unique and often new mode of perception. The proper word for it is *breakthrough*. Incremental improvements are indeed desirable. Leadership, however, like yoga, means taking charge of how the mind works—redirecting how you think and act. It is taking the oath of excellence.

The *Leadership Diamond model*, which this book explains, represents a mature analysis of the transformed leadership mind. It can help you achieve for yourself, and for your organization, precisely this new level of high effectiveness.

The Chinese sage Chuang Tzu said, in the fourth century B.C., "How shall I talk of the sea to the frog who has never left its pond?" Supporting you in reaching the goal of radically reforming how your mind works is the heart of the Leadership Diamond model.

7. To the leadership mind, greatness matters. Specifically, a leader is a person who is truly *effective* in achieving worthy results in any field, no matter what the obstacles and with unfailing regard for human beings. A leader is a person of unimpeachable *character*, an individual thoroughly to be trusted. Leaders are *open-minded* — good listeners, flexible, secure in the knowledge that they alone do not have all the answers.

There are four principal ways of expressing greatness in thought and action. They constitute the Leadership Diamond model, and the genuine leader is committed to greatness in *all* of them:

- *Vision:* a visionary leader always sees the larger perspective, for visioning means to think big and new.
- *Reality:* a realistic leader always responds to the facts, for realism means to have no illusions.
- *Ethics:* an ethical leader is always sensitive to people, for ethics means to be of service.
- *Courage:* a courageous leader always claims the power to initiate, act, and risk, for courage means to act with sustained initiative.

In learning to use the Leadership Diamond, one meets with resistances. They may be personal or internal psychodynamics (such as left-brain as opposed to right-brain thinking, paranoia, withdrawal, guilt, or envy). They may be external systems (company culture, ethnicity, national character, the work ethic). They may be economic constraints (colossal debts) or political realities (dictators). Finally, they may be philosophical or existential structures, obstacles in human nature that inhibit the ultimate creative act: the transformation of abstract thought into live action. A leader engages these resistances and perhaps overcomes them.

The Leadership Diamond model can help you honor your inner side of greatness. Through this model, you will end with an organization in which you yourself think and act in accordance with the desiderata of the Leadership Diamond model; in which you discuss with others their dimensions of leadership in terms of the Leadership Diamond model, and in which virtually every member of the total organization endeavors to think and act in conformance with this model, since everyone will have been invited to become a manager-educator, a leader-teacher, and an empowered learner. This ensures the genesis of greatness. To be a leader is first to be a leader in your own life. This is what separates the adults from the children.

8. This transformation, to be authentic, must occur in all five realms of life (referred to later as the five "Olympic rings of life"): work, family, self, social responsibility, and financial stability.

9. The "how" is always the most important question: you lead by empowering your people, by developing them, by educating them to be leaders. The leader is a teacher, and you lead not only by creating systems and assigning work but also by developing people. Effective *empowerment* is based on a simple formula, the product of *autonomy*, *direction*, and *support*: $E = A \times D \times S$.

Thus, leaders lead by teaching, that is, empowering, and what they teach is how to attain a different, uncommon, but highly specific form of intelligence: the Leadership Diamond method of thinking and acting.

In sum, leading is teaching leadership, which in turn depends on understanding the model.

And how does one teach this form of leadership? In the classroom, of course, with books, lectures, discussions, exercises, papers, and examinations. But you learn it best from experience, from practice—by doing it, for that is the greater knowledge. More important yet, before you teach leadership you must learn it yourself, making the *personal commitment*, as in an eternal oath, to think and act the way a leader does. In your whole life, you must model leadership.

But you also must expect leadership. You and your organization must feel the cognitive dissonance between your current reality and your leadership demands. If they are not congruent, the pain of the contrast mobilizes the necessary energy. Hold on to your oath of greatness, and nature will generate high-quality leadership performance for you and your organization.

Here, then, is your formula to lead the effective organization of tomorrow.

The Nobel Prize in Business

We need a Nobel Prize in business, awarded to organizations that demonstrate how business effectiveness (meaning survival, market share, profits, and stock value) results directly from ethical behavior. A society that is not built on ethics — on fairness, freedom, and mature hearts and minds — cannot survive for long.

This Nobel Prize would go beyond merely recognizing social conscience. It would go on to attest that profitability is an essential ingredient of social responsibility. Social responsibility without profit has failed the test of acceptability. The Nobel Prize in business would go to organizations that could prove that ethics make business sense, in all circumstances, for every business, for all cultures, and for all time.

I am not saying that we must be ethical because ethics lead to profits; quite the opposite. The Nobel Prize would go to enterprises that could prove that only if we observe ethics for their own sake, because of their intrinsic rightness, we will, as a side effect, show a profit. Profits must become merely a way to quantify the degree of ethics in a business. The ultimate economic and social responsibility of today's companies is to spell out in detail the meaning, for our time, of this crucial message. The proof must lie in practical success. This may not be the way we find the world, but it is how we must make it. We will build a world in which this is true. To the creators of that world, where ethics succeeds commercially and where we fail in its absence, would go the Nobel Prize in business.

As you and your organization internalize the Leadership Diamond, you can expect to double your leadership effectiveness on any measure you choose—and thus grow, from being good to becoming great. An understanding of the Leadership Diamond should also help alleviate the leadership burden for leaders and led alike. Intelligent "followership" may yet be the truest form of leadership.

PART ONE

The Search for Greatness

1

Confronting the Challenges

After one of my early philosophy lectures on the inner side of greatness, for upper-level executives at the Ford Motor Company in Dearborn, Michigan, a participant challenged me: "Doc, *I* make cars. What do *you* make?"

For a moment, he had me. But then it became clear that his was the wrong question. He does *not* make cars.

"Where is your wrench," I asked, "your screwdriver, your lathe? You do not make cars. You *communicate with people*— through your words and your behavior, clearly and obscurely, consciously and unconsciously, effectively and ineffectively."

The truth is, he is a *leader* among people, who themselves are leaders among their own people. Perhaps the people at the base of the pyramid are the ones who actually "make cars." But even at their level, almost everything occurs in the mode of human communication. They, too, are leaders—or they should be.

The fact is that the key issues confronting business today are leadership issues. The twin challenges that organizations must meet are to *develop leadership intelligence* and to *universalize that intelligence* throughout the organization.

The Fundamental Issue: Survival

Whenever I have the opportunity to meet business and political leaders at the annual gathering of the World Economic Forum, in Davos, Switzerland, I am reminded that one theme universal among participants—whether in business or government—is this: job one for business today is survival.

True, downsizing (although it can be slowed down by legislation, culture, and labor) is the inevitable outcome of technology. All human activities that are machine-replaceable will be replaced by machines. This process may be delayed, but it cannot be stopped. Nevertheless, it takes people to make the technology work in the service of an organization and its customers. The necessary consequence is that as the number of people goes down, the quality of the people who remain must go up.

Quality people are required for quality products and services. But, even further than that, quality people are needed for what is beyond quality—namely, *productivity*, or output per hour worked. It is easy to measure in manufacturing, but not in white-collar work (including the professions and management) or in human relationships, education, personal development, and the arts.

Newsweek, claiming that productivity is the only real solution to the United States' double-deficit crisis, reports that "in the 1950s and 1960s, the gross national product expanded at an average rate of about 4 percent. . . . Since 1965 productivity in the nonmanufacturing sector has risen only .7 percent annually" (Samuelson, 1988, p. 33).

In a *Business Week* cover story reporting on a nationwide survey of three thousand alumni from the twenty-three top U.S. graduate schools of business, a representative M.B.A. from Duke University writes, "My lasting regret is that I spent $40,000 to learn useless tools from academicians who never worked for a real business. I can crunch numbers to death, but I didn't learn anything about managing, motivating, and leading people" ("Where the Schools Aren't Doing the Homework," 1988, p. 84).

The same survey, speaking now of CEOs, reports that "of all the criticisms coming from the executive suites, perhaps the harshest concerns the short shrift that B-schools give to promoting effective leadership skills. 'The art and practice of managing people is a nonsubject,' complains Andrew S. Grove, chairman of Intel Corp" (p. 85).

Productivity is at the root of most of the concerns of those who are charged with ensuring an organization's survival. These concerns all involve issues of people—and leadership. The following paragraphs describe some of them.

Organizational Effectiveness. The perennial question is "How can we make the system that looks so good on paper actually work in the real world?" Members of the organization are not doing what they are paid to do (that is, they are not effective); consequently, teams get nowhere.

Morale. With good morale, everything is possible. With poor morale, nothing is. Organizations are people-driven. They exist for people, are designed by people, and work through people. Leave people out, and you drain the blood right out of the body.

Communication. Individuals and groups do not feel heard, understood, valued. In hospitals, to cite one common example, the usual complaint is that there is not enough dialogue among physicians, administrators, nurses, insurers, and patients. The criticism is that companies are cold and indifferent—as if they could in fact become parent substitutes. Nevertheless, it does seem strange that the warmth and personal loyalty that individual friendship offers is not possible when all these "warm and fuzzy" individuals get together to form one large, task-oriented organization.

Innovation. Capitalism is growth through innovation. To stay alive, let alone prosper, companies must innovate in products, in services, and in management. Each company has its unique cycle of innovation for survival; but innovate you must, in product as well as in process. To say "We've done it the same way for years" is a prognosis of an early death. Innovation also requires the unleashing of creativity and vision, as well as organizational support for the innovators.

Systems. The pervasive change in all areas of business today requires new systems. In the manufacturing industries, change leads to project management and continuous process improvement. It moves from "craft production" to "mass production" and then to "lean production" (MIT Staff, 1990). In the professions, it leads to radically new ways to deliver medical treatments—and to complicated and strained relationships between the private and public sectors. But these new, necessary, and highly complex systems cannot be implemented without breakthrough multidimensional new thinking about *people*, throughout the full culture of the organization. It requires new thinking about the personal side of leadership, about the transformed role that the human core plays in what John Naisbitt has called the reinvented organization.

Merger of Cultures. Restructuring often means that colliding cultures must now cooperate. The pain to organizations is great, and it is very difficult to allay anxieties and improve the morale of the reorganized company.

Consequences of Downsizing. Jobs are always in jeopardy when the terms *restructuring*, *efficiency*, and *cost management* are used. Middle management of a reorganized company is being destroyed, and the psychological contracts established long ago to help employees feel secure are now, by virtue of the new economic currents, being violated.

Future Thinking. Organizations must understand future markets and future products and have the good judgment and perseverance to produce long-term results in a short-term culture.

Quality Decisions at Lower Levels. To remain competitive, organizations today require speed. Hierarchy essentially means bureaucracy, where decisions are slow. In decisions, errors of either commission or omission are costly. Lower managers and people in the field are therefore called on to make more and more of the critical decisions. These demands necessitate that more and more employees become competent in leadership intelligence.

Retention of Good People. Good people are difficult to recruit, difficult to train and cultivate, and difficult to retain; yet strategies, products, services, financing, restructuring, and innovation are all accomplished by people who are mature human beings, motivated and loyal employees. Consequently, concern with establishing a culture that understands leadership thinking and behavior is paramount for organizational effectiveness.

Leadership: A Fresh Look

It is in the context of issues like these that we must view the complaint that leadership skills are notably absent from businesspeople's education and training. Further, a root problem of management is that technical achievement — research and development in products and services — is rewarded with promotion to management positions. But that is a lateral and not a vertical move, which means that managers are promoted out of their areas of competence. In this situation, the focus cannot be exclusively on systems and technology, nor even on quality products and processes. Developing quality in products and services means developing quality in people, and developing quality in people means developing leadership intelligence. It means identifying, recognizing, recruiting, retaining, cultivating, and rewarding the leadership mind. It means establishing a corporate environment where developing the leadership mind is modeled, expected, and facilitated. Here there can be no compromise.

It would be a mistake to understand this statement as implying a narrow concern with the technology of management or technical proficiency in "people skills," for to develop and motivate quality in people means to touch their depth, to sensitize their hearts, to unleash their creativity, and to challenge their character. It means to reach the human core. The leader's transformation must occur not at the level of skills but in the nature of the person.

To speak of the human core is to go beyond questions of technique, to fundamental questions — questions of philosophy—and here we come to one of the fundamental assumptions of this book: *what business needs today is a deeper—that is, philosophical—grasp of leadership issues.* Unleashing productivity of all sorts, not merely in technology and manufacturing, requires the full unleashing of all the leadership dimensions of the human soul. Lest this seem too far afield from the issues of survival and organizational effectiveness, consider the widespread problems of personal despair, job dissatisfaction, depression, lack of fulfillment, unhappiness, and burnout. Casualties abound, although the sufferers are not always clear that it is they who are the victims. The causes include career-family conflicts, lack of acknowledgment, incongruence between a company's values statement and corporate behavior, and so forth. The ultimate remedy for such profound ills is not in how management redesigns the workplace (although that helps) but in how each individual copes with life's boundary situations—death, destiny, anxiety, dependency, and guilt. That is what, in leadership, is meant by maturity and wisdom. The answers to questions of survival, then, are to be found in developing and universalizing leadership intelligence. Since the days of Socrates, this has been the task of education. Philosophy by itself does not solve problems but instead trains the minds of operations executives to solve the problems.

What differentiates philosophy in business and leadership from other management-development approaches is *depth*: philosophic profundity, wisdom; its commitment to greatness. For example, a high point of the inner-side-of-greatness seminars appears to be the "Oracle exercise" (discussed in my book *The Heart of Business*), in which participants anonymously raise their overwhelming leadership questions. These questions are then read aloud and discussed. The value of this exercise is both fascination and insight—fascination with the questions of others, and insight into one's own deeper self. Why the interest? Because every leader's ultimate question is philosophical. To face it becomes the noblest form of leadership, which is statesmanship. Consider the following two statements by participants in the seminars:

I was thrust into a leadership role at twelve years of age. I did not ask to be a leader, but circumstances dictated its occurrence. My mother, a paranoid schizophrenic, could not perform her normal duties, and my dad was a very weak man incapable of making decisions and leading. From cook to house-cleaning to caring for three younger siblings, I learned strengths of resolve, commitment, sensitivity, frustration, and how to cope. I married at eighteen, had five children by twenty-two, and worked my way through college, committing that I would sacrifice whatever necessary to become successful and be a leader.

As I approach fifty and look back upon those early days and twenty-five-plus years that have since passed, I can feel good about many things: a wonderful wife and five children, all basically responsible and good people; a position of substantial importance. But those successes do not come without a price. Many conflicting demands consume my most precious commodity: *time.*

My parents are still alive and, as would be expected, consume enormous amounts of time and, more importantly, emotional strength and resolve.

The children, for the most part out of the nest, require special attention to meet their needs.

The workplace continues to challenge with extensive work hours, overseas travel, and weekends away from home.

Health problems of some magnitude have come into our married life.

I have committed my life to being strong, being a leader, taking charge. Clearly, delegation and empowerment can help resolve time constraints at work.

Is it possible to successfully balance all the

conflicting demands that a leader encounters and *include time* for oneself—to fulfill one's own personal needs to grow in different directions?

I have watched for twenty years as various leaders have come and gone in our organization. Some things have changed as each has entered or vacated his or her chair. There has, however, been one enduring theme, and that has been the inability of their subordinates to feel free to be completely frank, open, and honest with them. You might surmise that this is due to fear, a desire to be nice, a wish not to be the bearer of bad tidings, and an intent not to jeopardize one's career.

Whatever, the result has been that the leaders have often not heard the truth—and the rest of the population has not been encouraged to offer it.

What is it that we can engender in our leaders to "demand" honesty and candor, and how do we do it?

The Inner-Side-of-Greatness Leadership Challenge

Today's leadership must convey a concept that is as simple as it is fundamental: *quality products and services must be supported by quality people.* Precisely the same meticulous effort and consummate professionalism that companies invest in creating quality products and services must be invested in developing quality people. Companies clearly understand technical solutions, but do they understand that technical solutions are accomplished by people who are human? Frequently, but how much do companies know about what it means to be human? How much professional attention to the purely human do they feel is useful for their own business purposes? How sophisticated, how open, are they in understanding the human? How much does business sabotage its own best interests?

Unless technology and philosophy march hand in hand toward the future, there simply will be no future, for current corporations—which within a generation will find a Third World woman as CEO of General Motors—are literally shooting themselves in the foot when they ignore depth in their leadership challenge.

This fundamental principle, the universalization of an inner-sense-of-greatness leadership challenge, is not adequately understood today. In business, we definitely know the meaning of quality products, but we are not yet nearly so committed to a commensurate in-depth understanding of the importance, even for pure bottom-line business purposes alone, of quality human beings. The management of *production* is quality in the objective and external world. The equivalent management of *people* means quality in the subjective and inner world. The same level of technological expertise used to ensure production quality is required for people quality. The weight of this critical point appears to be understood only by the most exceptional, forward-looking executives; yet where people grow, profits grow.

Shown this statement—that quality products and services must be supported by quality people—quite a few executives will say, "This is self-evident." Yet not much in the way of meaningful initiatives to implement this idea is ever taken. The future of industry demands employees and managers—white- and blue-collar workers alike—with highly developed character who understand loyalty, promote inventiveness, are at home with change, and are masters in the paradoxical craft of integrating results and heart, and do it for the sake of the growth of their own souls, for personal fulfillment, not because the business threatens them if they fail.

As a rule, the personal side of productivity is not seen as an issue. It is rarely developed systematically. It is always easier to do business as usual (react) than to take the initiative with truly future-oriented people programs (proact). The organization that first breaks through this inner-side-of-greatness barrier will clearly have the competitive advantage as company structures, employee populations, and economic environments change drastically in the next few years.

Breaking through this barrier means learning to combine results with heart. It also means developing an organizational culture of leadership. It means that developing quality people is at the top of the leader's agenda.

What do we look for in quality people? We look for *commitment*, which is ownership, loyalty, and the willing assumption of personal responsibility. We look for *communication*. We look for *creativity* and *initiative*. We look for *motivation* — that is, *love* and *validation*.

In general, what does one find upon entering an organization? The average organization is in some sort of *pain*. It varies from restlessness, uncertainty, and floating anxiety to severe despair. The pain, in its pure form, is not treatable. In some cases, an individual employee destroys the company; in others, a company destroys the individual. Fortunately, it is not difficult to find people who provide insightful diagnoses of organizations' ills. You need a good diagnosis to know what you are up against, what you have to conquer in order to win; now something can be done. What is less common, however, is to seize the *opportunities* in diagnoses. Business is the language of effectiveness, of getting things done. Thus, if the environment is polluted, there is a new business opportunity: cleanup. If mail service is unreliable, there are new business opportunities: worldwide courier delivery, E-mail, and facsimiles. If executive travel makes office work impossible, there emerge enormous new business possibilities for portable offices: cellular telephones, featherweight computers, tiny calculators and copiers, pocket dictating machines, and pint-size faxes. If an organization spends most of its time not on work but on complaining about its neurotic networks, there is the opportunity for releasing the leadership potential, the health, of its employee population. To make these ideas more concrete, let us consider a couple of examples.

Results Versus Heart. Leadership is the art of combining results and heart. Leadership means getting where you want to go. But leadership is equally concerned with matters of the heart. Human beings have feelings and a sense of worth and destiny. No one can live without self-respect. The balancing of these two needs of leadership is an enduring concern. It represents the conflict between the values of survival and love, between the need for harshness and compassion. It requires hard thoughts about soft subjects.

For example, consider what happens when a company's engineering and sales divisions have diverging interests. One of the world's most significant computer hardware manufacturing companies recently brought out, with much fanfare, a revolutionary new portable personal computer (PC) series. The company bet its future on the new product. It won rave reviews from PC magazine writers. "They've created a total design worthy of Leonardo da Vinci," gushed one. Meanwhile, a respected and influential international PC publication gave the new portable top-of-the-line PC model its coveted and unique Computer of the Decade award.

The computer company's top executives, however, were raving mad. The new PC portables had already, in their short lives, encountered several problems. The intended strength of the product was a demanding strategy, a strategy for which this company possessed the necessary engineering prowess: to produce an extraordinarily small, durable computer and to elevate its microchip power so high that it would not be obsolete for a minimum of five years. It was also to be one-half the weight of the lightest competitive model on the market. All this would be accomplished at a price one-third below the lowest-priced competitor. The engineers' promise to top management was that these sophisticated goals could be met, on time, and management trusted. The company invested heavily. This was to be the company's ultimate profit-making strategy.

The production models, to which the awards were testimony, were superb. But neither costs nor timing measured up to specifications, and with that failure went what top management felt was its fundamental competitive advantage. The engineers said that the definitive competitive advantage was the product's quality. The chief engineer said his team had achieved amazingly low weight, breakthrough computing power, small size, and unquestioned durability. Top management, however, supported by marketing and sales, argued that the competitive advantage lay 90 percent in timing, price, and profit margin.

The PC's brilliant design and its exceptionally high quality notwithstanding, overruns made it more difficult for the company to meet the intense shakeout competition of the portable PC market. The engineers said they had done their best and should have been acknowledged for it. Managers said they were lied to; they needed more reliable engineering support. Adding insult to injury, the top-of-the-line PC, the version named Computer of the Decade, was barely available to consumers at first because of manufacturing problems in producing a complicated key part.

These setbacks led to a very severe tongue-lashing of the company's product-development team by the company's tough top executive, together with all his senior officers. After this humiliating session, plans for an elaborate banquet to celebrate the Computer of the Decade award were summarily canceled. It was a difficult scene, humiliating and disturbing to everyone present. Eventually, the company was embarrassed by the publication, in a business paper with wide circulation, of this outrageous behavior.

The problems were eventually ironed out, and sales turned out to be excellent. The company enhanced its reputation and profits. Nevertheless, the chief engineer's career at the company to which he had devoted his loyalty and his life's profession had ended. Embittered, he resigned. The product's eventual success did not vindicate him for violating his promise to achieve precise results. This is not a question of right and wrong, but of results and heart. The chief engineer's story is repeated hundreds of times daily throughout business organizations in the Western world.

A lot of people in the company were upset by these events, which left ugly scars. Since much was at stake, commitment had been high. Some were angry because key business targets were not met. Others were deeply hurt because years of hard work, sacrifice, and devotion had been ignored. Both groups have a point, for the question is results versus heart. Results are important. Without them, no company can prosper, and workers have no jobs. But without heart, results simply do not appear. Feelings, loyalties, and the morale of the people are matters of the heart.

Figure 1.1. Results-Versus-Heart Matrix.

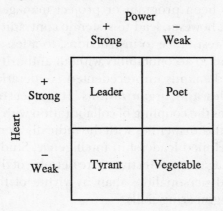

This example may be dated, but the emotions it arouses and the business wisdom it embodies are timeless. Which is more important, to punish people for not being fully committed to reaching bottom-line results, or to acknowledge them for their loyalty to excellence in product integrity? Leadership is the art of integrating results and heart. How would you have managed such a leadership challenge?

Twenty-five centuries ago, in one of the most celebrated passages from the history of ideas, Plato made reference to the conflict between results and heart—the need for dialogue, synthesis, and integration—in his *Republic*: "Unless either philosophers become kings in their countries or those who are now called kings and rulers come to be sufficiently inspired with a genuine desire for wisdom; unless, that is to say, political power and philosophy meet together, while the many natures who now go their several ways in the one or the other direction are forcibly debarred from doing so, there can be no rest from troubles . . . for states, nor yet, as I believe, for all mankind; nor can this commonwealth which we have imagined ever till then see the light of day and grow to its full stature." In short, leadership exists only when power and wisdom coincide in one person. The results-versus-heart theme lends itself to a matrix representation (see Figure 1.1).

Project Management. Western industry's answer to the Japanese challenge has been program or project management. Matrix organizations, however, lead to systemic contradictions: to role confusion, to resistance to instructions, to a lessened sense of ownership, and to accountability without authority. The matrix organization demands unprecedented cooperation within today's industries and organizations. If project management (which requires the coupling of collaboration with imagination) is to succeed, the answer lies with the radically alert mind — that is, with a developed leadership intelligence. Studies show that program managers are effective more because of their authentic and dedicated personalities than by virtue of their administrative and engineering skills.

Increasingly, corporations are no longer hierarchical, nor is there a sharp division of labor. The organization of tomorrow is a flat and flexible coalition (a team), not of workers but of leaders. It can have a coordinator or a facilitator who is also a spokesperson for the group (a transactional leader), or one who gives it direction and enthusiasm (a transformational leader). The status of positions and of jobs has also shifted. Motivations and rewards are different for leaders than they are for workers. Some CEOs are workers, and some laborers are leaders. In the well-led organization, all are mature leaders. The meaning of both work and the corporation must therefore be reinvented or at least redefined. In this new, "flat" organizational structure, "work" must give way to leadership. To work is to have one task, with instructions, a special turf, and a defined territory. It is to have a clear routine, an established process, a set way of doing things. Work now, however, is transformed, through a paradigm shift in the mind's thinking, into leadership. Leadership starts with ambiguity, begins with contradictions, goes through total lack of clarity, and must nevertheless end up with results.

Leaders are self-motivated, self-validating, and self-directed, whereas workers need spoonfeeding and parental substitutes. In authentic leadership, autonomy replaces dependency. In the new leadership, demands for individual maturity and responsibility to others are raised to new heights.

Today, the team no longer takes care of the individual. On

the contrary, the individual is responsible for the harmony and effectiveness of the team. It is the individual who must support the team. The team is no longer a refuge from accountability and personal responsibility, and yet it is now the team that is rewarded, not the individual.

The answer to accountability without authority is more authority. But more authority, in the real world, also means much more accountability, and this means that in the reinvented corporation your job, your career, and your future are literally on the line with every task you perform. But the rewards— emotional, developmental, and financial—must also be commensurate with the increased risk.

All these changes in project or program management are violations of an underlying "psychological contract." Workers (and students) entered the labor force with expectations, assumptions, and implicit promises that they now consider to have been fundamentally violated. The culture shock requires a basic redefinition of the meaning of work, of cooperation, and even of being human. Few measure up to the task. It is precisely this transformation that today's companies require in order to be competitive. To accomplish that is to lead.

The typical sequence of a project manager's career runs like this: At the outset, the employee is a first-rate line manager, with large responsibilities that are discharged successfully. Then the company needs this manager to carry out the project-management work, precisely because this manager is both good and experienced. This assignment is viewed as a sacrifice and accepted mostly for the sake of loyalty to the company. Later, the manager feels abandoned by the company, maybe even punished, for he or she has been held accountable for *team* results, requiring *top management's* support—neither of which was forthcoming. This problem is in the system more than it is the fault of particular individuals. The solution lies with top management, which has the ultimate responsibility to support its own objectives. It also rests with middle management, which must exhibit the breadth of the leadership mind and not be distracted by the damned-if-you-do-and-damned-if-you-don't vise.

In project management, characteristically, the system re-
inforces the opposite of what it says it wants. Officially, it endorses generalists—people who can take advantage of their
broad experience. In fact, however, it rewards specialists, people
who put their lifelong focus on only one type of organization.
For the nonleader, this paradox is insufferable. For the leader,
whose mind is spacious, there is ample room, since the leader's
mind thrives on paradox.

Project-management flow charts are complicated. To
make them work requires a high sense of personal responsibility
for teamwork success, a determined focus on the goals of the
company and not on one's personal needs. Systems are always
complicated, but attitudes are simple. Systems are lifeless machines, but attitudes are human intelligences. That is why everyone needs to pay attention to the inner side of greatness. For
program or project management to succeed, what is needed is
not only a better strategy and better organization but also, above
all else, managers and employees who are much more mature,
intellectually and emotionally.

As you will see when you study the dominant leadership
strategies, ethics means, among many things, also wisdom.
For example, the product-design and product-development division of the Volvo Car Corporation, in Gothenburg, Sweden,
was confronted with the typical problems of modern high-
technology organizations. Program management was introduced. One person became responsible for the total project, a
task that cuts across many specialties. This step diminished the
traditional significance of the specialties and, as usual, led to
many severely bruised egos. Pride, status, habit, territory—all
became high-tension factors. Matrix organizations make teamwork very difficult. Adding insult to injury, the critical workers
were highly trained scientists and technicians. They demanded,
understandably, a flat organization. They were independent
people and rather arrogant, often for good reason. Management
had the problem of supervising creative individuals. Furthermore, since all of them were highly trained engineers, the importance of human wisdom in the building of sophisticated auto-
mobiles was indeed a remote idea.

Exhibit 1.1. Volvo Car Corporation: Wisdom Statement, Powertrain.

1. I realize that I need to be a member of the Powertrain team, both professionally and personally.
2. To the best of my ability, I will
    a. support and encourage my colleagues,
    b. not hesitate to ask for help, and
    c. be open-minded about accepting advice.
3. I know that we together are committed to develop and optimize competitive Powertrain units according to the goals of the VCC, not discrete engines, transmissions, subsystems, or routines.
4. I am aware that, in order to benefit Powertrain, I will from time to time have to give up my own and my department's interests.
    These benefits to the whole must be developed and explained—to us and by us—with maximum clarity.
    The resulting sacrifices deserve understanding and human sensitivity.
5. I will use the Leadership Diamond as our philosophy for developing Powertrain leadership. I will assume the responsibility for taking the necessary follow-up steps.
6. I understand that *being a contributing member of a team requires more than technical competence: it demands, first and foremost, human wisdom.* I intend to act on this insight. And I know that therein lies the competitive advantage of the VCC.

The two divisions in question were engines and transmissions. The people in engines had the attitude that transmissions were mere afterthoughts to what really mattered—namely, the engine. The people in transmissions felt that they knew their business best and that the people in engines had no place telling them how to build transmissions. These arguments get emotional because they touch the core of the identity of long-term professionals in the engineering skills.

Management wanted to introduce the concept of one single "Powertrain." That meant a major reorganization of traditionally separate lines of authority and responsibility. It was therefore rather surprising when, after a stormy session on how to build teamwork among scientists in a hierarchical organization, the scientists ended up with a remarkable contract among themselves (see Exhibit 1.1). The contract was signed in a public ceremony, framed, and then widely and proudly displayed.

A Credo

What is the essential message of philosophy in business, of teaching leadership, and, in particular, of the Leadership Diamond model? First, organizations are successful to the degree that they think and therefore act with leadership greatness (that is, leadership intelligence). They must do so as organizations and as individuals. Leadership greatness applies not only to implementing strategy but also to the creation of strategy. Therefore, the challenge to leadership greatness is an organization's ultimate action tool. Second, the purpose of philosophy in business is to help individuals and organizations find and meet their objectives by challenging and supporting them in their leadership greatness. Third, leadership intelligence is a way of thinking, perceiving, and acting different from ordinary modes of consciousness. Fourth, leadership intelligence can be described, taught, and learned. It can be challenged, and it can be supported. Fifth, the how, the methodology, is to train executives to lead by teaching leadership. To teach is systematically to help others learn to think and act as leaders do and to integrate leadership intelligence into the achievement of organizational goals. Sixth, the what, the content, is the Leadership Diamond.

The principal critical success factor in meeting the competitive stresses of today's organizations is to meaningfully challenge organizations to greatness in leadership, and then to support them in that leadership greatness. This leads to a set of specific and ongoing behaviors, rooted in the depth of the human soul. These actions can ensure that, individually and collectively, organizations think and behave as leaders do. It is time now to look more closely at what it means to think and behave the way a leader does.

2

Developing the Mind

Leaders think differently. The leadership mind is radically different from the nonleadership mind or common sense. The leadership mind is different in kind and not just more of the same. The difference lies not in quantity but in quality, not only in incremental improvements but also in a paradigm shift.

I became interested in the leadership mind as a different mode of perception from the ordinary when, several years ago, I participated in a conference for CEOs. The speaker, a psychoanalyst, discussed how the Pentagon was searching for future generals; the armed forces wanted to learn how to identify young people who, in maturity, would make good generals. What kind of mind, if any, could be trusted with the vast destructive powers at the armed forces' command? One answer, it was suggested, rested on how these young people perceived time. Most executives experience time in terms of ten-year frames, which is a maximum. A general's mind, the speaker contended, must, at a minimum, perceive reality in terms of twenty-five-year frames, even if the individual in question is an old man. In other words, time, for generals, must be conceptualized in twenty-five-year chunks. A general's mind must have a sense of history. I have met generals at other times. Here are some of their observations.

One general said that you must care; it must hurt in the marrow of your bones if your men are not properly taken care of. Another said that you must learn to think the way the enemy does. Still another said (in response to the question "What is your leadership secret?") that, soldier or not, you must have a serious talk with yourself about death. You must make up your

31

mind that there are values more basic than life itself, that it is OK for you to die. In fact, our culture does not teach us how to die, and yet we must all go through it. A final general, a Marine, said that there are only two priorities for soldiering: get the task done, and take care of your men; nothing else is a matter of any serious consequence. Douglas MacArthur stated it quite simply in his admonition to West Point graduates: "Your job is to win your nation's wars."

You may not agree with the generals. These views may not apply to your leadership situation. Nevertheless, these answers illustrate the fundamental point: that the leadership mind thinks differently.

I began to think that leadership in general is not a talent, but rather a much more fundamental characterological and perceptual phenomenon, and I set out to describe it. As I met more and more leaders, I felt that I was able to establish some generalizations. I found that these observations fit nicely into basic philosophic categories of description and explanation of the world and of the person within it. As I fed back to leaders my philosophic observations, what I said appeared to deepen their perception of themselves and increase their effectiveness in motivating people.

Not that leadership is reserved for generals; the fact remains, however, that leaders think and act differently, and this difference can be described and taught. To draw the picture of the stretched mind of the leader is the goal of the Leadership Diamond model.

Leadership means control over the mind. The authentic leader does not accept the mind as he or she finds it but chooses either to construct or to "wake up to" the leadership mind: an inner space, unified, with room enough for conflict, paradox, and contradiction, committed to greatness in vision, realism, ethics, and courage.

How do you train yourself for a leadership mindset? For an analogy, we can look to athletics. Sports always provides us with good examples. Marilyn King, with a twenty-year athletic career that has included membership on two Olympic teams (as a pentathlete), writes, "I emphasize two things — internally moti-

Figure 2.1. The Leadership Diamond Model (1).

Lock This Image in Your Mind

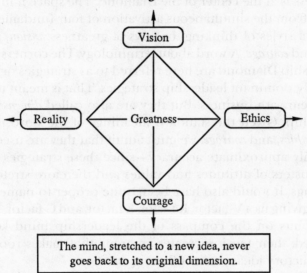

The mind, stretched to a new idea, never goes back to its original dimension.

vated commitment to a goal, and the ability to image that goal in detail. When a person says 'I *wish* I could become an Olympic athlete,' that is actually a negative image, emphasizing what I am not. It's a step forward to affirm that 'I *want*...,' and it is still more powerful to imagine that 'I *will* be an Olympian.' But the most effective process is to affirm and imagine, as though it were really happening, 'I *am* an Olympian.' This profoundly integrates both the qualities of commitment and imagination" (McNeil, 1987, p. 15). The image before you as a leader is not that of the Olympian in athletics but rather that of the Olympian in leadership: the Leadership Diamond model.

The Leadership Diamond Model

The Leadership Diamond model is the basic tool for training the leadership mind in leadership intelligence, for releasing leadership power and creativity in managers and employees. A preliminary view of the model is shown in Figure 2.1.

Leadership means, first of all, greatness. It is the effective mindset for high-quality leadership decisions. For this reason, greatness is at the center of the Diamond. The space it inhabits results from the simultaneous activation of four fundamentally different styles of thinking, or ways of greatness: *vision, reality, ethics,* and *courage.* A word about terminology. The corners of the Leadership Diamond are here referred to as strategies or, more precisely, dominant leadership strategies. That is meant to connect them with business. But they are also called *dimensions* of leadership. Given the standard meanings of the words *vision, reality, ethics,* and *courage,* we must admit that they are used here with only approximate accuracy—since these strategies designate clusters of attitudes and values and therefore stretch the meanings. It would also have been quite proper to name them *factors,* giving us a V-factor, R-factor, E-factor, and C-factor. These four points on the compass of the leadership mind keep it stretched; their tension creates an arena that makes room for contradictory ideas and conflicting emotions.

The greater the space thus created, the better the leadership. If even one strategy is dysfunctional, however, the amplitude of the space in the mind of the leader collapses totally. Hitler may have had vision, realism, and courage, but certainly no ethics. The result is no leadership mind at all. It is the collapsed leadership mind (see Figure 2.2). John Doe may have vision, a sense of reality, and high morals, but because he has no courage, no one has heard of him.

The concept of the collapsed leadership mind is important. Each strategy is like a resource. They are all needed, although not to the same degree in all circumstances. In an emergency, realism may be more important than vision; in great sorrow, ethics may be more important than vision; and so forth. As a rule, however, leadership means actualizing all four strategies. Problems, more often than not, are the result of neglecting one of the corners of the Diamond. In that case, solving the problem consists in building up the deficit or leverage corner. It will become immediately obvious that this is the way to work "smarter" rather than harder. If the business's bottom line is weak, more realism may not make as much of a difference as

Figure 2.2. The Collapsed Leadership Mind.

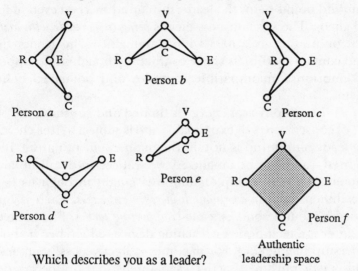

Person a

Person b

Person c

Person d

Person e

Person f

Authentic
leadership space

Which describes you as a leader?

more vision would. Problems with planning will not be resolved with more plans but with more courage.

Person *f* represents the ideal.

Person *b* has great visions, collects endless facts, and is a nice guy. But when it comes to courage — to initiative, to taking action — he is on vacation!

Person *c* should concern you. He is friendly enough and, unfortunately, also courageous. However, since he has no sense of reality, he is also dangerous. In fact, he is the one who spends all your money!

Person *a* is, practically speaking, an s.o.b. — great vision, relentlessly pragmatic — but people, what are they? People are numbers, objects, instruments, things — not souls and centers of feelings.

Person *e* is in too much trouble to benefit from further discussion.

Person *d* has the courage, the team spirit, and the facts for leadership but does not know where he or she is going! Complaints against this kind of a boss or organization are the most frequent.

The space created by the conflicting stresses of the four Diamond points helps the leadership mind succeed even in fog and chaos. The spaciousness means *being comfortable with ambiguity*, or finding greatness within ambiguity. The leadership mind contains within its space conflicting thoughts and opposing emotions, incompatible attitudes and polarized belief systems.

Whereas physical energy is limited and constant, the energy of consciousness is expandable and is subject to free choice. The leadership mind is not, in the main, a gift of nature. It is acquired—and can be taught. As we will see in detail in later chapters, the Leadership Diamond is taught through its four core dimensions or *dominant leadership strategies*. Each is buttressed by four resources, called *supporting tactics*. Each one of the latter is a technique or teaching device to help bring about leadership intelligence. For maximum effectiveness, each leadership tactic must be practiced separately. To train the mind is like training the body. It requires exercises, determination, self-discipline—and a coach. With a motivated student and a devoted and competent teacher, everything is possible. And you as leader must be both coach and teacher.

Individual leadership situations do no always fall clearly under one specific tactic. They can be composites of different supporting tactics. They are essentially loci where learning, teaching, and actions regarding leadership intelligence can be concentrated.

The Leadership Diamond thus organizes large amounts of material, suggestions, techniques, hints, tips, insights, theories, and processes conducive to a paradigm shift in leadership thinking. What differentiates the Leadership Diamond is its reliance on *philosophic depth*.

The four dominant strategies are, to repeat, greatness in vision or visioning (north), greatness in reality or realism (west), greatness in ethics (east), and greatness in courage (south) (see Figure 2.1). In order to be meaningful and make a difference, your understanding of these styles of thought and modes of greatness must be substantiated with *past examples* and must prescribe *future behaviors and actions* designed to have visible

influence. In this, we merely follow John Dewey's famous prescription of learning by doing.

The Contemporary Need for Greatness

Graham Allison, former dean of Harvard's John F. Kennedy
School of Government, "has been working to shift the emphasis
of the Kennedy School away from such courses as Strategies and
Tactics for Managing Information Systems and toward an emphasis on elective politics and more offerings such as Political
Leadership. . . . 'It's harder to teach vision and leadership and
the visceral elements of politics. But we have to do more of it, and
we will'" (Carlson, 1988, p. 19). In a similar leadership spirit,
former Massachusetts governor Michael S. Dukakis, in what the
International Herald Tribune (July 23, 1988) called "a moving
vision," said in his acceptance speech for the Democratic presi-
dential nomination, "Our greatest strength comes not from
what we possess, but from what we believe; not from what we
have, but from who we are."

Herbert Stein is a former chairman of the president's
Council of Economic Advisers and is currently an American
Enterprise Institute fellow. Comparing the economies of the
United States and Japan, Stein writes:

> The estimates used by the Central Intelligence
> Agency, the Organization for Economic Coopera-
> tion and Development and the United Nations
> show . . . for example, that Japanese per-capita GNP
> is about 75% of ours, and its total GNP is less than
> 40% of ours. . . .
>
> If the differential growth rates of the past six
> years continue, Japanese per-capita GNP will pass
> ours in 33 years and Japanese total GNP will pass
> ours in 189 years. . . .
>
> In a nutshell, being Number One is not nec-
> essary for leadership and is not sufficient for domi-
> nance. One could write off all this competitiveness
> and Number One talk as only talk. But it does have

some real significance. It is a distraction from our
real problem, which is not to get richer than someone else or to get richer faster than someone else
but to be as good as we can be, and better than we
have been, in the areas of our serious deficiencies,
such as homelessness, poverty, ignorance and
crime [Stein, 1990, p. A16].

Achieving greatness also means reassessing the work
ethic. Because of the stunning business successes of Japan and
other newly industrialized nations, the Western economies require, on an emergency basis, a return to what is usually known
as the work ethic. But the reality in the Western industrialized
nations is the exact opposite: alienation from work, increased
emphasis on leisure, widespread dependency on government
handouts, excessive self-indulgence, family pressures conflicting with career obligations, and, in general, decreasing commitment to hard work and diminished loyalty to organizations. The
International Herald Tribune reports, "*Prosperity has undermined
West Germans' 'zest for work,'* according to a study by the University
of Cologne. A survey of 1,000 people found that 43 percent felt
at their best when relaxing rather than working. This compared
with 27 percent in a 1962 study. The director of the survey,
Reinhard Haupt, concluded, 'The Germans have become lazier'"
(Jan. 13, 1989, p. 6). As a rule, when prosperity rises, the work
ethic disintegrates. Conversely, as unemployment rises, absen-
teeism diminishes. When prosperity is threatened, the work
ethic improves. Nevertheless, people spend at work the best
hours, days, and months—that is, the finest years—of their lives.
The results of work without meaning would be depressed, even
wasted, lives, and ineffective and therefore noncompetitive
organizations.

Today, we need greatness in reassessing the work ethic.
Every person faces the ethical responsibility to make a root
leadership decision: to create a life of meaning, a commitment
to worthiness, a devotion to excellence. If that person is a
manager, then only to the degree that he or she releases great-

ness, creativity, and excellence in his or her subordinates is that person doing the job for which a salary is collected.

The ethical leadership decision to bond meaning with work can go only two ways: resign from work and choose something else that leads to authentic meaning (even though also to poverty), or — and this is what really matters here — invest with profound and self-chosen meaning the work that you are now actually doing — or could be doing. That is the Zen of work, the decision to sanctify the work you do — not because the company requires it (which of course it does), but because the salvation of your soul demands that what you do every day be crafted like a poem, be composed like a work of art and illumined by a halo of profound significance. Herein resides the *renewal* of the work ethic. Kahlil Gibran ([1923] 1988, p. 30) said it well:

> Work is love made visible. And if you cannot work with love but only with distaste, it is better that you should leave your work and sit at the gate of the temple and take alms of those who work with joy.

In later chapters we use the model like a template or grid to analyze specific leadership situations.

Leadership as Teaching Leadership: TOTAL

Reactions to an inner-sense-of-greatness leadership challenge tend to be strong. Some individuals are enthusiastic and find it to be exactly what is needed. Others see it as irrelevant at best, interfering and offensive at worst. A common reaction is "This subject matter is deep. How do I use it? How do I make it operational? How do I make it work for one thousand people?"

The overall answer is that greatness in leadership consists in teaching leadership to others. It is to create a teaching chain. And teaching is Socratic. It involves empowerment. The fundamental leadership formula is to *t*each *o*thers the *t*eaching of *a*uthentic *l*eadership (TOTAL). It is to empower others and

The Toolbox

The Leadership Diamond Toolbox summarizes the Leadership Diamond theory — all you need to know about the leadership mind. Since to lead is to teach leadership, it is this model that you actually teach.

The Leadership Diamond Model
Practical Tools to Challenge the Inner Side of Greatness
(An International and Intercultural Value System)

Greatness: Definitions
What is greatness?

The problem: business is in a permanent "white water" condition (chaos — either randomness or laws, but with the added complexity of human freedom).

You must therefore *change* — work *smarter*, not only harder; *differently*, not only better; in *breakthrough* ways, not only incrementally.

The solution: develop a leadership mind. Leadership means greatness in all you do.

Pragmatic Greatness: Effectiveness

1. Be effective. Emphasize results, both through management by objectives and by process.
2. Understand that leadership is a mindset and a pattern of behaviors. It is to have made a habit of a new way of thinking and a new way of acting.
3. Be prepared to "wake up" and to change your perceptions and concepts radically (transformation, conversion), with respect to the human potential and to cultures (corporate, ethnic, national).
4. Lead by teaching leadership, by empowering (releasing people's volcanic energy and creativity) — by fostering autonomy, providing direction, and lending support. A teacher is an experienced and relentless learner.
5. Have faith that leadership can be learned and that it can be taught.
6. Know that the leadership mind can hold opposing ideas and contradictory feelings at one and the same time. It can achieve comfort with the tensions of ambiguity, polarity, and uncertainty. The leadership strategies are instruments of an orchestra, playing different melodies to create one symphony.
7. Be a leader in all five "Olympic rings" of life: work, family, self, social responsibility, and financial stability.
8. Inform your products and services with a leadership-teaching component. You do not sell a product or service; you help customers buy leadership in their affairs.
9. Use both reason or *models* (living from the "outside in") and instincts or *intuition* (living from the "inside out").

The Toolbox, Cont'd.

10.   Expect leadership to lead you and your organization to a higher state of health (associated with psychoneuroimmunology in medicine and with salvation in theology).

Philosophic Greatness: Character

1.   Honor life by striving for depth and for perfection (self-transcendence) and by devoting yourself to what is worthy and noble. Have standards, for their own sake.
2.   Stand up to death and evil.
3.   Be humble. Be open-minded. Listen. Understand the magnitude of self-deception, and identify your resistances to authenticity.
4.   Appreciate the mystery and miracle of being.

Greatness: Strategies
How do you achieve greatness?
(One single harmonious image, nevertheless rich
with the stress of internal contradictions)

Strategy: **Vision**

Formula statement: "A visionary leader always sees the larger perspective, for visioning means to think big and new."
Supporting tactics (tactical rings):

1.   Professional level: abstract reasoning and analysis
2.   Social level: systemic and strategic thinking*
3.   Psychological level: creativity and the unconscious
4.   Philosophical level: expanding and exploring inner or subjective space-time; awareness of your possibilities

Strategy: **Reality**

Formula statement: "A realistic leader always responds to the facts, for realism means to have no illusions."
Supporting tactics (tactical rings):

1.   Professional level: meticulous attention to practical details; attending to the precise needs of your immediate and end customers (use high technology)
2.   Social level: extensive information and objectivity
3.   Psychological level: survival (take care of yourself); relentless results orientation and market orientation*
4.   Philosophical level: direct contact and embodiment—with yourself, with other selves, and with how others perceive you (bonding and definitions of mental health)

* Critical success factors

The Toolbox, Cont'd.

Strategy: **Ethics**

Formula statement: "An ethical leader is always sensitive to people, for ethics means to be of service."
Supporting tactics (tactical rings):

1. Professional level: teamwork, loyalty to task forces*
2. Social level: meaning
3. Psychological level: communication, caring, love; commitment, loyalty
4. Philosophical level: integrity, morality, principle

Strategy: **Courage**

Formula statement: "A courageous leader always claims the power to initiate, act, and risk, for courage means to act with sustained initiative."
Supporting tactics (tactical rings):

1. Professional level: aggressive education and management of markets, product advocacy (stand for something)
2. Social level: aloneness, autonomy, and independence of thought (stand up to the world)
3. Psychological level: anxiety (face it, stay with it, explore it)
4. Philosophical level: free will and responsibility, energy and power, centeredness (confidence, hope)*

Expressed simply, the Leadership Diamond says this: *Greatness* means that you have standards. *Vision* gives you the larger view. *Reality* means facing the marketplace, the pragmatic facts. *Ethics* means people—that is, valuing feelings. *Courage* is the power and the freedom of the will.
The Toolbox is a map showing the resources of the leadership mind. Which tools are you using, and which are you not using? How do you think you can best grow as a leader?
Effectiveness becomes your personal choice.

* Critical success factors

create an empowerment chain. In countries where illiteracy is high, the price for learning how to read is teaching the same to others. So it is with the empowerment chain. And who is to do the teaching? The true teachers must be those persons who are in charge of the organization. The bosses, ideally, should also be the teachers.

Teaching is difficult. It can be done best by persons in

authority, and it is based mostly on the respect that subordinates have for the honesty and competence of their superiors. You do not sell; you help customers buy. In parallel fashion, you do not teach; you help people learn. And learning must be relevant. It must be quickly integrated, with visible results functioning as rewards in the organization's number one objectives and the individual's personal fulfillment needs.

The principal and most effective implementation tool is teaching others how to teach greatness in leadership. How do you teach leadership greatness? The focus is on others, not on you. You challenge people in the organization to leadership greatness—to think and act the way leaders do. You help others learn how to challenge. You release their leadership power and creativity. In other words, you empower people. You reveal their own possibilities to people. You model what it is to think and act as a leader does. You push the greatness-in-leadership challenge down throughout the entire organization. You create a critical mass of leaders, of culture bearers. You evolve an organization where people can legitimately make a commitment, where it makes sense to be loyal. In sum, you must teach people that *they* manage by teaching leadership. As a manager-educator, you achieve your organizational objectives by developing your people into leaders through releasing their inner side of greatness.

The TOTAL formula has important advantages. It is simple. It is practical and easy. It can be learned. It is not arrogant, for it does not presume to teach leadership (as if one knew how), but rather to teach how to teach, which is always easier. George Bernard Shaw said, in *Man and Superman*, "Those who can, do, while those who cannot, teach." But in leadership, doing and teaching are the same. Above all, TOTAL works.

A leader's responsibility is thus to *work* and to *teach*. Working means setting up systems and supervising. Teaching is mentoring and modeling how to lead people, which essentially means developing them. As you rise in levels of management, so will you need to increase teaching over working.

Teaching is transmitting information, through both mind and body. Information has been defined (by Claude Shannon) as "a difference that makes a difference." The information in the

Leadership Diamond model, its implicit philosophic depth, is
"different." If properly applied, it can make a significant difference in the productivity of your own life and that of your
organization.

We are now ready to embark on a more detailed analysis
of inner greatness.

PART TWO

What Is Inner Greatness?

3

Foundations of Leadership

"We are such stuff as dreams are made on, and our little life is rounded with a sleep," Shakespeare tells us in *The Tempest* (act 4, scene 1). So is the Leadership Diamond model surrounded with a context, with an environment, with a foundation, that must be understood before the model itself becomes fully clear.

The Leadership Diamond is a conceptual model to teach leadership intelligence. It consists of the *model* proper — greatness and its four strategies — and of the contextual *foundations* for that model. We get to the foundations first.

In brief, the heart of the model consists of the four dimensions or strategies of greatness, the so-called dominant leadership strategies, together with their supporting (that is, explanatory and amplifying) resources or tactics. (These will be explained in the following chapters.) Authentic leaders have branded these concepts on the very marrow of their bones. That is the message.

But before we are ready to embark on this analysis, certain miscellaneous preliminaries must be discussed. They are the ground, the basis, the assumptions, necessary to clarify the Leadership Diamond model. They are also the preparatory notions, the context, the peripheral ideas. These must be dealt with before the mind can be uncluttered enough to address the kernel of the Diamond itself.

Among these foundational matters is the concept of the breakthrough, for here we are not talking of merely getting better. We are concerned with new ways of leading, new perceptions, new conceptualizations. The metaphors of transforma-

47

tion are conversion, falling in love, revolution—in short, paradigm shifts.

The foundations also include the allied notions of polarity, paradox, contradiction, uncertainty, and ambiguity. The truth is not always simple or clear, nor do we seem to be able to change that. Even notions of logical truth, axiomatic when we grew up, occasionally need to be abandoned. And that is difficult and even dangerous, for your intellect and for your emotions. To the practical business executive, these points may seem excessive; nevertheless, that is part of today's groundbreaking leadership message.

The Pragmatic Definition of Greatness

Much of the material that is here called *foundational* is encapsulated in the pragmatic definition of greatness, which is the first part of the Toolbox (see Chapter Two). The Toolbox is the summary of Leadership Diamond theory, used to help executives think and act as authentic leaders do. It may be one man's opinion, but it is far from arbitrary. The Toolbox summarizes the learning, over a lifetime, from dialogues with successful leaders, fitted into the context of philosophy. The value of the Toolbox lies in its succinctness. It is easy to remember and therefore simple to apply daily. Its very brevity, however, demands that it also be explained.

The Leadership Diamond Theory is meant to be international and therefore intercultural. Whereas the West may appreciate the stress of contradiction among conflicting views, the East may need to see a higher harmony instead. We must be sensitive in both directions.

The outline of the Toolbox centers on greatness. There is a *what* and a *how*. What is greatness? What is its definition? How are we to achieve it? What are the techniques and strategies?

The Toolbox uses such words as *strategies* and *tactics*. There is some question about the wisdom of using these terms. The rationale is to integrate philosophy into business, and in this context, terms like *strategies* and *tactics* are easily understood.

That is why they are retained here. Strategies are also "dimensions," and tactics are "resources."

There are also terminological difficulties with such words as *greatness, ethics, autonomy, inner space, anxiety, contact,* and others. That is the risk one runs when endeavoring to be pithy. Since it is the concepts that matter, not the language, the hope is that words will not stand in the way of ideas. Therefore, it should be helpful to present, in annotated form, some major points of the Toolbox.

The problem: business is in a permanent "white water" condition (chaos—either randomness or laws, but with the added complexity of human freedom).

The fundamental business problem is stated in terms of chaos: a world difficult to understand and impossible to predict. Chaos not only means randomness but it is also compounded by human free will. Even if we have a theory of randomness, the free choices of men and women can always invalidate our most sophisticated predictions and probabilities.

You must therefore change—work smarter, not only harder; differently, not only better; in breakthrough ways, not only incrementally.

The solution: Develop a leadership mind. Leadership means greatness in all you do.

What paradigm shift will give you the competitive advantage? To work "smarter" means to make the commitment to the leadership mind. It is as if you were to take an oath, the oath of leadership, that henceforth your mind shall always function in accordance with the criteria of the Leadership Diamond.

There is a pragmatic and a philosophic definition of greatness. The pragmatic consists of ten propositions that seem to work in practice. If you think that way, the promise here is that your leadership capacity will at least double, on any terms you choose for measurement. The key word here is *effectiveness.* The deeper, philosophic definition of greatness centers on character—that is, human authenticity and depth, the fully developed mind.

1. Be effective. Emphasize results, both through management by objectives and by process.

This is the overall meaning of leadership. If there is one word, it is *effectiveness* — results. Rather than choose one style of management over another, the suggestion here is to utilize both. Whether you plan exactly how to achieve a precise goal or concern yourself with ongoing improvements may matter little. Each approach has its merits and is radical in its own way.

2. Understand that leadership is a mindset and a pattern of behaviors. It is to have made a habit of a new way of thinking and a new way of acting.

Leadership is a way of thinking and a way of acting, and it is new. It is an attitude, a mindset. The Leadership Diamond suggests not so much specific leadership practices as a definite direction to the mind. It is like health. Medical practice does not tell you what to do with a healthy life; it promotes health, period. But that is enough. So it is with a philosophy of leadership. You will be a leader in all you do. Specifically what you do is less relevant, for you will figure that out yourself. But you will do it better.

3. Be prepared to "wake up" and to change your perceptions and concepts radically (transformation, conversion), with respect to the human potential and to cultures (corporate, ethnic, national).

Leadership is a conversion experience. It is a new alertness. It is a "snap" in the mind to a fresh reality. This is the breakthrough theme. Its models are religion, art, politics, and love. The focus is on breaking through to new worlds, on thinking differently, in dramatic ways.

4. Lead by teaching leadership, by empowering (releasing people's volcanic energy and creativity) — by fostering autonomy, providing direction, and lending support. A teacher is an experienced and relentless learner.

5. Have faith that leadership can be learned and that it can be taught.

Too many people say that leadership cannot be taught. That may be true, but it is irrelevant. It may be better to agree that leadership cannot be taught — but insist that it can be learned!

You do not give up on yourself or on the subordinates you need. There will always be people not interested in leadership, but they will be replaced with machines. Many modern businesses cannot afford to hire managers not interested in developing a leadership mind. There is no room in modern organizations for people not prepared to make the decision to think and act as leaders do. More and more CEOs are saying just that and letting their organizations know that they mean it.

The helpful technique is to know that you lead by empowering people, and empowerment is a form of teaching—in fact, it is the best way. It started with Socrates, who helped the truth be born from the minds of his students. They were pregnant with the truth, and he was the midwife.

To *empower* (E) means to release the volcanic energy and creativity in employees. Specifically, it means to challenge them to *autonomy* (A)—to taking full responsibility. Expect them to be adults. Challenge them to understand the meaning of human freedom, the importance of initiative, and the "meaty" realism that arises from their knowing that nothing happens unless they make it happen. It is to give them *direction* (D)—that is, goals. And then it means to *support* (S) them, to validate who they are. Give them attention and care. Know what they are doing, and let them know that their efforts are important to you. The leadership teaching or empowerment formula is therefore

$$E = A \times D \times S$$

We multiply the leadership virtues with each other to show that a zero in one gives you a *product* of zero. All three—autonomy, direction, and support—are essential for empowerment to take place. To forget one is to invalidate the entire process. The precise structure of the empowered mind is described by the Leadership Diamond. It can be enhanced, even acquired, as the case may be. That is good news, and very practical.

6. Know that the leadership mind can hold opposing ideas and contradictory feelings at one and the same time. It can achieve comfort with the tensions of ambiguity, polarity, and uncertainty. The leadership strategies are instruments of an orchestra, playing different melodies to create one symphony.

For many executives, this point is central. This is the

principle of polarity. It comes as a relief to know that confusion is in the nature of things. Lifelong efforts to remove frustrating contradictions suddenly cease to be a worry. A weight is lifted. Managing is no longer arduous but actually becomes easy and is even fun.

7. *Be a leader in all five "Olympic rings" of life: work, family, self, social responsibility, and financial stability.*

This seems to be exceptionally important. Leadership is holistic. It is, in your life, a global need. Many people have an *Aha!* experience when challenged with this point. Why financial stability? Is that not out of character? Perhaps. But we are dealing here with business, and business is all about money. And for most people in this world, financial stability is the number one concern. If that part of their lives works, then so can everything else. But if that fails, then the rest is of little use. Most students go through school without learning financial literacy. They become literate in their own language, maybe also in another. They are likely to learn computer literacy, essential for today's business and science. But few if any learn financial literacy, the meaning of money and the instruments available for its management, and the price they pay for this ignorance is a lifetime of anxiety that could have been avoided.

8. *Inform your products and services with a leadership-teaching component. You do not sell a product or service; you help customers buy leadership in their affairs.*

Selling anything means helping customers buy leadership in support of their own values. That is the first principle of business. Teaching leadership, empowering, is not only a principle of management. It goes deeper. It is a principle of marketing. It is the heart of the business. If you teach leadership to your customers, then you will prosper, for you will have created a satisfied customer. If you merely sell something to your customers, they will feel exploited and will become hostile.

9. *Use both reasons or* models *(living from the "outside in") and* instincts or intuition *(living from the "inside out").*

Let us be fair. To create a model of success and then control your mind—train it—is surely effective. It is the yoga of business. The mind's discipline is the body's success. This approach is used in the performing arts, in athletic competition, in public speaking, and in salesmanship. But if we are to be truly multicultural, we must acknowledge that there is another way. "Going with the flow" may be too simplistic, but it means not imposing anything on your mind—not disciplining it (that would be too Victorian), but presuming that it has its own secret inner voice, silenced for too long. Once the chatter ceases and the interference stops, the mind may talk back with its original pristine needs. These may be quite different from what business has learned to prize. Intuition means that you listen to this inner voice.

   10. Expect leadership to lead you and your organization to a higher state of health (associated with psychoneuroimmunology in medicine and with salvation in theology).

   This point is controversial. Your state of mind influences your body's health. Few doubt it, but even fewer can show any exact correlation. The hypothesis offered here is that the Leadership Diamond, based as it is on the tradition of the humanities, delineates the way you must think if your mind is to influence your physical health. The subjective power of a healthy mind is translated into the objective power of your immune system. But this connection presumes an in-depth understanding of the Leadership Diamond theory of personality, and that is not easy to accomplish. This is an important hypothesis, and it must not be presented irresponsibly. This last point is stated here with as much caution as fervor.

Philosophic Definition of Greatness

At the center of the leadership mind is *greatness*, statesmanship. Greatness may not be a sufficient condition for effective leadership, but it surely is a necessary one. In effect, you lead people by modeling greatness. Before we delve further into the Leadership Diamond model, it is important to pause and reflect on what *philosophic* greatness is.

   Philosophic greatness is the commitment to relinquish mediocrity forever. Greatness is not sought because it furthers other values. It is not an instrumental good. Greatness is an intrinsic value, an inherent good, a pure virtue. It is good in and of itself. It is to be sought for its own sake. It is chosen as a way of life because it is right, because it ennobles the human spirit, because it honors the fact that we are alive, and because it is our meaning for being on this earth. The fact that the commitment to greatness is good for politics and business, medicine and literature, and everything else it touches is almost incidental.

How do you motivate people? By giving up techniques, and by risking—you, yourself—a personal, lifelong commitment to greatness. Can this pursuit of greatness be taught? It can be *challenged* into existence.

Greatness is the struggle against mediocrity. It is the upgrading from good to excellent. At a profound level, greatness is the struggle against nihilism (what philosophers call the descent into "nothingness"). Nihilism involves accepting an inner emptiness as tolerable, even natural. This inner emptiness is then covered over with sensory hyperexcitation, with the supersaturation of the organs of perception—thrills for the sake of thrills, thrills to extinguish any remnants of spiritual depth, thrills to hide the horror of the hollow darkness. It is because of nihilism that there is evil in the world, the cruel indifference to human suffering. Ultimately, nihilism is the unwillingness to confront the painful mystery of death.

In this way, the general's remark that the leadership mind must confront death is not so remote from leadership in business as it might seem. Death makes one honest. It gives one the sense of time. Death is the source of anxiety and the motivation for seeking depth. John Donne refers to "the Democracy of Death: It comes equally to us all, and makes us all equal when it comes." Shakespeare puts it more pathetically in *Henry VIII* (act 2, scene 3):

> An old man, broken with the storms of state,
> Is come to lay his weary bones among ye;
> Give him a little earth for charity.

To be great is to stand up to nihilism. It is to live out the belief that perfection matters, that excellence—as in sports and the arts — is worth pursuing for its own sake. Leadership means that transcending the self is an inherent value.

Greatness means more than facing death and confronting evil. It also means appreciating the mystery of being, the miracle that things are, the inexplicable truth that there is a world, and the wonder that there exist consciousness and perception — for they are the only miracles we shall ever need. To acknowledge them is to step into a separate reality. Greatness is having a sense of the esthetic and a feeling for the religious. Greatness is appreciating the value of art and the religious sensibilities of mankind.

Attempts to live out greatness inevitably summon resistances. The resistances to greatness (discussed in more detail later on) fall into three categories. First are the *psychodynamic* resistances, the unfinished childhood business, the neurotic behaviors. These are modes of coping appropriate to the different reality of an earlier age. They are atavisms, residues from long ago, encrusted in the soul's perceptions and in the body's behavior patterns. They must be shed, and not — what is usual — exaggerated. A good example is dependency, the unwillingness to take personal responsibility. Children are taken care of; adults take care of themselves. That is a key principle for successful competition in the marketplace.

Second are the *systemic* resistances. Systems essentially do not change. Their inertia stops movement. People, regrettably, act out the system's resistance to change. They are marionettes. They rationalize. From a helicopter point of view, their behavior is transparent, but from the myopia of their own inwardness, the irony is virtually imperceptible. People often espouse political positions that they believe are the result of independent thought, when in truth they are but the automatic parrotings of what society has taught them.

Third are the *existential* resistances we find to the radical transformation of world views that is required when we move from reflection to action. Since many people do not believe that leadership requires conversion, they hope that theory will automatically be translated into action. They ignore the anxiety of shifting world designs, the fear induced by change. Change leads to uncertainty, to insecurity. It leads to anxiety and then to isolation. We feel out of touch, and it hurts. That is why our century has been called the Age of Alienation.

The concept of self-deception is an entry into the realm of the unconscious. The unconscious is *prima facie* a contradictory concept, but it is essential to carry out a successful transformation. In-depth change is not possible without touching and exploring unconscious material. Resistances to authentic personal and organizational existence express themselves differently in each one of the dynamic corners of the Leadership Diamond. Resistance to vision is *blindness*. Resistance to reality is *denial*. Resistance to ethics is *indifference*. Resistance to courage is *fear*.

To repeat, greatness means to

- Honor life by striving for depth and for perfection (self-transcendence) and by devoting yourself to what is worthy and noble. Have standards, for their own sake.
- Stand up to death and evil.
- Be humble. Be open-minded. Understand the magnitude of self-deception, and identify your resistances to authenticity.
- Appreciate the mystery and miracle of being. (See the Toolbox.)

To these four characteristics of greatness correspond the four levels of depth that we will explore in the tactics of all the dominant leadership strategies. To honor life by achieving something noble with it is an everyday task. It is the background for all of life. That is the *professional* level. To stand up to death and evil represents one's contribution to the social order. This defining trait of greatness therefore describes the *social* level. To identify resistances is to touch the unconscious — to reach out to intuitions, to the roots of feelings. This refers to the *psychological* level. Finally, the miracle of being stands for the *philosophic* level par excellence. Individuals who cannot relate to these themes of greatness are not the kinds of people we want for our leaders.

Greatness and Ultimate Questions. The opposite of greatness is *depression.* Greatness is the decision to live, to say yes to the life force, to choose to be constructive. Depression is not only to have given up the will to live (not "lost" it, for you are responsible) but actually to have chosen its converse—to want to die, to be destructive, to obstruct progress—for the depressed person is not only sad but also chooses not to be helped.

Shakespeare, in *Twelfth Night* (act 2, scene 5), writes, "Be not afraid of greatness: some are born great, some achieve greatness, and some have greatness thrust upon them." How much attention do *you* give to greatness? In *Henry VIII* (act 5, scene 5), Shakespeare gives an even stronger eulogy to greatness:

> Whenever the bright sun of heaven shall shine,
> His honor and the greatness of his name
> Shall be, and make new nations.

Greatness, however, is not limited to famous figures. Every year, *Newsweek* publishes an edition saluting "everyday heroes." The July 10, 1989, issue mentions Tom Whittaker of Idaho, whose right foot was amputated after an auto wreck: "Whittaker, who wears a prosthesis and walks with a slight limp..., was invited to join an expedition to climb Mount Everest. He reached 23,500 feet but in May was forced back, after three attempts to climb the rest of the mountain, by fierce weather and illness" ("Everyday Heroes," 1989, p. 46). It also mentions Lorena Casey, a seventy-five-year-old woman, from Missouri, who spends fifty hours a week as a volunteer running a thirty-bed shelter for battered women and children: "Her work for the shelter... is balm for an old psychological wound. As a girl, Casey often saw her father beat her mother, who stayed in the marriage for the sake of the children. 'There was nothing she could do,' Casey says. 'There was nothing like this for women back then'" (p. 49). Gwen Rust of North Dakota was an incest victim. Rust "was unable to discuss with her family—or even with her husband— how she'd been abused: 'I covered up my pain totally.' Only at the age of 37... did Rust discover how much anger and bitterness she'd repressed. ... Rust now works toward prevention of abuse, as well as for treatment of the victims, through open discussion.

Rust runs the Incest Awareness Project and publishes a newsletter for incest victims called *Breaking the Silence*" (p. 50). As Willie Maxwell, a fifty-nine-year-old man from South Carolina, "lay in bed in 1982 recovering from cancer surgery on his vocal cords, he vowed that if he pulled through, he would do more to help others. . . . Five mornings a week . . . he makes 'house calls' in his van, gathering scrap paper and aluminum cans to raise money for Camp Kemo, a local summer retreat for kids with cancer. In six years he has collected more than $16,000. Maxwell also finds out which children in the hospital need cheering up, and he talks with them and brings them books, cards, flowers and fruit. . . . 'If they die, I'll try to make it to the funeral. I follow them to the end'" (p. 50). "In 1986 Shelby Long's 30-block neighborhood in Richmond [Virginia] suffered three murders, two rapes and 134 burglaries. . . . Long . . . developed a 'telephone tree' to get the word out. She calls 35 neighbors and they each call 35 neighbors until everyone is alerted. Long, 49, works nearly full time as a voluntary crime fighter. 'No other citizen works as many hours trying to stop crime,' says Richmond Police Lt. Herbert Nichols. Last year . . . there were no murders, no rapes and only 20 burglaries" (p. 54).

Pauline Gomez, a sixty-nine-year-old woman from New Mexico, "lacks sight, not vision" (p. 60). She was born blind. She helped found the National Federation for the Blind of New Mexico. She is self-supporting, and she devotes her time to teaching blind people self-confidence and self-acceptance.

The eternal questions emerge also in the concerns of executives. Asked what their one root leadership question is, executives in my inner-side-of-greatness seminars are led through a Delphic Oracle exercise. Like the great and powerful of antiquity, they "ask" the god Apollo. After considerable reflection, they formulate anonymous questions. In so doing, they demonstrate deep sensitivity to the eternal questions (some of the questions used in this book have been rendered into English from other languages), which arise camouflaged in many forms (for instance, there are many symbols of death, such as rejection or retirement). Here are some examples:

I *love* my present job within the company structure.
I can see that the realization of my life's work is
coming within reach. My colleagues and staff represent the closest personal relationships (contact
with my family is loving, but quite infrequent). I
may need ten to twenty years more to bring home
the needed changes in process, systems, and people. My question: How do I reconcile the implicit
dichotomy? I want to spend all my time on my
dreams, time that I enjoy most, and every day, yet
retirement will terminate my work and leave me
stranded in a vacuum of not having an intimate
relationship and/or alternative goal.

How do you balance the need to be loved with the
loneliness of leadership?

What is the purpose of the intense efforts toward
self-improvement and development, if the end result is death?

I have, in my life, been burdened with a series of
personal tragedies, which have left a certain residue of bitterness. From a philosophical point of
view, how can one rationalize that such experiences
were "useful" in developing one into the person he
is now?

Although I am relatively comfortable with my present perception of self in pursuit of greatness, I
don't believe the real me has emerged. How do I
find the real me in such a way as to enhance the
value of the rest of my life?

Dear Oracle: I have three questions.
1. How can I achieve a higher level of self-
    development while so encompassed by mental
    struggles with impersonal data?

2. What does God want from me?
3. How do leadership qualities work or apply to
    life after work (retirement)?

How do I discover the real purpose of my life?

I am, perhaps, at the midpoint of my life. I have
been successful so far, as many would judge success — married, and happily so; a parent, happily
so; and engaged in fulfilling and challenging work.
But if I ask whether what I am doing will take me on
a trajectory of being all that I can be — of contributing something to the world that will truly mean I
made a difference — then what I am doing presently
is not enough. My question: How do I choose where
to go to offer my gifts? No one issue, as yet, beckons
me in a compelling way, no one people speak to me
to join my strengths to theirs. Will I know the issue
when it comes? Will I recognize my people when I
pass among them? Or is it the leader's task to
choose — now — despite the uncertainty?

Now that we have finished discussing greatness in both its
pragmatic and philosophic aspects, we are ready to consider the
more emotional elements of a commitment to greatness.

The Breakthrough

The leadership mind is radically different from the ordinary
mind. The shift from the latter to the former is a conversion, a
transformation, a breakthrough. The leadership mind, mindset,
or intelligence is a *radical departure* from ordinary, everyday
consciousness. The "leadership turn" is a *paradigm shift*. It is a
transformation. It is like enlightenment. Other and related expressions for this new leadership awakening are *expanding our
possibilities, developing the human potential, the exhilaration of discovering one's freedom, enthusiasm,* and *positive thinking*. All add up
to one thing: the joy of a leadership mind.

The radical transformation or paradigm shift—the mind's "snap" into something different—can be horizontal, or it can be vertical. Horizontal transformation means that the leadership mind expands by challenging itself to brilliance and creativity. Vertical transformation is deep and high. Here, *high* means that in transforming the personal side of leadership, we get in touch with the eternal questions. *Deep* means we touch the unconscious and assiduously dare to go to where the pain is.

We find examples of similarly radical transformations in conversions following a religious experience, in reconstructive psychotherapy (such as psychoanalysis), in culture shock, in artistic inspiration, and in Plato's famous allegory of the cave. Plato writes about prisoners in a cave, watching shadows that they accept as real. One of them frees himself of his shackles, leaves the cave, sees the sun, and returns to the darkness, temporarily blinded by the star's brilliance. His fellow prisoners think he is crazy, yet he knows they live a life of illusion. That is the transformation of the enlightened person. It shows itself when we fall in love and in the sudden shift of perspective in humor. Transformation is philosophy's raison d'être. Philosophy's hope is to penetrate the depths of being and to provide the magic of radical newness. Leadership intelligence is such a transformation. Plato, in the *Timaeus*, compressed the idea of radical transformation into a stunning image: "Light is the shadow of God." Similarly, Shakespeare, recognizing the existence of a separate reality, makes Hamlet say, after seeing his slain father's ghost, "There are more things in heaven and earth, Horatio, Than are dreamt of in your philosophy" (act 1, scene 5).

Experience demonstrates that when the Leadership Diamond model is applied to actual breakthrough decision making, it becomes necessary to make some basic distinctions. Each dominant leadership strategy must then be challenged on three levels: the *pragmatic* (practical, incremental, lower) level, the *breakthrough* (advanced, transformative, higher) level, and the level of analysis of the *resistance* (and the form that it takes) to self-awareness and to change.

Most people, executives included, do not have adequate access to the full range of their possibilities. Authentic leadership is not only to be better but also to be different. It is to work "smarter," not harder. We seek transformation, not just improvement.

What is the precise nature of the important interface between the pragmatic and the breakthrough levels in each of the four dominant leadership strategies? How do we transcend and transform our leadership performance from the merely pragmatic to genius-level breakthroughs? There are four elements.

First is *reflection*, the foundational skill—not just to look, but to look at the act of looking itself; not just to think, but to think about thinking itself; not just to learn, but to learn about learning itself; not just to feel, but to examine the act (or "passion") of feeling itself. We must go beyond what the light illuminates (like the dark wall of a cave). We must look at the light itself and attempt to understand it.

Second is the *existential crisis*. This crisis involves the willingness to surrender yourself to anxiety and other negative emotions (guilt, depression, disorganization, anger, indignity, ignorance, lack of intelligence, tragedy), in the knowledge that, once you reach the other side, you find strength of character, a new level of power, and a new depth of happiness. In other words, the distinction between higher and lower or pragmatic and breakthrough levels of leadership exhibited in each strategy is keyed to anxiety and other negative emotions. The existential crisis uses the energy of anxiety positively; it finds constructive uses for anxiety. For example, lower-level leadership decisions, as a rule, are routine (if sometimes tough) business decisions, but they are business, period. For the experienced executive, they are relatively easy. In contrast, sensitive personal decisions deeply affecting your life and your relationships tend to produce serious anxiety and guilt. Whereas business decisions are responsive to logical analysis, personal decisions rarely are. A modest degree of anxiety and guilt indicates that you are operating on the practical leadership level. High or intense levels of anxiety and guilt, however, are likely to be produced by operating in a breakthrough leadership capacity. And, of course, many business decisions are so difficult and involve so much of your ego that they become personal decisions. It is the mark of a leader to *manage* the anxiety and guilt of making business decisions while retaining the willingness to *experience the maximum* anxiety and guilt of unique, life-transforming personal choices.

Third are *genius levels*, vertical and horizontal expansions of the mind. Vertical expansion means, in height, to reach the eternal questions; in depth, to go to the unconscious and to where the pain is. Horizontal expansion means to aim for transformational brilliance and perfection in creativity.

Fourth is *esthetic intelligence* — the use of metaphor, symbol, and abstraction, rather than concrete and literal language.

With these four complex and sophisticated competencies you are ready to move from the pragmatic to the breakthrough level of the leadership mind. If you understand this interface, then you will have an opportunity for an authentic breakthrough in your leadership performance. These four competencies are critically important because they distinguish the common from the uncommon mind.

As we shall see in detail later, to be satisfied that you adequately understand this material, you must be prepared, in the end, to produce at least four complete diagnoses of the *organization's* leadership performance and of *your own personal* leadership style. In each case, you must distinguish between *what is* and *what could be*, between harsh reality and imaginative ideals.

Ask yourself, "What do I get paid for?" The usual answer is "To work," but the correct answer is "To lead," and leadership is not work. Work is performing a manageable task. Leadership is seizing an impossible situation and either wrestling it into a breakthrough solution or releasing its dormant greatness.

Context

The Leadership Diamond itself, with its dominant leadership strategies, rests on a contextual foundation, some of whose individual elements are described in this section.

The serious study of the *humanities* is neglected in the education of our business and professional people. The application of the humanities to everyday affairs, axiomatic in earlier ages, is today virtually forgotten. For the sake of society as well as of business, this trend must be reversed. Human depth is the key ingredient of success, including success in business and the professions. To fill this vacuum is one of the goals of the Leadership Diamond model.

And what are the humanities? The disciplines that tell us about the human core, the prerequisites for mature leadership, are philosophy; religion, theology, and mythology; literature and the arts; and the study of history. We must also mention aspects of the behavioral sciences, ranging from psychiatry to anthropology and from medicine to sociology.

The Leadership Diamond is differentiated from other leadership approaches in that it is based in part on philosophic insight and wisdom. Philosophy is the world's oldest science. Today's proliferating leadership techniques are adjuncts to the tradition of philosophy.

Why philosophy? The answer is *depth*. We are concerned not with skills but with the seat of the self, the foundation of the soul. Character means depth, not technique. Integrity means substance, not form. In our business affairs, we must allow our consciences to call us back to the things that matter most.

A corollary to the model's dependence on the humanities is the focus on *education*, which is increasingly becoming a function of business. Our colleges and universities, said a well-known CEO recently, are delivering "defective products." Peter Drucker has frequently asserted that a company is to be measured by the extent and quality of its training. Education for leadership is comprehensive. It excludes nothing but must be grounded in a heavy dose of the humanities and the liberal arts.

The leadership mind is *awake*, rather than asleep. It is alert, conscious, aware, in touch with reality (both internal and external), proactive, autonomous, brilliant, energetic, and sharp. The leadership mind is never in a trance. It does not have a blank stare, nor is it purely reactive, passive, dependent, or dull. The specific business implication is that the leadership intelligence is always conscious of the pervasive need for marketing (each employee must earn for the company at least twice what he or she expects to get paid—that is, believes he or she is

worth—*after* overhead). The leadership mind always engages in
CEO- or chairman-level thinking. It knows and cares about the
total business, not only its small turf. It never says, "I just mind
my own business," "I do what I'm told," or "This is not my area."
Always ask whether your work can be replaced by automation. If
the answer is yes, then you are not doing a leadership job. Only
when the answer is no are you a leadership mind.

A leadership mind is characterized by *hope*. The world is
full of frustrations. They produce stress, which *can* be healthful;
but too much frustration leads to despair. People give up. That is
depression. What is needed is hope, the realistic perception that
there is a way out, that there is a future, that there is a solution.
Others manage, and so can you. You have a right to feel good
about yourself. That is why you need hope. But the hope must be
realistic. It must work. It cannot be a manic delusion. The line is
thin. Making the distinction between a manic-depressive personality and an authentically hopeful one is an art, not a science.
But so is leadership an art, and not a science.

The leader has the capacity and the will to take charge of
generating hope. Two clichés are applicable: "Managers do
things right, leaders do the right thing" and "Managers drain
energy away from organizations, whereas leaders infuse energy
into organizations." In practice, this means that (for example)
you frame your meetings (begin and end them) with images of
greatness in leadership intelligence, and that you will accept no
less than peak leadership performance from yourself and your
team.

The leadership mind is *democratic*, not elitist. Everyone is
capable of it, and everyone needs it. A well-led organization
consists of nothing but leaders. This is a short point long on
significance.

Leadership is *teachable*. It can be facilitated or challenged
into existence. This is the Socratic method. Some say that leadership cannot be taught, but that it can only be learned. Plato
wrote that human beings are born with wisdom. Teachers do not
tell anything new to their students, because the knowledge exists
already, pregnant within them. Instead, the authentic teacher
helps the truth to be born. The teacher facilitates, challenges—

in short, empowers. The idea that teaching is empowerment comes from the first teacher of Western civilization, Plato's very own mentor: Socrates.

Executives must train themselves and others in the leadership mind and leadership intelligence. They need to open themselves to all the mind's possibilities. Then they must teach the teaching of leadership to others, for an organization is no better than its weakest leader. The educator Jerome Seymour Bruner wrote, "Any subject can be taught effectively in some intellectually honest form to any child at any stage of development."

That the leadership mind can and should be taught may be one of the most significant contributions of philosophy to the community of executives. It is not only that leaders with responsibility must be taught leadership; they must also, if they can, do the teaching. The young now starting in business, government, and the professions — the leaders of the future — must be taught the leadership mind, so that they can make their contributions to society. And teaching means challenging — provoking people to bring out their best, motivating them to be all they can be.

In sum, no one should think of himself or herself as a born leader. Leadership ability, skill, and even charisma can be acquired and, if already present, can be improved and put to more effective use. The higher the quality of the raw material, the more effective the leadership challenge. Consequently, everyone can become a leader. Leadership, by distributing responsibility and according the highest respect to every person, is the fulfillment of the democratic ideal. In a well-managed organization, everyone is challenged to CEO- or chairman-level thinking. Three demanding steps are required, however: *choose* to be a leadership mind; *train* to be a leadership mind, preferably with a mentor (who, ideally, will be your boss or supervisor); and grasp the *obstacles*, resistances, and defenses that inhibit the release of leadership energy.

That leadership can be taught to everyone, and that everyone can become a leader, may be an exaggeration. Theoretically speaking, leadership *is* for everyone; in practice, however, only a few understand it, and even fewer choose it. Having chosen to study this material, you have preselected yourself as a leader.

What ordinarily happens is that individuals are promoted to leadership from nonleadership positions, positions that required technological and not managerial expertise. This point, raised earlier, warrants repetition. Good lawyers, good financial people, high-quality engineers and mathematicians, and superior biological scientists eventually become scions of industry. Promotions to leadership positions are not necessarily upward moves but may be lateral shifts. Eventually, even the greatest technical expert will know less than the people over whom he or she has been promoted. It then becomes clear that leadership is a sui generis calling even more than it is a profession. It is different in kind from positions in which technical competence is required. Engineering, chemistry, law, medicine, finance, and teaching are taught; leadership is not. In management, that situation leads to a leadership vacuum. We must not only start teaching leadership but also *manage* by teaching leadership.

Leadership is taught by releasing leadership energy, by helping others learn to lead. But understanding leadership does more. It helps you *recognize* leaders, helps you *select* those whom you wish to cultivate. Furthermore, the world will in time demand that you be proficient in all of the leadership dimensions. You have no option other than to respond by leading.

Another point worth reemphasizing is that operational problems are best managed by training the *minds* of operations executives. This means training for leadership intelligence and challenging leaders to their inner side of greatness. Developing leadership intelligence is a high-level solution to technical operational problems. Coaching in the *personal* side of quality, competitiveness, productivity, company survival, restructuring, and organizational effectiveness is the missing link in making strategies work.

Your company may have state-of-the-art technology (which, in Leadership Diamond theory, is called the *technical architecture* of a company). Your company may also have the

Figure 3.1. The Positioning of Leadership Intelligence.

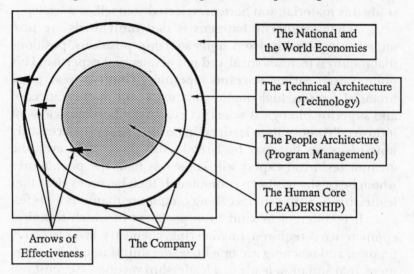

streamlined organization to match it (which Leadership Diamond theory calls the *people architecture*), but if inadequate attention is paid to human issues, to the inner side of greatness (what Leadership Diamond theory calls the *human core* of a company), even enormous expenditures will avail you little. Effectiveness starts at the center and moves outward. The human core influences the quality of the people architecture, the systems by which organizations work. The people architecture in turn influences the quality of the technical work of a company, the products and services produced and developed. And the technical architecture—the buildings, the factories, the technology, the production processes—shows itself to the world, affects the national and global economies. These are the "arrows of effectiveness" (see Figure 3.1). Without caring attention to the human core, an organization's people architecture is not of significant value. In Leadership Diamond theory, this principle is considered to be a root fact.

In other words, most practical problems in business ("What is our marketing plan for our next acquisition?" "How can we reverse the deterioration of quality production at the plant?") have one answer—leadership (that is, challenging and training the leadership mind). That may sound simplistic, but in practice it is a real solution because we know how to develop leadership intelligence. It works. It gets results.

As organizations get flatter, more responsibility falls on what used to be the lower levels of management. Speed has also become a critical success factor. Mistakes are costly. The answer is management that is better trained in strategic thinking and in other tactics of the leadership mind. The more I travel around the world and talk with recognized leaders, the more I see the deep truth of this position confirmed. And it is good news, for companies are people-driven, and attention to the personal side of human existence is recognized as leading to win-win solutions for bottom-line business problems.

The Leadership Diamond is a field, a symbol of *spaciousness*. The leadership mind comfortably embraces paradoxes and contradictions, polarities and ambiguities, conflicts and incompatibilities. The leadership mind holds many thoughts and attitudes at once (see Figure 3.2). Specifically, the distended or spacious leadership mind is not troubled by contradictory ideas. Nils Bohr said it well: "The opposite of a great idea is another great idea." In youth, we may believe that the truth is simple, that complex questions have but one simple answer. As we mature, we realize that consistency is a mindset, one that may be very important but that does not correspond to all realities. Leadership requires a mindset where ideas compete democratically, where opposing ideas can be friends and get a safe hearing.

The same is true of emotions. Emotions conflict, but they can coexist as well. We love and are angry at one and the same time. We are attracted and repelled at one and the same time, and by the same person. The leadership mind is generous, and a generous mind can compassionately entertain emotions that appear to be mutually exclusive.

It all adds up to the ambiguity of the world. The world is susceptible to many interpretations, several of which may be correct. Some are simpler than others. When we question the world and ask it to reveal its secrets, we get many answers. These

Figure 3.2. The Leadership Diamond Model (2).

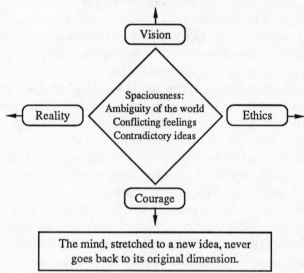

Lock This Image in Your Mind

Vision

Spaciousness:
Ambiguity of the world
Conflicting feelings
Contradictory ideas

Reality   Ethics

Courage

The mind, stretched to a new idea, never
goes back to its original dimension.

are known as myths, cultures, world views, belief systems, metaphysics, world designs; they all serve a purpose. If there is one
thing that philosophy teaches, it is that the world has many
explanations, and they can live with each other. That is the
ambiguity of the world.

Science and religion may not be compatible, nor can we
say that one is right and the other wrong. Both reflect reality,
with a different emphasis. Economic and political theories conflict. Rather than argue that one is right and the other wrong, it
is often possible to realize that they represent different perceptions of a single reality. The perceptions differ because the
values we wish to extract from reality may differ. This is known as
the *pragmatic theory of truth.* There comes a time when one must
take a stand, but that need not be done precipitately or
prematurely.

In short, the world is ambiguous. The leadership mind
understands this real-world fact and is fully adapted to it. The
leadership mind is spacious enough to accommodate conflict-

ing emotions and feelings, as well as contradictory concepts. Being comfortable with polarization, paradox, and dialectical interactions—in the world, emotions, and ideas—is the hallmark of the spacious leadership mind. Since authentic leadership is needed mainly in conditions of chaos, we can call leadership the *Hydra phenomenon* (you may recall Hercules' confrontation with the snake; each time he cut off its head, it grew two new ones). The challenge of leadership is to cope with intense and (for most people) essentially unmanageable frustration.

What does the spaciousness of the leadership mind mean, besides openness to contradictory ideas, to conflicting emotions, and to the ambiguities of the world? It means the willingness and the capacity to learn—to know the joy of learning, the youthfulness that comes with ceaseless learning. For example, imagine a CEO-owner who has been very successful in building a multimillion-dollar business. Now several conditions impede further progress. The members of the company's executive committee feel secure and no longer exhibit the leadership required to deal with an expanding company. The owner knows little about the stock market and other matters regarding financial markets, for going public or leveraging his big investment is not something he takes seriously. He wants to leave his growing business to his son. That strategy may not be viable in the current competitive climate. He understands that his business, in its present form, will last no more than ten years, and that is a maximum. Major changes are needed. And his son, who is still very young, may inherit an albatross instead of a thriving enterprise. Leadership, for this executive, rests squarely on his ability to learn, to understand what it is that he does not know and then learn about it. The open mind learns constantly, for it has learned how to learn, and it gains pleasure, joy, meaning, and fulfillment from learning. Specifically, the learner knows what he or she does not know, knows how to find out, has the will to do it, and gains energy from learning.

The space of the leadership mind is kept distended through the centrifugal tension of all four Diamond points, which, like springs, push in opposite directions. The leadership mind is defined by all the points on the compass: while each one is independent, together they create one geographic field.

The four Diamond points are not connected by a common thread. They are independent variables, like factors in a statistical analysis. Think of a juggler handling four balls, or of four crewmen on a yacht performing different tasks for one winning team. Think of a string quartet—each voice different, yet one piece of music—or of a cantata, where soprano, alto, tenor, and bass sing different notes and beat contrasting rhythms, all for the sake of one expansive harmony.

Reality is *polarized*, as symbolized by the spaciousness of the Leadership Diamond itself. That is a general philosophical description of the very essence of reality. Polarity is the yin-yang principle: that everything has its opposite, its counterpart, that nothing is either black or white. For every masculine trait there is a feminine counterpart; opposed to matter there is antimatter. For every right there is a contradiction that is also right. Leadership means coping in that kind of world, a world where answers are actions, decisions, commitments, and risks, not the unambiguous conclusions of mathematical calculations. Everything of beauty has its flaw, and all that is flawed has its aspect of beauty.

Polarity leads to some highly practical rules for the conduct of leadership life. Hackneyed phrases may serve us best: "What goes up must come down," to which one must add, "What goes down will go up"—and, no matter how well prepared you are, "life will always surprise you." Just look at any newspaper, virtually any day; what sells newspapers is precisely these surprises. In politics, there always arise developments that are unexpected, unpredictable, inconceivable. The positive and the negative always go together. Expect failure while you are in the middle of success, but also expect success when in the depths of failure. Business planning must always be cognizant of this metaphysical principle of the universe.

Consider these examples. In 1989, while *glasnost* and *perestroika* were in full swing, there were riots and demonstrations for democracy in Poland, Hungary, East Germany, Estonia, and Czechoslovakia. Indeed, the Berlin Wall finally came down toward the end of that year. The prosperous United States suffered two of its greatest natural disasters in a century: Hurricane Hugo, which caused serious damage to Charleston, South Carolina, and the October 17 San Francisco earthquake. On top of all this, the stock market gyrated wildly, casting a pall over any attempt to make sense of the economy. Perhaps, in theory, all these events had been vaguely predicted, but their actual occurrence, as well as the psychological impact of living with them, had all the aspects of unpredictability and complete surprise. And then, at the very same time, some people are the victims of crime. To them, it is always horrendously unexpected, for it always happens to the "other guy." Good and bad are always joined.

Here is an important practical principle to keep in mind: authentic leaders make superhuman efforts to be prepared. When business is good, they make plans for the downturn. *Business and politics are a series of overlapping but rising bell curves—* that is, they rise if they are well managed. During good times, leaders prepare for new products, new ventures, and restructurings for the inevitable downturn. The width of the curves, from two years to twenty, will also be a surprise. In your leadership, you must factor in the element of surprise, the inevitable disaster, to such a professional degree that the only thing that can surprise you would be the absence of surprises. It is like planning for death: you know it will come, but you never know when. Make your plans, but also know that they will fail.

Know that specific events will occur and that they are completely *unpredictable*. Additional recent examples, all of them surprises to the general public, are the political changes in South Africa, the secession of the Soviet republics, the invasion in August 1990 of Kuwait by Saddam Hussein, and the surprising United Nations reaction.

Know that life proceeds in cycles, but know also that the nature of the cycles themselves is unpredictable. Know that the leadership mind, which is a product of evolution, can cope well with these realities. The world is made for the leadership mind. Such realism is a mindset. It is translated into continuous action. And as the leadership mind acts on these principles, the world

Figure 3.3. Life as a Series of Cycles.

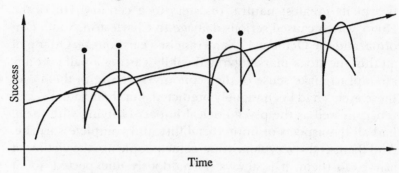

● Key leadership decision points:
  the start of new businesses, products, or processes.

responds. It becomes familiar and congenial. A virtually mystical bond is established between leadership intelligence and the power of the cosmos (see Figure 3.3).

The principle of the pervasiveness of polarity often impresses people with its explanatory power. Most of us feel compelled to choose between opposites. That may sometimes be appropriate. But, just as often, it may mean we are stuck in a rut. To live in a world of opposites is a transformative step upward, a new way of perceiving an old reality. We do not need to choose. We can be big enough to live in paradoxes. That is an artistic solution, not a scientific one. Consider some common and unresolvable paradoxes: society and the individual, liberty and equality, the masculine and the feminine, mind and matter, justice and forgiveness, art and science, whole and parts, perfection (craft) versus profit (business), vertical management (line responsibility) versus horizontal management (project responsibility), pro-choice versus pro-life advocacy. The realization that no solution is found either in taking a stand on these opposites or in balancing them opens up the possibility of a higher level of perception, which integrates or synthesizes both and renders a fatuous choice between them unnecessary. This is called *maturation*, mellowing. It springs from wisdom. You can live with contradictions because there is room for a democracy of feelings, perceptions, and ideas.

The leadership mind is *unitary*, integrated rather than fragmented. While there exist contrasts within the spacious leadership mind, the total effect, as in contrapuntal music, is harmony. Fragmentation, which is akin to the more serious condition of disintegration, debilitates the mind. Unity, on the contrary, reduces anger and anxiety and releases dormant energy.

Effective organizations understand *teamwork*. In effective organizations, *every individual also takes responsibility for the total group*. In this connection, there are two quick measures of how well managed a company is. First, are the teams acting as teams? Do we find in the teams a combination of individual initiative and commitment to the success of others? Second, does every employee know and care about what goes on elsewhere in the organization? Does the bank teller know the history of the bank? Does the cardiology nurse understand the psychiatric services of the hospital? Both measures can show proof of "ownership," of personal interest in and responsibility for the total business. These two are necessary but not sufficient success measures.

The leadership mind is the key to mental and physical health. Indeed, the leadership mind can be described as a hardy personality. In the successful struggle against diseases of stress and of the immune system (cardiovascular problems, cancer, colds, lupus, arthritis), the key may be here, in the leadership mind.

What makes for a healthy body, for effective protection against disease? Many researchers believe that physical health depends, at least in part, on how you cope with your psychosocial life problems (a theory developed in a discipline known as *psychoneuroimmunology*). Leadership intelligence—with its emphasis on full self-disclosure, freedom, autonomy, encounter, and respect for the existential crisis—tries to teach the precise mindset that makes for a sound mind in a sound body.

The Leadership Diamond theory, especially at the philosophic and breakthrough levels, addresses itself to the mindset required to achieve psychosomatic health. To be a leader is ultimately to be in command of the lymphocytes and macrophages of your own immune system. Consider these findings reported by the *International Herald Tribune* (Apr. 21, 1989, pp. 1, 6):

- The immune system may be strengthened by mild stress and the excitement of living at a mildly hectic pace.
- The relief and challenge of confronting traumatic memories has salutary effects. Research found that the exploration of deeply upsetting episodes in a person's life that goes on during psychotherapy may have direct benefits for the immune system. Writing about upsetting topics, which many research subjects had never discussed with anyone, led to a significant increase in the level of T cells, which fight infection and virus.
- Cancer patients coached in defeating pessimism and self-defeating beliefs, and in learning to look at life with more optimism, had more active natural-killer cells, which protect the body against tumor growth, than did patients who received only standard medical care.
- Men in a program that combined aerobics and relaxation, combined with other training in managing stress, showed an increase of 10 to 14 percent in T-4 cells, which fall as infection with the AIDS virus progresses. Earlier studies have found benefits for the immune system from such practices as exercise, relaxation, and laughter.

Major institutions, including the National Institute of Mental Health, are financing research in psychoimmunology, and Norman Cousins's *Anatomy of an Illness* (1979), in which he describes literally laughing himself back to health from an incurable illness, is an extraordinary illustration of the powers of authentic leadership thinking and acting over physical disease.

The tie between the Leadership Diamond theory and all this is not casual. Medicine has not found a precise answer to the question of exactly what mindset is correlated with physical health. I propose here that the answer is found in the kind of thinking reflected in the *philosophic* level of tactics characterizing leadership intelligence. A developed leadership mind is more intimately connected with first-class physical health than with any other trait. But leadership is more difficult to measure than ordinary personality characteristics, for leadership follows from the resolute will and the awakened mind, rather than from measurable behavior and responses to a psychometric instrument. The reason for this claim lies in an understanding of the meaning of human freedom. Freedom is a "nonnatural," nonscientific, nonbiological reality. Freedom connects us with our subjective reality, one not measurable by scientific instruments. But that freedom is also the source of consciousness and of life, and it has become more or less accepted that mental and physical health arise as a result of integrating the material world of objects, susceptible to scientific assessment, with the subjective world of our will and our imagination.

Effective leadership springs from the *unconscious*, which is also the source of creativity. The unconscious is the body's silent voice, speaking from the wisdom gleaned from billions of years of experience. Transformational leaders inspire, mostly through what they are in their depth, and not by virtue of calculations, which are of rather late evolution in the brain. The unconscious responds to strong images as if they were realities. Consequently, a strong vision of the leadership mind becomes a lasting imprint on the unconscious. Your world will then reflect the new programs in your unconscious. Herein lies the power of the Leadership Diamond model.

A number of separate points need to be recorded here before we move on to the next major issue. First, to activate your leadership intelligence and make it permanent does not require work or effort; on the contrary. As in a nuclear reaction, it releases dormant energy. Second, leadership is added value to yourself. You become a leader because you have a deep personal need for it, not because the company's stock value or the national economy depend on it. Third, what happens under stress? What happens to the Leadership Diamond mindset when you meet a serious crisis that undermines your values and disorganizes your world? The Leadership Diamond must be useful not only in happiness and peace but also and especially when the world you know is shattered. Times of distress are when the greatness-in-leadership challenge is most sorely needed. The leadership challenge is particularly important during hard times. When companies are wealthy, they say they want to set up leadership programs to steel themselves for the tougher times to come, but the bureaucracy often drags its feet, so that not much of significance happens. When hard times finally come, as they always do, leadership programs are cut, since cost reduction emerges as the top priority. But the opposite would make sense: when the patient is sick, medicine is the most serious need.

Social and Political Issues

The effect of leadership intelligence on the world population is to divide societies into leaders and nonleaders. Part of the reason for a "decision" in favor of a condition of nonleadership is culture; part of it is individual choice; part of it is economic injustice and lack of resources. There are poor nations, and there are the poor in rich nations. A life that has gone too far into choosing nonleadership may be locked into a pernicious vise, never to extract itself.

Nonleaders are, in the last analysis, the homeless, the urban underclass. They are the hungry. A society or a world that permits their degradation degrades itself. The nonleaders would be dangerous but for their lack of knowledge. Society's leaders are compelled to care for them. We are moving not toward one homogeneous society but toward two incompatible ones.

Misunderstood and misused technology is a partial cause; every job that can be automated will be automated. The only nonautomated jobs left will be leadership jobs. There will be no more work for those who do not make the leadership choice. This dilemma will be a key problem facing humanity at the beginning of the Third Millennium.

Too many people cannot cope with life today, nor can today's society cope with those who cannot cope. The failure of the prison system in the United States is only one of many examples. Consider these figures from the *New York Times* (Malcolm, 1988, p. 6):

- State and federal penal institutions now house more than 604,000 prisoners, and the number increases daily.
- The care of one young prisoner costs $23,000 per year. For older ones, the cost rises to $70,000 per prisoner per year.
- Florida's Department of Corrections receives 100 new prisoners a day. One new federal or state prisoner is sentenced every twelve minutes, and each new cell costs more than $70,000.
- After forty years inside, prison is home, and other prisoners are family. It could be considered cruel and unusual punishment to turn a seventy-year-old loose with some clothes, a few dollars, and a good-luck wish.

Or examine the following statistics on our children, the leaders of tomorrow: One-fourth of adolescent boys and 42 percent of adolescent girls said that they had seriously considered committing suicide at some point in their lives; 18 percent of the girls and 11 percent of the boys reported actually trying. These are findings from a 1987 nationwide survey of adolescent health knowledge and behavior, conducted by three national health-education organizations. The survey involved more than 11,400 eighth- and tenth-grade students from 217 schools in twenty states. More than three-fourths of the eighth graders and almost 90 percent of the tenth graders said they had used alcohol. More than one-fourth of the eighth graders said they had had five or more drinks at least once during the preceding two weeks. About 5 percent of the tenth graders reported using marijuana in the preceding month. Almost a third of the boys and half the girls said they had not eaten breakfast more than twice during the preceding week (Otten, 1989, p. B1).

There is the danger that the lack of leadership may become institutionalized. Here, more than virtually anywhere else, worldwide leadership—in every sense of that word, and in its very best application—is mandatory.

Management today—in industry and government, in education and the military—has reached an unprecedented impasse. Perhaps only 15 percent of organizational effectiveness and corporate competitive advantage can be attributed to the systems and the technologies designed to cope with current economic realities. The rest, the remaining 85 percent, is leadership and people. While this disproportion may always have existed, it can no longer by sustained in today's competitive environment. In the past, however, and in many companies today, the actual working ratio has been an 85 percent emphasis on technologies—these are the architectures, both a technical architecture (automation, machinery) and a people architecture (human engineering, quality circles, self-managed work teams, matrix organizations)—and a 15 percent emphasis on the human core (which means intense focus on personal—that is, emotional and intellectual—maturity). This pervasive structural situation is the *15/85 formula.* Japan does not have the problem of the Western industrialized nations, for it has a ready-made culture, one that already gives attention to the human core and thereby automatically supports the technical architecture.

Many leaders today agree, especially in view of the Japanese competition, that 85 percent of organizational effectiveness and industrial competitiveness is to be attributed to morale, spirit, heart, to the commitment and loyalty employees give their companies, to the inventiveness, imagination, and creativity they devote to their jobs, and to the understanding they have of the real world within which their companies exist and operate. That new 85 percent represents the development of the human core, the promotion of leadership intelligence.

A basic feature of the new leadership is thus *the inversion of the old 15/85 formula.* While 85 percent of executive energy had been invested in applying the principles of analysis and technology to systematizing machinery and people for more effective production, only 15 percent had been devoted to understanding the human core, the inner issues (loyalty, patience, cooperation, sacrifice, autonomy, respect) required to support the existing systems. When things go wrong—for example, program management is often simply not a good return on investment—the tendency has been to increase the pressure on technology and human systems: more expensive equipment and more intensive skills training; turning up the volume instead of changing the station. The solution is in fact a path of diminish-

ing returns. That is another reason why the leadership challenge is of such grave importance to business and, in general, to
the management of the social and economic orders. The competitive advantage is now with those companies that invert the
ratio and invest 85 percent of their energies in supporting the
people who need to support the complex systems. It is sufficient
to use the remaining 15 percent to improve the systems incrementally and keep them finely tuned.

The senior vice-president in charge of all technology in
one of the world's leading technology-application firms was
asked, "What percentage of effort should executives devote to
technology, and what percentage on teaching leadership to your
people?" Without blinking an eye, he replied, "The technology
takes care of itself: 2 percent on technology, and 98 percent on
leading people!" This inversion means that time must be spent
on leadership, and not just on work. Spending time on leadership means learning leadership and teaching leadership; and
teaching is carried out by giving lessons, by providing experience and a practicum, by challenging people and confronting
them with their possibilities, and by personal example.

Is there a more dramatic example of the need for leadership training than the tragic downing of the Iranian civilian
airliner on July 3, 1988, in which 290 civilians perished? At first,
the tragedy was attributed to technology. According to an article
in *Time*, "The plane identified by the [U.S.S.] *Vincennes* as a 62-ft.-
long F-14 Tomcat fighter turned out to be a 177-ft.-long Iran Air
Airbus." The reason for the error, the article speculates, was that
technology-dependent nations may "have become prisoners of a
technology so speedy and complex that it forces the fallible
humans who run into it into snap decisions that can turn into
disaster" ("Technology and Tragedy," 1988, p. 4). It is easy to
blame the technology, but quite the opposite was the case, as
other reports attested. The failure was not in the technology; it
was in the leadership—in not preparing a partial-war–partial-
peace strategy, in not training troops properly for the stresses of
first engagement, in not feeding civilian air schedules into naval
computers, and so forth. The true failure was one of courage, of

maintaining the leadership mind intact under stress, and of vision (in not anticipating the obvious).

A well-known study (Wallace and others, 1987) points out that of a total of $6.8 million in expenditures from nine software-development contracts, only 2 percent ($120,000) of the software was used as delivered. A stunning 47 percent ($3.2 million) was delivered but never used, 29 percent ($1.98 million) was paid for but not delivered, 19 percent ($1.3 million) was used but extensively reworked or later abandoned, and 3 percent ($200,000) was used after changes. It is clear that the 85 percent of leadership intelligence that was so desperately needed was nowhere in view.

The situation is similar in the military. Officers' leadership training is 85 percent weapons and tactics, and 15 percent people. But when you ask an officer how his time is actually spent, it is 85 percent people and 15 percent tactics.

The inversion is difficult, for it requires a shift in our perception of leadership; hence the Leadership Diamond model.

Having now covered a host of peripheral, contextual, and foundational issues, we shall move on to an exposition of the mindset required for thinking and acting as a leader—a discussion of greatness and of the four strategies for being great, which make up the heart of the Leadership Diamond model.

4

The Leadership Diamond:
Four Strategies for Greatness

Greatness is expressed in four dimensions, or strategies: vision, reality, ethics, and courage. Each strategy is explained and amplified through four resources, or tactics.

In each strategy, the tactics form a sequence: their order is important. They start with the simple, the practical, the measurable, and move down more and more deeply into the undergirding philosophic structures of the leadership mind itself. Each tactic represents a different level: professional, social, psychological, and philosophical, respectively. As we go down these stages, their leverage to improve leadership effectiveness increases, *for depth equals truth, and truth begets results.* The deeper we go, the more we reach down to the roots of problems, and the more successful we shall be in resolving them.

The *professional level* represents the skill expected on the job. It is the realm of everyday activities. The *social level* is that of maturity. It involves the social skills expected in the larger setting of the community. The *psychological level* is the psychodynamic one. It is the realm of intuition, of a lifetime of experience sedimented in the heart and the mind. It touches the often unconscious functions of the psyche, with roots in childhood. The *philosophical level,* the deepest of all, represents a fundamental structure of being human, an element of the universal human condition. We find references to these roots not only in philosophy but also in theology.

In each strategy there are four supporting tactics, one of

which is the *critical success factor*. You cannot hope to be a leader
of some magnitude without competence in this tactic (although
you may, at least for a while, "fake it" along with the others).

In this chapter, we consider the four dominant leadership
strategies and their supporting tactics. More extensive discussion of these strategies will be found in the following four
chapters.

Vision: The Strategy and the Tactics

Vision, speaking now in general terms, means thinking big,
maintaining perspective, relentless alertness, and clarity. Vision
is valuing intellectual brilliance. Vision means thinking for
yourself, maintaining a clear image of your distant goals — in
short, being not only reactive but also resolutely proactive. It
means having a sense of legacy and destiny and at all times
keeping that sense in view.

Vision is not so much *what* you think as *how* you think.
Vision is less a matter of content than of process. It is thinking in
a very special way, tuning your mind. Vision is moving away
from micromanagement, from "flyspeck management," to
macroleadership. Vision is not necessarily having a plan, but
having a mind that always plans.

In terms of formal definition, visioning means to *think big
and new*. This then becomes the *formula statement* for vision. It
means to think big — that is, always from a high level of perspective. It means thinking even bigger than that, for there is always a
perspective beyond the one we have adopted. This is vertical
thinking. But there is also thinking new — horizontal thinking,
thinking sideways, as it were. Creative people have new ideas,
new insights, new intuitions, that come virtually from nowhere.
Jokes and humor are based on throwing a lateral interpretation
at you just as you, unsuspecting, are moving instead in a straight
direction. The Texas farmer looks contemptuously at the Maine
farmer's land: "You call this a farm? In Texas, we call this a flower
pot! In fact, sometimes when I step into my car early in the
morning I can't reach the limits of my property even by night-
fall!" Shifting his toothpick from one side of his mouth to the

other, the Maine farmer reflects, with some compassion, "I've got a car like that, too!" Such is the essence of humor: surprise. And this abrupt shift in your world design also represents the nature of creativity. That is what is meant by *thinking new*. In sum, vision means to be in touch with the unlimited potential and expanse of this marvelous instrument called the human mind.

The visionary mind's supporting *tactics*, from simple to complex, from common sense to philosophy, are these:

1. The visionary mind is good at abstract reasoning and analysis. This capacity is usually known as intelligence, but in Leadership Diamond theory it is called, specifically, *logical* intelligence. It is to be skilled at making logical connections and breaking a problem into its many subsidiary issues, so that they can be addressed one at a time. This tactic exists on the professional level.

2. The visionary mind is skilled at systemic and strategic (that is, integrative) thinking—meaning, basically, *thinking big*. This tactic is on the social level. It is the capacity to see larger and novel patterns, to imagine clever scenarios. This skill contrasts with and complements analysis. It is a key to success at high levels of leadership responsibility. Fully developed, this skill is among the rarest and most highly paid gifts. It is the critical success factor in this strategy.

3. The visionary mind exhibits a high degree of creativity and has ready access to the unconscious. Visionary intelligence is rich in the production of newness, stimulation, incremental and breakthrough innovation, and lateral thinking, including the use of the unconscious and the intuition for developing new insights. This tactic is on the psychological level. It rests on developed intuition in the leader's mind. It is thinking that is truly new. Creativity, with its source in the unconscious, is the synthesizing function of the leadership mind.

4. The visionary leadership mind is capable of expanding and exploring the experience of inner or subjective space-time. This means having an awareness of your possibilities. Here you are in touch not only with what you actually are but also

with the whole rich range of your human possibilities, the full spectrum of your human potential. This tactic is the study of pure consciousness, found in the religious and philosophic sensibilities of both Eastern and Western thought. This tactic exists on the philosophical level. It is the deepest of them all. It has the greatest potential for expanding your mind and for stimulating the brilliance of genius. It is also the most difficult.

In sum, an informal statement of this strategy is that a visionary leader sees the larger perspective. That is then incorporated into the formula statement: that visioning means to think big and new. The following Oracle exercise question provides an example of the need for perspective:

> It seems as I grow older my intellectual response to day-to-day discouragements at home and at the office is "Does it really matter in the whole scheme of life?" Who will know or care ten years or one hundred years from now if my secretary is late for work, my son doesn't clean his room, or my wife scrapes the car? Unfortunately, if we take this line of reasoning to its logical conclusion, one wonders what really matters—virtually everything can be discounted as unimportant in this context. Should one attempt to overcome this frame of mind? If so, how?

Reality: The Strategy and the Tactics

Reality, the second dominant leadership strategy, stands in sharp contrast to the strategy of vision. Realism is the pragmatism of being in touch with the market, with the facts, with the truth. It means that you do not lie to yourself, that you do not live in a state of self-deception. To be realistic means to think rather than feel; to be objective, not subjective; rational, not irrational.

Realism means being connected with your external realities, and that means principally the economy, the laws of the land, your surrounding culture, the competition, and, above all, other people. Realism means that you understand, accept, and cope with the realities of your specific business, professional, or governmental organization—that you know your customers and your suppliers, your stockholders. But you must likewise be thoroughly familiar with the larger social culture within which you live or where you do your business. Societies' cultures differ sharply, and it often takes years to fully feel that and learn how to manage the conflict. In short, to be realistic is to be in touch with the market.

But realism also means being in touch with people. You are conscious of how others perceive you. Their perceptions of you need not be accurate; in you, they may see only themselves. But they will act on these perceptions. Understanding that is realism. For most managers, reality must be people, not things. How others see you—and, even more, how others limit you—these are the fundamental realities. Some managers prefer things and systems to human beings; there is less backtalk and ambiguity. People, however, are the most important reality in virtually all leadership situations, but people also offer the most frustrating constraints to leaders. To internalize this truth is part of what we mean by realism.

Realism also means being in touch with your internal realities, such as ideals, values, feelings, and attitudes (here, it may overlap with ethics, the third dominant leadership strategy). Finally, realism means being conscious of the acceleration of change. In planning, it is not enough to be prepared for change; events will usually overtake your best planning.

In adopting reality as a strategy, you are fully in touch with all aspects of the "real world." When you say, "I am a realist," you probably mean that you want to be in contact with the external world. But that is not enough. You must make equal connection with your realm of inwardness. Beyond that, realism includes existing comfortably at the interface between your inner and your outer worlds. That, philosophically speaking, is the language of your body, which includes the language of your mouth and fingers (that is, of course, the language of the spoken and the written word).

Realism, therefore, means that you are competent, that
you are in command of the hard facts of the business. There are
hard business facts and soft people facts. The market represents
natural economic forces, and people are irrational. You must
have no illusions about either. And realism means that, instead
of complaining, you find solutions. Realism in general, and by
way of definition, means to *have no illusions*. That is the formula
statement for reality. The supporting resources, or tactics, that
teach the leadership mind and develop realism in leadership
intelligence, in order of their increasing philosophic depth, are
the following:

1. Realism means, first of all, meticulous attention to practical
    details, attending to the precise needs of your immediate
    and end customers. Realism means that you focus on what is
    right for the customer, not on what is convenient for the
    business. This tactic exists on the professional level. It is the
    minimum requirement for professional behavior. It is the
    source of quality.
2. Reality as strategy is a commitment to obtain extensive
    information and maintain a stance of aseptic objectivity. It
    means adhering to professional standards. It stands for
    detachment, research, facts, and calculations. It means that
    you know the business thoroughly, and the more you know
    about what surrounds it, the better. You never stop increas-
    ing your competence with the business and its context.
    This tactic is at the social level. As you use this resource, you
    are also in contact with your social reality, with the ma-
    ture expectations of your business and professional
    communities.
3. Realism is sharply focused attention on survival. It signifies
    a relentless results orientation and market orientation. This
    tactic represents the psychological level. It shows how you as
    a leader perceive reality, and the terms are primarily in the
    form of survival. This mindset is the critical success factor
    for this strategy, for no one can be a CEO of a significant
    organization whose mind is not riveted, always, on survival

in the market. The best analogy, unfortunately, is to a predatory jungle animal.
4. At the philosophical level, a strategic commitment to reality
    means direct contact and embodiment: with yourself, with
    other selves, and with how others perceive you. This tactic is
    the ultimate philosophic statement of what it means to be in
    touch with reality, to exist healthily in the world. To be is to
    be intertwined and interconnected with reality. Self and
    world are in steady dialogue; they are one field. In psychia-
    try, this pervasive attitude is the very definition of health. In
    philosophy, this is called a *dialectical relationship*, an
    encounter.

An informal summary statement of these tactics is that a realistic
leader responds to the facts. This is incorporated in the formula
statement: that realism means to have no illusions.

Ethics: The Strategy and the Tactics

Ethics, as a dominant leadership dimension, or strategy, means
primarily that people matter to you. You reach out to them.
Ethics means that morality and integrity are really important to
you. You treasure your character because you *are* your character.
Ethics also means that you know the power of love and that you
act on that wisdom. Ethics means, furthermore, that you appreciate the personal enrichment that comes from being of service.
The New Testament is not short on this wisdom: "Whosoever
would be great among you must be your servant" (Matthew
20:26). Ethics means that you can be and are interested in seeing
the world from another person's point of view. Ethics means
mentoring: you know that, as a boss, you have the responsibility
to develop, train, and make your subordinates more marketable.
As a subordinate, you have an obligation to train your bosses as
well. Ethics means that you are conscious of the central role that
values play in making a business profitable. Ethics means that
you are now mature enough to have stepped off your adolescent
"ego trip." Power is no longer an end in itself, but a means to do

good. Ethics means that you understand the depth of a human being—you understand others as well as yourself. Ethics requires respect for the study of the human feelings and relationships you find in literature, the arts, and all the other sensitive descriptions that plumb the profound mysteries of the human heart.

Ethics means having the wisdom to be authentic—that is, yourself—in human relationships. In fact, ethics is close to wisdom, and the latter notion also covers many of the meanings implied in the use of the concept of ethics as a dominant leadership strategy. Ethics as a form of wisdom means that you are experienced in the ways of this world and that you are exceptionally sensitive to all human issues. Wisdom means that you have lived enough to know what pleases and what hurts, and that your compassion for how people struggle to solve the problem of existence ranges over the full spectrum of human frailties.

Plato reminds us that leadership is the combination of power and wisdom—that without wisdom, power is tyrannical; that without power, wisdom is vacuous. Greatness in ethics means also that you pursue your inner health, the soul's fulfillment, which transcends what most of us deem possible. Simply stated, and by way of a formula definition, ethics, as a dominant strategy for leadership, means *service*.

In business and the professions, the term *ethics* often refers to quality in products, services, customer contact, and management. The four supporting tactics, or resources, in order of their increasing depth and leverage, are as follows:

1. Ethics means teamwork, understanding that effective leadership involves accomplishing tasks through people working together. It means loyalty to task forces or ad hoc teams (that is, it refers to the concept of flexible teams). This tactic exists at the professional level. This skill is the critical success factor in the dimension, or strategy, of ethics.
2. Ethics is meaning. There must be meaning in your work, and there must be meaning in the work you create for others. Meaningful work means interesting work. Meaning

is also making a commitment, finding a loyalty that gives significance and worth to your existence. In life, it is necessary to find something worthy to which one can make an unconditional commitment. The search for meaning is to reach that human profundity without which a leader lacks credibility and cannot hope to earn the loyalty of his or her people. This tactic is a resource that exists at the social level. The question of the meaning of life, although of course fully relevant here, applies even more specifically to greatness itself, the very center of the Leadership Diamond model.

3. Ethics is also, and centrally, love. Love means service, mentoring, seeing the world from others' points of view, making others successful. It means compassion. Love also means validation. Love is two selves entering a single, and common, world. In love, one self witnesses and mirrors another self. Such a noble virtue must be expressed also in the workplace. This tactic exists at the psychological level, at the level of feeling. To love is to care. If others suffer, so do you. You cannot help yourself, since concern for others springs from the very marrow of your bones. Love is closely related to communication. Strictly speaking, communication means accurate data transmittal. But at this psychological level, communication means in-depth human contact. It means understanding, with sensitivity and compassion, the emotional needs of another person. Love, also, is a matter of commitment, of loyalty, and of attachment. Betrayals of these promises are always painful.

4. Ethics means integrity, morality, and principle. It is adherence to core values. In particular, to be ethical is to understand the nobility of the Socratic ethical message— that the moral person is motivated by what is right, and not by what feels good. This tactic exists at the philosophical level, at the level of principle. Perhaps more than any other virtue, the ability to be ethical, the perception that values have a claim on you, distinguishes the human from the nonhuman, persons from animals. An unfailing mark of ethical leaders is their attitude toward promises. Credible leaders remember their promises, keep them, and expect the same

of others. In sum, and stated informally, an ethical leader is sensitive to people. That insight becomes part of the formula statement: that ethics means service.

Courage: The Strategy and the Tactics

Courage, as a dominant strategy, or dimension, for acquiring the leadership mind, is the willingness to risk. Security, as the stoic philosophers told us, lies only in your courage and your character, not in dubious guarantees from the world of business and of government, not even in your private life. The courageous leadership mind understands that you cannot live life without courage. And the leader knows that courage does not avoid anxiety and guilt but uses them constructively.

To lead is to act. To have courage is to take charge, first of one's own life, for the true hero is not the person who conquers others but the one who conquers himself or herself. Then you are ready to take charge of organizations.

Specifically and formally, in Leadership Diamond theory, courage means *to act with sustained initiative*. This is the formula statement. Use it to remember your courage and apply it. This strategy leads to four supporting tactics, or resources:

1. Aggressive education and management of your markets means stretching markets, not merely understanding and responding to them. It means designing and introducing leadership products. It means *product advocacy*, product championship. Whatever you offer, that is your product. To make a commitment to one product over another is also to take a *risk*—the risk of a necessary solution to your need to survive in the business. This tactic occurs on the professional level.

2. Courage is the ability to exhibit personal autonomy and independence of thought, to take the initiative, to be a self-starter. Courage means that you are willing to stand alone. As a mature leader, you freely choose your identity. You define yourself. You "invent" who you are. You are responsible for who you are, regardless of your origins—your par-

ents, your education, your ethnicity. You freely accept your
origins, or reject them, or modify them, or supersede them.
This tactic occurs at the social level. The leader often is
painfully alone, necessarily distant, for the leader knows
that certain responsibilities can never be delegated: being a
parent, a spouse, caring for your health, your money, and
ultimately your organization. In brief, you cannot delegate
being a leader. If you do delegate the undelegatable, you will
live to regret it. Companies are sometimes run by powerful
consultants. No CEO can allow such delegation, tempting as
it may be, for that also, as when someone else takes over in
private life, invariably ends in disaster.

3. Courage is the free decision to tolerate maximum amounts
   of anxiety, to manage your anxiety constructively, to understand that being anxious is what it feels like to grow. To
   understand anxiety is to have touched the heart of courage.
   The fact that anxiety is the natural condition of human
   beings, rather than a pathological aberration, is the pivot of
   Leadership Diamond theory. This so-called tactic represents the psychological or feeling level of courage.

4. Courage requires a clear comprehension of the fundamental and difficult philosophic concept of free will. You are "a
   freedom." Your nature is to choose, always and in all circumstances. You are never free *not* to choose. Freedom is a fact,
   although not a scientific one. The pervasiveness of freedom
   in your soul is a "philosophic fact"—that is, a subjective
   reality, subjectively confirmed. When it comes to human
   freedom, that is the only confirmation possible. This tactic
   therefore occurs at the deepest, the philosophic, level. Your
   freedom is a resource that exists in the kernel of your soul.

Courage, like freedom, is the decision also for energy, the
decision to be positive and enthusiastic, the decision not to be
depressed, the choice to live with greatness. It is also the discovery of centeredness, the still point in your core that is the source
of peace and thus of self-confidence and mature strength.

Leadership is the use of power. But power, to be ethical,
must never be abused. To ensure that, one rule cannot be

broken: power is to be used only for the benefit of others, never for yourself. That is the essential generosity and self-sacrifice of the leader. In the modern organization, the reality of power must be integrated with the need for teamwork. After years in power, one CEO was asked what the secret of his success was. "I learned to share my power with my people, and they learned to share it among themselves," was his profound reply.

Power is like a globe. Some CEOs hold on to it exclusively; then there can be no teamwork. Others, however, split the globe of power. Half they keep, and the rest they give to their senior officers. The currency in which the senior officers pay for the power is teamwork. If the CEO gives power and does not get teamwork in return, then he or she has been cheated, exploited. Conversely, if the CEO, not having given away any power, receives loyalty and teamwork from subordinates, then the senior officers are the ones who have been cheated and exploited.

Transferring power is also transferring responsibility and accountability, a point often overlooked. Accountability without power is as empty as power without accountability. When a subordinate is held accountable but does not have the authority to implement decisions, that is as ridiculous as a corporate officer's having power but not feeling personally responsible for the success of the organization. These are some of the systemic and psychodynamic problems that characteristically arise when the question of teamwork is posed.

To sum it all up, you know that to choose energy is to be always action-oriented. The authentic leader knows how to act. Likewise, the one word that summarizes initiative is *action*. The leader acts and does so at all times. To be action-oriented is to be physical and extroverted—the opposite of being introverted and reflective.

In short, the courageous leader claims the power, at all times, to initiate, act, and risk. This summary is incorporated into the formula statement: that courage means acting with sustained initiative. This skill, which is the tactic of will power, is the fourth critical success factor, the others being systemic and strategic thinking, survival, and teamwork.

Will power means taking full personal responsibility for a

specific state of affairs, holding oneself fully accountable for the consequences of one's actions. This critical success factor, like survival under reality, is the harsh dimension of leadership. Moreover, what immediately characterizes persons as leaders is that, in the midst of ambiguity, they nevertheless know what the problem is; they do not need anyone to tell them. They know how to solve it and need not be instructed. They have the resolve to do so and need not be externally motivated. This is action. This is initiative.

Leaders are not dismayed by obstacles, for they know that in successful business and politics one finds nothing but obstacles and frustrations. Their joy comes from confronting these obstacles and wrestling with them to a winning conclusion. The satisfaction is in the challenge, for challenges energize: they are like a brisk walk in fresh air.

It should be clear that to have courage is to act with sustained initiative, an initiative that never stops. An informal statement of this tactic is that a courageous leader always claims the power to initiate, act, and risk.

Strategy Is Not Enough

The strategic side of leadership, as usually conceived—the abstract and rational analysis of corporate direction, especially in its larger financial aspects, and which, of course, is one element of authentic leadership—is not enough. It is on the personal side of leadership—in the sense of greatness and inspiration, focus on people, their meanings, their souls and hearts, their destinies—that the next breakthrough in business will occur.

Strategic buyouts, leveraged buyouts, financial wheeling and dealing, mergers, acquisitions, divestiture, debt restructuring—all these strategies may improve Western business by making it meaner and leaner. But the true future, after all the strategies have been exhausted, is the human factor, the core of the person. That is why business exists: the person is the blood that fuels the business. And it is people who in the end will make, or undo, the business. This is the personal, not the strategic, side of leadership (see Figure 4.1).

Figure 4.1. Leadership Matrix (1).

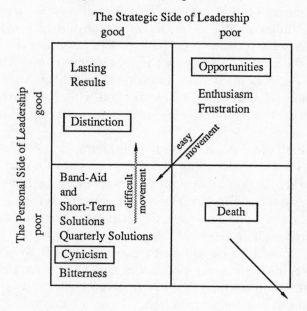

Entrepreneurial businesses often start with high leadership and questionable strategy. Management and investors soon find out. They presently acquire better strategy. Sometimes it is purchased through consulting firms; sometimes a better strategic planner is employed. Sometimes there is a change in the executive suite. This process may be difficult, but it is manageable. Regrettably, in the process of improving strategy, the personal side of leadership is often neglected. Many CEOs do not have time for the personal side of leadership, even to spend informal hours with their people, or they do not understand its overwhelming importance, or they painfully lack the capacity. And CEOs frequently feel guilty of neglect that they perceive as unavoidable. As strategies improve (unfortunately, at the expense of the personal side of leadership), the company discovers, to its dismay, that its culture does not adequately support these strategies. An enormous amount of waste, in the sense of irrelevant and unproductive work, takes place. The bureaucracy has taken over.

Moving the company now, however, up from good strategic but poor personal leadership is a staggering undertaking. From the perspective of gaining competitive advantage and survival itself, however, such uplifting absolutely must be done. Part of it can be accomplished through consultants—the part that empowers people. Consultants can help employees upgrade their potential. But sponsorship from the top, commitment from above, and exemplary behavior on the part of senior management can be achieved only by the designated executives themselves. The challenge to empowerment can be delegated, but inspiration from above cannot.

A recent poll showed that, in response to the question *Compared with ten years ago, are companies today more or less loyal to their employees?*, 25 percent of respondents said "more," but 57 percent said "less," and in response to the question *Compared with ten years ago, are employees today more or less loyal to their companies?*, the answer was a depressing 22 percent "more" and 63 percent "less." Thus, "all that leanness and meanness has left companies more profitable, but management experts fear that in the process, business may have sown the seeds of a more enduring and costly problem: company loyalty is dying. . . . Companies are just beginning to appreciate the damage that these changes can do to morale and productivity" (Castro, 1989, pp. 53–54). Kanter and Mirvis (1989, pp. 55–56) write that many managers and professionals "have become 'free agents' in the business world, selling their services to the highest bidder. . . . These cynics believe that only saps and suckers are loyal to their companies today." Meyer and Gustafson (1988, p. 85) quote a letter from an hourly worker to a high school classmate who is a manager: "Knowing that I never had a chance to be anything within the company, the next obvious move was for me to become active in the local union, and I did. I now had a cause . . . to screw the sons of bitches in management that had been too good to recognize me as another human being. . . . I picked on bad management people and good management people. It made no difference." The worker then describes his conversion to the cause of cooperation, after he realized that the animosities were taking the company right down the tubes: "We have to truly change if we are to survive. We have to care about the stockholders. We have to care about the people we represent. But most important, management people and workers have to care about each other" (from review in the *Wall Street Journal*, Sept. 20, 1989). Rarely has the case for the personal side of leadership, in the total context of a company's productivity, been stated more clearly.

Generalizing now, we can see that the dimensions of the Leadership Diamond are well illustrated in observations about Napoleon: the spacious mind, holding several ideas and feelings simultaneously; the all-encompassing visionary time frame; the simultaneous use of the strategies of vision and of reality—the visionary strategic and systemic patterns, and the minute details at one and the same time; and leading as teaching, which in turn is releasing energy, empowering. Nanus (1989, p. 72) quotes Napoleon's contemporary biographer, Louis Madelin: "He would deal with three or four alternatives at the same time and endeavor to conjure up every possible eventuality—preferably the worst. This foresight, the fruit of meditation, generally enabled him to be ready for any setback; nothing ever took him by surprise. . . . His vision . . . was capable of both breadth and depth. Perhaps the most astonishing characteristic of his intellect was the combination of idealism and realism which enabled him to face the most exalted visions at the same time as the most insignificant realities. And indeed, he was in a sense a visionary, a dreamer of dreams." Napoleon himself has been quoted as saying, "The art of choosing men is not nearly as difficult as the art of enabling those one has chosen to attain their full worth."

Positioning Philosophy in Business. We are now ready to locate, formally and within the complexity of the marketplace, the specific role of philosophy. There are four distinct areas of business: world, strategy, culture, and the individual leadership mind (see Figure 4.2). *World* is the global political and economic situation—historical and market forces governing the world within which every enterprise must operate. *Strategy* is a company's response to that world situation. Strategy is how businesses survive in the real world. Strategy is essential. A com-

Figure 4.2. The Areas of Leadership.

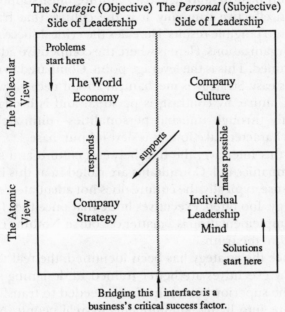

The *Strategic* (Objective) The *Personal* (Subjective)
Side of Leadership Side of Leadership

The Molecular View

The Atomic View

Problems
start here

The World
Economy

Company
Culture

responds

supports

makes possible

Company
Strategy

Individual
Leadership
Mind

Solutions
start here

Bridging this | interface is a
business's critical success factor.

Do not use objective measures to manage the
subjective side, just as you would not use
subjective methods to manage the objective side.

pany's success rests heavily on the brilliance of its strategic market response, and good strategists receive the highest pay.

These two areas of business, the practical world and the company's reaction to it, are "objective" phenomena. They comprise the *strategic side of leadership*. The proper logic (or language) with which to address these two areas is *objectivity*: precision, mathematics, science, and analysis. This appears to be what is emphasized in most business schools.

The third area is *culture*. It is the intangible that defines what people feel and how they behave. Culture means loyalty and commitment to the organization—how much of themselves people are willing to give. Culture consists of unspoken expectations and invisible contracts, but it packs enormous emotional power, both positive and negative. Culture must support strategy. In an effective company, it is the culture that translates strategy into tangible results. Here lies the critical success factor in most organizations. Here is where the competitive advantage is to be gained. This is the leverage point. Compared to culture, strategy is easy. Strategy is mechanical and, if necessary, can be bought. Culture, by contrast, is personal and is brought into being only through unusual personalities—ultimately, only through character. Like love, it is beyond purchase.

In this interface, the link between culture and strategy, many companies fail. Consultants are called in at this intersection, because, typically, the culture does not adequately support the strategy. Too often, executives hope that once they have the strategy, implementation is a matter of course. Nothing could be farther from the truth.

Once the strategy has been identified, the real work begins. Many executives are better trained in designing strategy than in the superior human qualities needed to transform abstract plans into living commitments by real people. Not that executives are limited people; it is a matter of expectations and training. It is how business traditionally has been run, and here we are dealing with breakthroughs, with breaking new ground, with paradigm shifts. These two tasks, rooted in the subjective and objective sides, respectively, are different not only in degree but in kind.

We come now to the fourth area: the quality of the *individual leadership mind.* Culture is made possible through a critical mass of individuals who think and act as leaders—individual executives with leadership minds. Only to the extent that individual managers choose to make this personal transformative decision to the leadership mind can a company expect to be truly competitive in the tough years ahead.

The opportunities are unprecedented, but so are the difficulties, for competition is more intense than ever. The critical success factor is individual leadership development, the quality of a company's leadership minds. Authentic individuals, mature and committed, will make possible the kind of culture

capable of supporting the business objectives of the organization. This subjective side, culture and the individual leadership
mind, comprises the personal side of leadership.

The Two Realms. Culture is different from strategy. Whereas a
company's strategic response belongs to the strategic side of
leadership, its culture is part of the personal side of leadership.
Here, we use the logic of subjectivity.

The world is divided into two realms, objectivity and
subjectivity. Both contain infinite space—there is outer space,
and there is inner space. While similar in many respects, these
two worlds have their own languages and logics. The thinking
and the methodology for each is different. Outer space requires
science; inner space, intuition. The outer world needs measurement; the inner world, poetry. The interface between the two, the
connecting channel, is your own body. Only through it can the
inner world reach out and the outer world penetrate the inner
realm. (That is the metaphysical significance of your body.)
Techniques for strategies that manage the world economy are of
a different order of being from approaches effective with
culture and individuals.

These statements may sound odd. We do not usually think
in these terms. But they are profoundly true and are the key to
any deeper look into leadership. To understand this difference
is to unlock your mind's lost leadership powers.

Strictly speaking, to have a "strategy" for culture is to
perpetrate a "category mistake"—to use the language of objectivity for subjective phenomena—and that is no more appropriate than to use the language of subjectivity to cope with objective phenomena. In brief, scientific love is as irrelevant as poetic
engineering, yet it is amazing how many executives are encouraged to use objective techniques to manage subjective states.
Courage and initiative, creativity and caring—these are not the
strategic side of leadership. On the contrary, they exemplify the
personal side.

True leadership, of course, means addressing all four
areas. Nothing can be left out. Philosophy, however, can help the
subjective side cope better with the objective areas. The precise

focus of Leadership Diamond theory is to understand and develop, mostly by challenging and empowering, *the individual leadership mind*. That is where it all begins. Effectiveness with culture, strategy, and world all start with the individual. Here you have the greatest leverage. Achieving results in this manner is truly working "smarter," not harder. Such is the way in which philosophy can best be positioned in business.

The reader may be puzzled about why the words *strategy* and *tactics* are used here to discuss the personal side of leadership, and perhaps that is not ideal terminology. Nevertheless, it is felt strongly that the theory must keep alive the business flavor, the organizational language. Using these words bridges the gap between the objective and the subjective realms, a connection that is the critical success factor for the effective organization. As suggested earlier, in Leadership Diamond theory *strategies* are also the *dimensions* of the leadership mind, and *tactics* are also the *resources* of the leadership mind.

A distinction is sometimes made between the different meanings of truth in the civilizations of Athens and Jerusalem, the two sources of Western thought. Athens defined truth as a universal theory. Jerusalem defined truth as an individual courageous decision. Truth for Athens lies in a scientific proposition. But truth for Jerusalem, exemplified perhaps most dramatically by the life and death of Jesus (although Judaism and Islam have a central stake there, too), lies in risking, to the death, a personal decision about what this world is, what right and wrong are, and how a human being is to live—and we are given only one chance.

In psychiatry, when patients are confronted with important but difficult life choices, what works is not the objective approach of Athens (that is, theories of personality) but rather the subjective challenge of Jerusalem. It is the personal commitment of the therapist to the patient, and the willingness of the patient to suffer courageously through the anxiety of making choices, that brings success. Rollo May has put it well: the goal of psychotherapy is not to make people happy or healthy but to set them free. Herein lies the difference between the strategic and

Figure 4.3. The Two Sides of Leadership.

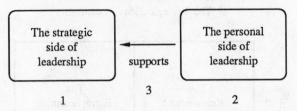

personal sides of leadership. If you want to be competitive in your business, then you need to make sure that you have managers who fully understand, live, and teach this personal side of leadership. Business problems may start with general theories about the world, but the answers are first found in individual decisions of leadership minds. To get results, that is where you must place your energy.

The Leadership Diamond methodology is devoted to understanding and teaching the personal side of leadership. Its goal is to train the individual leadership mind. Results are measured by the business objectives achieved. A simpler way to see this is to look at Figure 4.3. A company has three key elements. It has strategy—which means mergers, acquisitions, alliances, products, positioning, organizational charts, future scenarios, and so forth. The personal side means loyalty, culture, commitment, sacrifice, morale, enthusiasm, energy, joy, innovation, initiative, and courage. The third element, perhaps most important of all, is the degree to which the culture supports the business objectives. Here lies the critical success factor for achieving the sustained competitive advantage. This is where the work usually needs to be done. This is the frequently neglected area. It is therefore also the best niche for promoting progress in a company—and that requires leadership.

Look at Figure 4.4. Companies can be classified according to their leadership competence. The average problem with the relatively successful company is the lack of cultural support for business objectives. Any step taken to strengthen that connection in a company—a task requiring special skills—is perhaps the greatest possible return on investment.

Figure 4.4. Leadership Matrix (2).

The Strategic Side of Leadership

	+	−
+ (The Personal Side of Leadership)	The Reinvented Corporation	The Entrepreneurial Corporation
−	The Fortune 1000 Corporation	The Bankrupt or Takeover-Target Corporation

If to lead with greatness is really to teach how to lead, to empower, then what can we do to become leaders with greatness? This will be the subject as we examine each of the dominant leadership strategies or dimensions in the next five chapters.

5

Vision: Thinking Big and New

As we have seen, each of the dominant leadership strategies is amplified and supported by four tactics, each one of which in turn consists of many elements. Together, these elements draw an informal portrait of each strategy, to help you diagnose and improve your leadership skills.

Each chapter on the strategies concludes with a number of practical applications. There is, for example, reference to the sense of time at the end of the vision chapter, to sales at the end of the reality chapter, to team at the end of the ethics chapter, and to democracy at the end of the courage chapter. There are other applications as well.

Elements of the Tactics

Specifically, and for the sake of amplification, what are the leadership elements of vision?

Abstract Reasoning and Analysis. This is what you find in intelligence tests. It is logical intelligence, which, after money, is the most widely used measure of success in our society. College and university admissions, job recruitment, promotions, and the like depend heavily on one's performance on the kind of intelligence tests with which everyone is familiar. Some test questions are essentially puzzles. To make sure that the mind stays in shape, it is interesting to stretch it periodically with such puzzles. Here are a few examples (see the end of this chapter for the answers; questions 2–5 were suggested by Sternberg, 1988):

1. On Monday, a scout climbs a mountain. He starts at approximately 6 A.M. and reaches the top by evening. He makes his camp on the mountain top and returns by the same path early the next day, Tuesday. He arrives at his starting point by about noon, for going downhill is easier than uphill. Is there on the path any one single spot that he would have reached at exactly the same time on both Monday and Tuesday? (yes or no)
2. The Russian calendar does not show Washington's birthday. Does it show the Fourth of July?
3. A bottle of wine costs $12. The wine costs $10 more than the bottle. How much does the bottle cost?
4. Can you plant 10 trees in 5 rows of four trees each?
5. How can two men play five games of chess and each win the same number of games, without any ties?

Scholastic Aptitude Test (SAT) questions measure abstract reasoning and analysis. Sample questions are always good practice for the leadership mind as it endeavors to strengthen its capacity for visioning. Try these (taken from Gruber, 1990):

1. ROBBERY : THIEF as
   (a) diamond : vault
   (b) crime : prison
   (c) hostage : kidnapper
   (d) capture : convict
   (e) forgery : counterfeiter
2. CLOCK : TIME as
   (a) minute : hour
   (b) dimension : space
   (c) distance : meter
   (d) thermometer : temperature
   (e) gravity : weight
3. The opposite of OSTENTATIOUS is
   (a) lazy
   (b) motionless
   (c) contented
   (d) ambitious
   (e) modest
4. The opposite of ASSIDUOUSLY is
   (a) incorrectly
   (b) brilliantly
   (c) stupidly
   (d) heedlessly
   (e) willingly

As a component of abstract reasoning and analysis, visionary intelligence is strong on *gestalt completion*. There are pictures that are indecipherable—seemingly amorphous dark blotches against a white background—until a sudden perspectival leap reveals a person, an animal, or some other figure. You have also seen the sort of ambiguous picture that changes, if you find the right (almost indescribable) shift in your perception, from being one figure to being another altogether. One cube can be seen in two ways, if we know how to shift our point of view. In parallel fashion, the leap from seeing or thinking to *reflecting on* seeing or on thinking is equally dramatic, probably even more radical.

Systemic and Strategic Thinking. Let us take a look at *strategic intelligence* and *systems thinking*, as a style in which the mind thinks. This is the critical success factor of the strategy of vision. For example, to think big is to see your world from a satellite—to be like Martians arriving on Earth for the first time. It is, first, to fly by helicopter over a medieval city and see all houses clustered around the big church, and not a little church perched among the tall skyscrapers that are today's banks and corporations. It is, second, to fly to the world a hundred years from now, a thousand. What do you see? You can get a possible glimpse by looking back into history and seeing how things have changed. Let your mind wander, and reason into what lies ahead and what you can do to bring that about—better, bigger, and new.

Systemic thinking, coupled with abstract reasoning and analysis, gets at assumptions. Always *examine the assumptions* behind your actions. Be sensitive to the unconscious, the social, the ethnic, and the economic forces that silently lead you and that may prevent you from seeing what might have been. We find suppressed assumptions in jokes, for a good joke catches you making assumptions that you did not know you were making.

To have vision is also to have developed strategic intelligence and systems thinking. These skills or mindsets are the trainable ability to digest large portions of information at once, as in speed reading, and quickly create images of how they might be integrated and systematized. It is to perceive large trends and recognize (or invent) their interconnections. A highly developed strategic intelligence is as rare as it is in demand. The more effectively you train yourself in that skill, the more dramatic will be your success and your organization's.

Your reality is like a large mosaic. The tiles can be arranged and rearranged in many ways. Reality is like a set of blocks, like modular furniture and movable walls in modern offices. Reality, as perceived, consists of sets of modular tasks. These can be organized into many different arrangements. The strategic mind, like a good chess player, can imagine and anticipate many moves because of the high-level perspective from which the vision-centered leadership mind thinks.

Strategic intelligence, like systems thinking, takes a fluid reality and reperceives it as cut into units, or congealed into solids; or it reconceptualizes perceived reality into a set of processes. Strategic intelligence then manipulates these units, just as a painter uses individual colors. This procedure is the analytical, logical, conceptual, and scientific way to control the environment. It becomes a pragmatic way to manage change, to achieve mastery over the future.

For training in the strategic-intelligence component of visioning, it is best to seek out examples—in business, economics, politics, and military history, for instance. Since the strategic mind always thinks of new and surprising angles to routines, learning occurs by imitation, by example, by living in a context of strategic intelligences and ceaselessly searching for ways to be like them.

Competent orchestra conductors can encompass, in one glance, an immensely complex score—and play it immediately on the piano. Advanced speed readers can take in a full page (or at least one single paragraph) at a glance—they see not the individual words but one massive statement. A good strategic thinker divides world politics, or economics, or history into manageable units and, moving them like chess pieces, creates different scenarios. These valued skills are needed in such diverse concerns as finance, speculation, planning, and production, as well as in getting unstuck emotionally, and so forth. The prerequisite to strategic intelligence is to have enough space in the mind to see a plethora of possibilities from the perspective of an inner satellite.

Systems thinking also means developing new languages. A language organizes experience, and that can be done in innumerable ways. But the organization must always be both coherent and consistent. This means that concept formation corresponds to empirical facts—the concept must be true to what is real. And it must be logically consistent: one cannot assert contradictory propositions. Using systems thinking, therefore, means inventing new categories. For instance, the Australian aboriginal language Dyirbal has a category, *balan*, that includes, in one image, women, fire, and dangerous things (Lakoff, 1987).

Language creation is a breakthrough achievement of the visionary mind. It is a skill that can be encouraged and developed. It is also the joy of the mind. Language is power. It suggests new avenues for investigations. It is control over nature. It is adaptation to circumstances. It is survival. It is mastery over destiny.

Systems thinking is the ability to use language to create new realities. The word *systems* itself makes you aware of the importance of connections to which you may have paid no attention in earlier times. The word *process* suggests that we have been focusing on things—that is, on isolated and stationary entities, rather than on flowing continuities. A continuum might never have entered the perceptual field had it not been for the invention of the word *process* and the contrasting of it with *thing*, *stasis*, or *results*.

Intuitively speaking, causation means direct contact in space and time. But new thinking, systems thinking, points out that causation is often not connected, either spatially or temporally. This is truly causation at a distance. What is counterintuitive in one age (the spherical earth, the gravitational pull, relativity) becomes intuitive in the next.

In everyday life, new conceptual systems, new ways of organizing experience, emerge as we force ourselves to ask certain questions: What are some of the fundamental strategies we use to cope with life? What myths do we live by? Which do not work for us, are not serviceable? Are we able to give up strategies that do not work for us? Are we able to discover what they are in the first place?

Basic psychological categories, such as those found in the theories of Freud, Adler, Jung, Horney, Sullivan, and Kohut, are examples of systems and strategic thinking, for they search out and find major patterns of attitudes and behavior. They talk of an Oedipus complex, an inferiority complex, archetypes, the anima and the animus, and so forth. The same holds for the discovery of historical and economic patterns, explained in such theories as those of Hegel, Toynbee, Adam Smith, and Lord Keynes. To have this ability is to be good at systems thinking. These thinkers did, and reading their books makes that clear. The concept of knowledge industries is another such example. The discovery of the concept creates a new organization of the business universe. That mental restructuring increases our power over the business environment. For instance, we can say that knowledge companies are distinguished from industrial companies by four factors (Sveiby and Lloyd, 1988): nonstandardization, creativity, high dependence on individuals, and complex problem solving. Industrial companies may need that kind of help, but that is not their business, nor is it their product. Furthermore, knowledge companies, for their own purposes, translate concepts from industrial companies, so as to increase their management effectiveness. That is how systems thinking and strategic conceptualization provide new controls over business and the professions. The following illustrates the use of systemic and strategic intelligence (Sveiby and Lloyd, 1988, p. 21):

Industrial company	Knowledge company
Revenues, flow of goods	Information
Machine	Human being
Capital, fixed assets	Knowledge
Maintenance	Education
Investment	Recruitment

Disinvestment	Departure
Production	Data production
Raw material	Time

Revenues, in an industrial company, become information in a knowledge company. The machine in an industrial company is replaced by a human being in a knowledge company. What an industrial company calls *raw material*, a knowledge company calls *time*. What matters in these transformations is our understanding that, by thinking in this fashion, we create a new world and new power over our environment. That is why it is useful for a realtor to say, "I do not sell homes, I help customers buy them."

Those who have a strategic sense get rewarded handsomely. When strategic and systems thinking is applied to understanding finance, the generous remuneration is obvious. For example, the highest-paid professor in a university may be the business professor who understands strategic finance.

Visioning also means thinking internationally and conceptualizing globally. This is a natural consequence of systems thinking. The whole world is one business, one enterprise, one *integrating* (but not yet integrated) *reality*. Technology got us there and will continue to fuel the journey. Science has kept up with globalization, but human attitudes have not. Until our perception of the world catches up with what technology is doing to it, we will suffer the pains of the irreal and the agonies of being out of phase. Here is a further example of the 15/85 formula, for without new leadership, technology cannot get us out of this painful dilemma.

Since visioning means to *think globally*, always consider the relationship between your own problems and actions and the events in the rest of the world. In your inner mind, see the hustle and the bustle of neighboring communities, competing businesses, other nations. Speaking more narrowly now, one can say that an organization is effective to the degree that each member knows and cares about what others are doing. Employees who say "It's not my area" reveal their business to be poorly managed.

Where is the sense of home, of territoriality, of grounded-ness for the Third Millennium leader? It is in the world, on the full globe, not in any secreted house, hidden valley, lost cave, or uncharted coastline. Where are the students, the school, the university of the Third Millenium teacher? They are in the whole world. The world is the true university, not any one school in particular. Third Millenium therapists will no longer talk only of individual patients but rather of company therapy, university therapy, national therapy, global therapy, whole-earth therapy, and so it is with markets. The whole world is your market, no matter how small your business.

A further aspect of the visionary mind is creative problem solving. It is a characteristic of systemic and strategic thinking. It is the ceaseless focus on what the real issue is in a problematic situation, what the wider context of it is, what you need to do to come out on top in the long run, what questions you ask in order to make a difference. This type of mind will ask, "Who is in charge? What is the right thing to do? What are the implications? Are we adhering to our core values, or are we getting lost in details? What have we ignored, forgotten? We are acting like managers, but how would a statesman deal with this situation? How would a genius with vision act?"

The trademark of this kind of visionary quality is results-oriented speed and efficiency in resolving tough issues. This means not only quick decisions but also the right decisions (as perceived by those affected). But it means even more than that. It means to choose to be the kind of mind that makes quick decisions, to choose to be the kind of intelligence that makes decisions that go to the core and come from the highest possible relevant perspective. The visionary leadership mind knows that time is precious, and, like a top engineering or mathematics student who solves problems speedily, the visionary leader works fast.

There is a results orientation, which is a matter of vision, not only of simple realism. To achieve results, you must strategically envision the total system. Aristotle distinguished between efficient and final causation: the former is the finger that pulls the trigger and propels the bullet, and the latter is the target that caused the sportsman to fire in the first place. Results can be achieved by inverting our ordinary perception of the vector of time, from "I am now *here* and will, in the future, go *there*" to "I am already *there*, I came from *here*, and now I must recall how I did it." You must shift your mindset from plodding efficiency to visionary final causation, and you will live on results rather than hopes. In short, think of the future as *now*, clearly (visualize it while you are in a state of alert relaxation), and you will automatically choose to move toward it. The Metropolitan Life Insurance Company used to advertise "The future is now." That is how leaders think.

It is not subject matter or content that determines whether your thinking is big; it is the way your mind works. You can think big about a pebble, and you can think small about world history. You must also persistently scan your mind for new possibilities, new opportunities, new solutions.

Creativity and the Unconscious. This moves us into the tactic of creativity and the unconscious. Always monitor, review, and assess what you are doing, and ascertain how you could do better and what you could do differently, especially when you think you are doing well. Think in terms of continuous improvement. Think like Thomas Edison: "There is a better way, find it!" *Innovation* is the key capitalistic tool, according to Joseph Schumpeter, the celebrated Moravian-born U.S. economist and sociologist. He combines the breakthrough dimension of the leadership challenge with creativity when he writes that innovation "is that kind of change arising from within the system *which so displaces its equilibrium point that the new one cannot be reached from the old one by infinitesimal steps.* Add successively as many mail coaches as you please, you will never get a railway thereby" (Schumpeter, 1934, p. 64). The visionary leader's mind is intuitively systemic: "Economic and political life are shaped by human beings who have the ability to get things done, to overcome habitual thinking and perceive objective possibilities hidden to others" (Tinbergen, 1951, pp. 59–60). In Japan, constant, continuous, incremental improvement is known as *kaizen*—enhancing the process daily, rather than worrying about specific results.

The relentless concern with outcomes and results—where the mind focuses on ends rather than on means, and where you understand that life does not forgive the person who is not riveted to results and to results only—is as much realism as vision. It must also be considered as a component of the latter strategy. Here the two strategies overlap.

You must expect all you do to be fresh, crisp, exciting, imaginative, creative, new, innovative. In other words, the visioning mind is always conscious of the need to be creative. It always reminds itself that it must be creative; it never descends into sloth. Creativity is too vast a topic to be covered here responsibly. Creativity does involve the unconscious. The unconscious is real, even though it is invisible, and there can be no significant psychology, psychiatry, and psychotherapy without granting this premise. The unconscious is like the body of the soul: it has a life of its own, which nevertheless is you. The unconscious treats you as you treat it. Thus, if you believe in its existence, it will believe in your existence—and take good care of you. If the reverse is true, if your unconscious neglects you, then you may well be involved in an accident or succumb to an illness. Openness to your unconscious is simply a safe wager.

There are many who have little access to their unconscious, or at least for whom that is neither an important project nor a significant factor in how they manage. The following Oracle question is a typical example of this attitude:

> I am used to making quick, logical conclusions relative to work-related issues and approaches. How do I deal with day-to-day frustrations that are generated by others who do not see the same logical conclusions? They continue not understanding what the real approach is or should be.

The writer seems to overlook the fact that people are governed by unconscious motives, not just logical considerations.

The creative process is thought to go through five stages.

These are the steps that people usually perceive as practical actions they can take:

1. *First insight:* This means playing your hunches, following up your intuitions.
2. *Preparation:* Do your homework. Saturate yourself in the problem. Learn everything there is to know about your creativity concern. Saturate the mind with information. Get a very clear picture of what you wish to create. It must be important to you, something to which you are deeply committed.
3. *Incubation:* Trust the unconscious processes. Change your pace. Allow the unconscious to work undisturbed. Have faith in it. A good time for it to work is while you sleep. Tell yourself that you will dream the answer to a question sharply fixed in your mind as you drift into slumber. Be alert to subliminal messages from the unconscious.
4. *Illumination:* Hope that you will get an answer—but your mind must be open and receptive to it. It is claimed that great discoveries in science have been made through the use of this method of harnessing the unconscious for creativity. Examples are Kekule's discovery of the benzene ring, Mendelev's discovery of the periodic table, and Descartes's invention of his famous philosophical, mathematical, and scientific method.
5. *Verification:* Test your hypothesis. The worst that can happen is that it will turn out to have been a false start. You may find that, with modifications, it is a real solution to a problem that was intractable earlier. "Sleeping on it" does seem to make sense.

Creativity (which, in this tactic, is closely allied to the unconscious) can also be enhanced by your following the principle of *inversion:* reverse what you do or think. If you post orders in the morning for your employees, try posting a blank sheet, inviting them to make requests of you for the day. If you live to acquire power, try giving power away. If you find someone disagreeable, think of yourself as disagreeable. If you are shy, think

of someone else as being shy. In this way, you may reawaken the
lost parts of your personality.

   Another way to reach the unconscious is to view life as a
journey, one that is repeated by all generations and has been for
all time. History itself then becomes a precedent for the evolution of the person. You can predict your next stage of personal
development by your knowledge of history. (Here, reference is
more to the collective unconscious than to the personal or
individual unconscious.) Many executives have found this interpretation of their life's journey insightful and stimulating. We
say, in biological evolution, that ontogeny recapitulates phi-
logeny. We repeat the history of the race—both as biological
evolution and as human history, including the history of ideas—
in the journey of our own lives. For example, review for yourself
some of the major and better-known events of history, such as the
discovery of fire, the invention of writing, the exodus from
Egypt, the Crucifixion, the fall of Rome, the Great Plague of the
fourteenth century, the Spanish Inquisition, the invention of
science, the Reformation and the Counterreformation, the invention of printing, the Renaissance, revolutions (American,
French, Russian), the two world wars, the Great Depression and
so on. Then ask yourself which crisis you are going through now.
Which crises have you passed? Which are still to come? And
what does it all mean to you personally? Where do you find
yourself in the journey of your life today? What still lies ahead?
How will you meet it?

   The following case illustrates how decisions are made
unconsciously and how, when we discover that, we receive reas-
surance that the difficult decisions we have made were the right
ones:

> A company we shall here call Constructo is a three-
> man company in France that received a $250 mil-
> lion contract to develop, by remodeling several
> historic buildings, a complex convention center.
> The original buildings were owned by a large insur-
> ance company, and it was this insurance company
> that gave Constructo its massive contract. Con-

structo was responsible for obtaining and supervising whatever was required to complete the job:
hiring the architects and overseeing the drawing
up of plans, carrying out all negotiations with the
authorities, engaging contractors and construction
crews, rebuilding the structures inside and out,
furnishing them, restoring the old art, creating the
desired public image, properly advertising the services of the convention center, and so forth. The
construction itself would take three years. After
that, Constructo would also be responsible for running the convention center. Constructo therefore
also signed a five-year operations contract.

The construction was completed — with em-
inent success, on time, and to much praise from
the press, due partly to Constructo's well-
established and well-deserved reputation as a first-
rate construction-management firm.

Administering the convention center was a
different story. The center had four "legs" to stand
on — restaurants, theaters, a convention hall, and a
hotel. One enormous restaurant was capable of
feeding over a thousand people every evening. Another, open for lunch as well, could serve two hundred people. The several theaters had to be kept
active nightly. It had a large convention hall. Con-
ventions had to be kept coming. And it had a one-
hundred-room hotel. All these buildings were
finished on time, to the highest standards of quality. But operating such a huge establishment was
quite a different and very complicated matter.

Constructo found it impossible to hire managers adequate to all these tasks, nor were the
owners of Constructo smart enough to do the job
alone; they simply did not have the experience.

With great effort, they did find another company, Foodco, that owned one of the most efficient
and experienced restaurant chains in Paris and

other French cities. Constructo could not hire away
any of Foodco's key people, however. Even if the
Constructo owners had succeeded, they would not
have found any hired person who could give them
the commitment and the initiative they needed, or
so they felt.

The only way for Constructo to get experienced management was to create a new company.
That would mean to become equal partners with
Foodco. A partnership would mean loss of control
over the huge project because the partnership
would have to be evenly divided. Constructo would
have to give up the project in order for the project
to succeed, and that was an agonizing decision.
Eventually the decision was made, and the new
partnership was sealed. In this major decision for
both companies, much money was at stake.

Both companies had been run by single, very
dominant personalities. François, the chairman of
Constructo, was a strong leader, a person who com-
manded instant respect. The same could be said of
Jean-Pierre, the CEO of Foodco. Both men were
used to full control, and they were very good.
Needless to say, their relationship as partners
soon became strained. Problems then quickly
mushroomed throughout the newly formed
organization.

The critical decision now before the two men
was this: they had been individual bosses; now, to
grow, they made a fundamental decision—to become a team. The decision created psychological
stress and business controversy. Had they made the
wrong decision? Should they separate, something
that would be not only very difficult to do now but
also dangerous for the future of the business? Or
was there a deeper message? Perhaps the unconscious would offer a clue.

The following analysis, unorthodox as it may

be, appears to have resolved some of the deep-
seated conflicts that were so seriously disrupting
the business. Their unconscious chose for them, as
it were, to *force* on them the next step of growth —
from their intemperate and somewhat self-
indulgent behavior as individualistic leaders to
their functioning as truly integrated and mature
team players rationally oriented toward meeting
organizational business objectives. Teamwork, in
this case, was a higher state of human growth and
maturity than individual indulgence. The two
dominant men, François and Jean-Pierre, had not
merged their businesses because of logic (although
that was in plentiful use but was applied more as
rationalization). They had merged, ultimately, because of instinct. Their unconscious and intuitive
processes somehow told them that this is what they
wanted to do, and the reason for it was growth in
the journey of life, not business calculations. The
soul's growth required that it be forced from isolation to encounter, from aloneness to integration,
from being cut off to "being with," from monarchy
to democracy. Over the months, both men grew to
this, their next level of maturity. They moved from
anger and depression to new heights of satisfaction
and efficiency, and the bottom line reflected it.

The unconscious is the source of creativity, which is particularly well illustrated in the following story.

A company long recognized for being masters of innovation, for keeping new products coming, is 3M. They have been
successful in integrating some of the philosophic principles of
the visionary mind into their daily operations. Here is their
story of creativity (*Business Week*, Apr. 10, 1988, pp. 58, 62):

It was 1922. Minnesota Mining & Manufacturing
inventor Francis G. Okie was dreaming up ways to
boost sales of sandpaper, then the company's pre-

miere product, when a novel thought struck him. Why not sell sandpaper to men as a replacement for razor blades? Why should they risk the nicks of a sharp instrument when they could rub their cheeks smooth instead?

The idea never caught on, of course. The surprise is that Okie, who continued to sand his own face, could champion such a patently wacky scheme and keep his job. But unlike most com-panies then—or now—3M Co. demonstrated a wide tolerance for new ideas, believing that unfet-tered creative thinking would pay off in the end. Indeed, Okie's hits made up for his misses: He developed a waterproof sandpaper that became a staple of the auto industry because it produced a better exterior finish and created less dust than conventional papers. It was 3M's first blockbuster.

The precedent set by this initial idea then became the creative pattern for the future of the company.

Through the decades, 3M has managed to keep its creative spirit alive. The result is a company that spins out new products faster and better than just about anyone. It boasts an impressive catalog of more than 60,000 products, from Post-it notes to heart-lung machines. What's more, 32% of 3M's $10.6 billion in 1988 sales came from products introduced within the past five years. Antistatic videotape, translucent dental braces, synthetic liga-ments for damaged knees, and heavy-duty reflective sheeting for construction-site signs are just a few of the highly profitable new products that contrib-uted to record earnings of $1.5 billion in 1988.

How, in practice, is all of this achieved? What are the leadership behaviors and expectations that are institutionalized in this company?

3M relies on a few simple rules...

Keep divisions small. Division managers must know each staffer's first name. When a division gets too big, perhaps reaching $250 to $300 million in sales, it is split up.

Tolerate failure. By encouraging plenty of experimentation and risk-taking, there are more chances for a new-product hit. The goal: Divisions must derive 25% of sales from products introduced in the past five years. The target may be boosted to 30%.

Motivate the champions. When a 3Mer comes up with a product idea, he or she recruits an action team to develop it. Salaries and promotions are tied to the product's progress. The champion has a chance to someday run his or her own product group or division.

Stay close to the customer. Researchers, marketers, and managers visit with customers and routinely invite them to help brainstorm product ideas.

Share the wealth. Technology, wherever it's developed, belongs to everyone.

Don't kill a project. If an idea can't find a home in one of 3M's divisions, a staffer can devote 15% of his or her time to prove it workable. For those who need seed money, as many as 90 Genesis grants of $50,000 are awarded each year.

Intuition and instinct, nourished by experience and ambition, reflect another component of creative and innovative leadership intelligence. The visioning mind, the intelligence that thinks big, takes many forms, perhaps as many as there are high-level executives and leaders. The visioning mind has sharp intuition and sound instinct based on experience. The experienced, instinctive, intuitive leader stands out from the crowd and survives endless crises because of a trail of successes. Since they have worked in the past, the value of the instincts and the reliability of the intuitions are reinforced. And from the point of view of important business and political decisions, the right intuition means a successful decision. Should we invest $1 billion in developing a new aircraft, or will it suffice to update and improve what we now have? Shall we invite the hostile foreign minister of nation X, or shall we snub that person instead? What are the implications of these actions? Market research, polls, and information about historical precedents, necessary as they are, will add only one more set of data to fill in the details of a complex picture. The final decision belongs to the person with the instincts and intuitions, based only on long experience, that tell what will work and what will not.

How can you cultivate intuition and instinct and encourage experience? Be alert to these qualities in yourself and in others, so that when they appear in you, you recognize them. Strive for these qualities and practice using them. Be conscious of what else occurs, inside the person and in your own environment, when you see a sound decision being based more on experience, instinct, and intuition than on analysis and research. Just as you can imitate physical behavior and create a parallel environment, you can also stimulate a similar inner state into existence. You see others trusting their intuition, and you imitate that yourself. Then you examine the results and learn from them. It is partly a simple matter of practicing. Let us consolidate these ideas by saying that *a visionary leader* is *instinctive, intuitive* and *experienced*, and let us remember that such leaders are not born (although some may develop naturally and with ease, as talented musicians and athletes do) but made. Who makes them? They make themselves. You can turn yourself into this type of leader by the choices and decisions you make over your lifetime.

Experience can be developed only through more experience. The authentic leader always looks out for new experiences. You cannot anticipate exactly what a new experience will teach you (that is precisely why it is new), what your feelings will be, or where the newness will take you; a bachelor does not know the inner feelings of marriage, nor does he (if he has no children) know the emotions of fatherhood. *Leaders grow by accelerating experience.*

Another aspect of the visionary leadership mind is ambition — not the kind that feeds on other people, that takes away in order to get, but the kind that is constructive, helpful, useful, has a certain charm, is worthy of imitation, and endears others to the leader rather than making them envious. There is ambition that offends and ambition that endears. There is ambition that is greed and ambition that serves; the latter is true leadership. The leaders' ambition towers above that of others because through it others can be served — and not because the leader craves riches, which can lead only to isolation from the world.

Ambition is constant. Its source is inexplicable. It is a form of the instinct to survive. It is a manifestation of the life force, an expression of the soul's striving for perfection and transcendence. It is an ongoing dissatisfaction with what is and an insatiable appetite for realizing potentials that, by definition, can never be fulfilled. Persistence in vision is characteristic of the leader. The light of the final goal rarely flickers. Effortlessly, the mind focuses for a lifetime on a single ambition — cloudy at times, perhaps, but clear when found. Ambition keeps people young and energizes society. Look for ambitious people whom you find attractive, and imitate them.

Expanding and Exploring Inner or Subjective Space-Time: Awareness of Your Possibilities. Vision means to be at home in the infinity of inner space and time. There exists a vast expanse of inner space, just as there exists an endlessness of inner time. Mathematicians (through what is known as *a priori knowledge*) have traditionally believed that the *thoughts of inner* space and time are also the *laws of outer* space and time — that is, of the universe (the laws of causation, mathematics, logic, and geometry).

Meditation may help you achieve access to and control over inner space and inner time. To concentrate on them is also to expand your mind. As you get a sense of the infinity of your inner world, your mind will also expand its creative and innovative potential. Train your binoculars on your inner landscapes and your telescope on your subjective galaxies.

Roger W. Sperry, Nobel laureate in physics, writes, "Current concepts of the mind-brain relationship involve a direct break with the long-established materialist and behavorist doctrine that has dominated neuroscience for many decades. Instead of renouncing or ignoring consciousness, the new interpretations give full recognition to the primacy of inner conscious awareness as a causal reality." In fact, the winners of the 1972 Nobel Prize in physics and chemistry, when asked what awards would be given in their fields in the year 2000, replied, "The study of man's consciousness. This is the new frontier" (Sperry, 1987, p. 6).

Go back to the puzzles and the SAT questions at the beginning of this chapter. To get the answers requires abstract reasoning; but to understand the processes by which your mind reaches those conclusions is quite another matter. Abstract reasoning means being involved mostly in thinking, engaged with the objects of thought. But to understand how your mind works as it tries to arrive at the answers means detaching yourself from the thinking process itself. First you think as we normally think, but then you also think about how you think. You think, and you also reflect on your thinking. You do both at the same time. That requires expertise in the last tactic of visioning—namely, the ability to exist within the infinite space-time expanse of your mind and, from that exalted perspective, review what it is that you do when you think.

Visioning is enhanced by an attitude of *nonattachment*, of being detached from emotional identification with the issues at hand. Nonattachment, as a philosophy of life, has been both a stoic practice and a key step in Eastern philosophies. Nonattachment is a fundamental skill required for the creation of visionary leadership intelligence.

Visioning is the ability to shift from the *natural* to the *reflective* attitude, from *being* who you are to *reflecting on* who you are, from acting out who you are to observing and evaluating who you are, from seeing the world from within your subjective ego to seeing yourself objectively within the world, from acting to examining your actions.

Visioning means to reach the next-highest level of perspective. When you view what you do from the next-highest level or point of view (observing yourself enjoying a party, for example, or surveying the life of your city from a satellite), your consciousness itself goes through a fundamental transformation. To know how to precipitate that shift is one of the secrets of breakthrough creativity. Whenever you reach an insoluble problem, try shifting your consciousness from the natural to the reflective attitude, and suddenly you will receive innovative and higher-level solutions.

This higher-level perspective becomes the leadership key to solving otherwise intractable problems. Whenever you feel stuck in your leadership concerns ("Why is this group not a team?" "Why do some people refuse to follow orders?" "Why can some people not accept a majority decision with which they disagree?"), raising your consciousness to its next level of perspective can promise you solutions. Some questions cannot be settled with ordinary logic. They require a metalogic: a logic *about* the logic you are using. You then discover deeper personal psychodynamics and invisible systemic social forces. In making a conscious shift from agent to observer, your attitudes and intentions change, and what was once a problem no longer exists as such. Speaking literally, you may not solve anything, but the problem itself dissolves. It turns out to have been a pseudoproblem, or infantilistic behavior. The principle of the higher perspective frees the mind for its next action. The higher the perspective, the easier the solution; the narrower the perspective, the tougher it is.

(There are two chapters on this fourth vision tactic in my book *The Heart of Business*, where this type of thinking is called transcendental intelligence.)

Vision as strategy also means transcendence. You see only a cloud, but you know that behind it is Mont Blanc. Your mind sees into the farthest distance. Reflexivity means to look *at* yourself. Transcendence (or self-transcendence) means to look *beyond* yourself—beyond what your eye commonly sees, past the horizon, and through the fog. The visionary leadership mind always looks farther than the eye can see and asks what is beyond the horizon, above the clouds, under the waters, inside the mountains, within the atom, inside the black hole.

Critical to visioning is always to be proactive. The leadership mind anticipates what will occur; it is always ahead of its time and always forward of its space. Reactive thinking and behavior may be necessary, for life is full of crises. But the mind that is responsive exclusively to environmental stimuli will also have lost its integrity. (As one manager said, "If I did not have a crisis when I went to work, I would not know what to do!")

Your mind is always split between existing in the here-and-now and existing elsewhere in space and time, on the globe and in the future. You lead a dual existence—you are fully here, engaged, involved, and you are also not fully here; you are distant, objective, observant. The leadership mind holds such contradictions within it.

Finally, visioning is greatly improved with stimulation. Welcome and seek stimulation. Do not think, even for a moment, that you have the answers, or that you need not learn from others. Socrates' great wisdom was that he acknowledged his ignorance. And choosing to make these types of decisions—leadership decisions, visionary decisions—is a mindset that can be found, described, imitated, and practiced until it becomes habit. That is one further and teachable aspect of leadership intelligence.

You can set up for yourself a series of exercises, activities, experiences, commitments, and processes to practice each one of these leadership tasks. You must treat these mind-control protocols as you would any other set of exercises for skill building, whether for swimming or solving quadratic equations, playing tennis or performing on the oboe.

Remember vision when you think of George Bernard Shaw, to whom is attributed the following: "You see things; and you say, 'why?' But I dream things that never were; and say, 'why not?'"

Time

"All my possessions for a moment of time."
— Queen Elizabeth I, with her dying breath, 1603

In 1967, testimony before a Senate subcommittee indicated that by 1985 people could be working just twenty-two hours a week, or twenty-seven weeks a year, or that they could retire at thirty-eight. That would leave only the great challenge of finding a way to enjoy all that leisure. In fact, however, "according to a Harris survey, the amount of leisure time enjoyed by the average American has shrunk 37% since 1973. Over the same period, the average work week, including commuting, has jumped from under 41 hours to nearly 47 hours. In some professions, predictably law, finance and medicine, the demands often stretch to 80-plus hours a week. Vacations have shortened to the point where they are frequently no more than long weekends. And the Sabbath is for — what else? — shopping" (Gibbs, 1989, p. 58). Needless to say, for today's executive the concept of time, or the experience of temporality, requires special attention.

Time is included in the last of the four tactics under the dominant leadership strategy of vision. This last tactic or resource is the most philosophical of all the vision tactics. As we explore the subjective sense of time — and to the extent that we understand that subjective time corresponds to objective time — we recognize the practical importance of exploring this concept. The exploration of time expands the mind. This endeavor has been a traditional and major task for philosophy.

Pervasive and inescapable executive complaints are the lack of time and the pressure of time, producing stress, burnout, and illness. Executives rarely feel that they are adequately organized or that they measure up to the demands of their priorities. For persons in positions of responsibility, success and failure in business are in truth success and failure in the mastery of time.

Time management starts with an *understanding* of time. The sense of time is produced by the anticipation of death.

Animals do not feel the pressure of time. They do not have the concept of time, because they do not possess the idea of their own death. Time can be experienced or thought of as an external fact—a reality outside of me, within which I exist, and which limits and constricts me. This kind of time is called clock time or spatialized, mathematical, linear time. The only solution to the pressures of clock time is to fragment it, to set priorities, and to marshal fierce self-discipline. Such effort, although laudable, nevertheless leads to the mechanization of the self, the technocratization of human existence. It logically promotes regimentation and bureaucracy—that is, technical efficiency. That may be necessary, but it is neither living nor human.

The greatest source of time pressure is bureaucracy. Bureaucracy is a disease, a toxin, that infects the modern age. Bureaucracy is the direct result of mass everything: production, communication, marketing, standardization. It is a necessary consequence of size, and the individual must guard against its demoralizing and otherwise destructive effects. Bureaucracy occurs when an organization becomes large and therefore impersonal. It invariably regards its people as objects, things, machines, instruments, tools. In a bureaucracy, people can be replaced by robots and other high-technology devices (with significant improvements in productivity, one might add). Bureaucracy requires that people submit themselves to the needs of the organizational machine. People must regiment and document their lives, both of which activities are seriously anti-ergonomic, for life is to be lived from within, not from the outside. We are life's agents, not its spectators or victims. Every human being demands and deserves personal attention, not mass, standardized, often irrelevant, and always heartless management. To overcome bureaucracy may require radical decisions, sometimes of extraordinary courage, like recognizing it, naming it, removing its causes (size, the concentration of power)—eventually even emigration. A person who lives inside an organization, not inside himself, must surrender his creativity and integrity to the needs of the organization. That means he lives *in* time—a time that is neither himself nor a time that is his, but rather a time that is imposed on him from some external source and alien reality.

Time is also an internal fact: I am time; time is I; time is the very essence of the self. The inward ego is a time-generating organism. This attitude toward time—supported by philosophers from Saint Augustine to Bergson, and from Plato to Kierkegaard and Heidegger—means that a person lives from the inside out. I can never feel pressure from what I am or from who I am, only from what I am not. The solution to time problems lies in exhibiting one's most profound integrity, authenticity, and courage, for time and integrity are one.

Problems with time cannot be resolved at the level at which they are experienced, for they are experienced at the level of being *in* time, and they can be solved only at the deeper and more real level of *being* time itself. That level means being totally true to oneself. This truth about time becomes increasingly apparent as one rises on the ladder of executive responsibility. To the degree that one's life is fully authentic—clearly in tune with what one experiences as one's destiny, manifestly originating from within one's deepest inward source (consistent with the fundamentals of mental health and ethics)—one has no problems with time, for then there is meaning in everything one does, and there is fulfillment in every expenditure of time. One lives life naturally, from the inside out, *as* time (and not, unnaturally, *in* time, from the outside in).

Problems with time are ultimately problems with authenticity (which is also to say that authenticity is the correct experience of time), with being true to one's meanings, with responding to one's existential guilt, and with maintaining a total perspective. It is here, in the character dimension of the human core, that time problems are both formed and solved.

To believe that time problems can really be resolved at the level of being *in* time—through discipline and organization—is, in effect, to manage the destructive impact of bureaucracy on the individual with additional, bureaucratic measures, a traditional "scientific" and "technical" business solution. It is an objective answer to a subjective question, an "outside-in" response to an "inside-out" dilemma.

In practice, to *be* time rather than to live *in* time means to *find your meanings*: What can you do that no one else can (such as fulfilling the expectations of a specific loyalty or relationship, or performing one specific task for which you have superior skills)? Listen to your unconscious, and ask yourself what acts of courage are still required of you before you can die with dignity and honor.

The pressure of time is really the pressure of existential guilt. You feel under stress because you do not yet live fully up to your meanings. As C. G. Jung has wisely said, a psychoneurosis is the suffering of a soul that has not yet found its meaning.

Work, for the average employee, is external to his or her life; therefore, work is experienced as a constraint imposed from outside the self. The self must cope with a medium that, like a foreign protein, is alien to itself—and that is time, for it exists *in* time. Here, the self lives from the outside in.

Note the paradox. You are time. When you live like that, you have no problem. But you think you are inside something else that you *call* time. Then you are in fact outside yourself! No wonder you are then confused and under stress! Leisure, pleasure, entertainment, fun, fulfillment, ecstasy, joy are *internal* to life. They arise from the seat of the self. Here, the self *is* time and lives from the inside out. Bureaucracy can thrive only in the condition of one's being *in* time.

What can you do? Direct your life (and your organization) so as to make work part of your life—part of living from the inside out, part of your inner production of time. Do not separate work from home or leisure. Do not compromise your full self-disclosure. Know your meanings, and commit yourself to them. Existence is not an easy task. It takes a lifetime to come even close to achieving authenticity. But as you move in that direction, your problems with time management will resolve themselves. *This works; nothing else does.* Do not stop organizing your time, but know the difference between a true solution and an anodyne.

You will never be totally true to yourself, but to the degree that you make a commitment in that direction, and to the extent that you approximate that ideal, the world will respond. This means that your health will improve—your physical, spiritual, intellectual, emotional, relational, educational, and financial health. You will attract from your environment the people, systems, and financial support required to fulfill your deepest essence, for what you do is also the most natural thing to do. This new health, springing from within, will express itself in diminished problems with time because life is now your own, and so is time. To accomplish this is the slowly unfolding project of a lifetime. Each day that you embark on this process can feel like a success.

In sum, if you have real problems with time scheduling (problems that lead to "symptoms"), it means that in some fundamental way you do not like your work, that you are not leading your work life (or your life in general) as you deeply need to lead it, and that you are not assuming full and mature responsibility for your own life. Time problems that lead to burnout suggest that a fundamental decision about who you are and how you shall lead your life has not yet been made and is overdue. And that is a decision that takes great courage to face. Unless you address this need for *decision* and for *courage*, your scheduling problem cannot go away.

The Structure of Lived Time. Understanding time *alleviates* problems with time. The first distinction, mentioned earlier, is between clock time and lived time. The former is measured, and its steadiness depends on mechanisms external to the self. The latter is *felt*, experienced, perceived, lived, and thus "real" in the more basic philosophical (specifically, epistemological) sense. *The human-core approach to time management is, first, to know the difference between authentic and inauthentic experiences of time and, second, to achieve control over lived time.*

Control over time is achieved not by what you do but by your decisions about attitudes and perceptions. You are a time-generating organism (time does not exist without your creating it, through your living). You can change your perception of time. To do so will give you the best chance yet to cure your problems with time pressure. Here are various modes of experiencing lived time.

Time in General. Time, when perceived and lived authentically, consists of three dimensions: the lived or experienced *future*, the lived or experienced *past*, and the lived or experienced *present*. We normally live essentially *in* the future and *for* the future. Our inner eye is focused on what lies ahead; our sense of self is "ahead" of ourselves. But that future must be connected intimately with the present, which in turn is the zone of real life, of activity, of action. We use the past as a resource to exist in the present — to orient ourselves and make decisions in the present that will move us into the future.

There are frequent disruptions of these fundamental structures of lived time. As we correct these disturbances, we also correct our lives.

The Future. The White Queen says to Alice in Wonderland, "It is a sorry memory that works only backwards."

When healthy, the future is open, flexible. It is the realm of possibilities. But it can also be structured and predictable, to the extreme of being fixed and rigid. That becomes obsession and compulsion. Or the future can be totally blocked, closed: there is no way to reach it. That is depression. The future can also be empty, bereft of the sense of consequences. We can feel no power over it, no sense of efficacy; the future then is not us, not an extension or projection. We do not live in it and therefore do not feel *responsible* for it, and this is the key.

Another consideration is how the future is related to the present. The future can be connected with the present. It can evolve out of the present, be caused by the present, or it can be disconnected, alienated from the present, perceived as not caused by the present.

The Past. It can be accessible, available, reachable, retrievable, usable, or inaccessible, unknown, unusable, or unused. The past can be experienced as causing the present, as developing into the present, as unfolding into it. It is then characterized by feelings of continuity, causation, and consequences. It provides a sense of history, of journey, and of narrative. The past is valued. If the past is not connected with the present, does not lead into it, it is cut off from it. The past is not valued, and history is of no significance.

The Present. When authentic, the present is experienced as both alertness and as self-disclosure—as anxiety, guilt, freedom, decision. It is the source of action and the zone of courage. Or the present can be experienced as a trance, as sleep, denial, inaction, and cowardice. The present uses the past, with which it is intimately connected, to move toward the future. This is an integrated life. Or the present functions independently of its past and future or is disconnected from either. This is a fragmented life.

Transcendence. There is a final position: the transcendence of time, the experience of and existence in the eternal now (or, more accurately, the eternal here-and-now). It is life outside time. It means seeing time as a phenomenon external to the self. It is a mystical vision.

Velocity. Lived, subjective, or experienced time has a speed. If time passes slowly, it can mean boredom, an unpleasant task, pain, anxiety, or guilt. If it passes at moderate speed, then it may mean satisfaction or indifference. But if time passes quickly, then there may be joy and intense happiness, distraction, entertainment, or absorption—that is, *meaning*.

Unit. The unit of time or the time frame in terms of which we experience or measure lived time can be related to intelligence and to leadership. Up to a point, the unit is connected with self-concept, age, maturity, and the capacity to plan. Typical units are one day, one week, one and six months, and one, three, five, seven, ten, fifteen, twenty, and twenty-five years. You do not merely look twenty-five years ahead, you also see the total twenty-five-year span as one unit. You have a sense of history. Which unit is yours? Can you change it? How would that improve your leadership effectiveness? How would your health improve?

Projection. Related to the unit of time is projection in time. Where do you focus when you think ahead (or just plain think)? Where is the focal point of your existence? In the present? In the past? In the future? At precisely what point? Can you draw a lifeline and mark it with an X, the point on which your consciousness is focused? How would changing that point affect how you lead your life?

There is the immediate future. That covers tomorrow, the schedule of meetings, classes, minor jobs, tasks, assignments, errands, calls. There is the mediate future, which refers typically to such slightly more distant matters as vacations, weddings, graduations, anniversaries, major tasks, or projects. Then there is the distant future, covering such matters as one's financial planning, final educational degree, license, or certificate, final promotion, life's ambition, career planning, and so forth. Finally, there is the terminal future, which refers to the image of being a very old man or woman, being on one's deathbed, being an aging grandparent or great-grandparent, thinking of oneself in a home for the aged or a hospice, and so on. Where are you? What are the implications? What happens if you change the focal point in your sense of time?

In sum, feelings of hope, anxiety, guilt, depression, and confusion are all connected with how you perceive time. As you can change your sense of time, so also will you change your moods.

Communication depends on understanding one's own and another person's sense of time. "We'll start our project in one year." To one person, who may be young, such a wait may be perceived as short (as 2 percent of time before death). To another, who may be older, one year may be a long time (7 percent of time before death). For the second person, therefore, the same amount of time may be experienced as 350 percent more valuable than it is for the first.

In conclusion, we can say that a healthy sense of time is connected with other aspects of authenticity and forces us to deal with them—claiming our freedom, initiating action, insisting on alertness, and maintaining perspective (always seeing the total picture). Such a sound attitude toward time is a precondition for organizing life—organizing it in every sense of the word, and keeping it that way. (A delightful little book on time is Servan-Schreiber's *The Art of Time*, 1988).

How do *you*, as a leader, live the time of your life? T. S. Eliot, in his poem "Little Gidding," expressed well the structural integration of subjective time:

> Time present and time past
> Are both perhaps present in time future,
> And time future contained in time past.

An authentic leader is not only a visionary but also functions in the way a helicopter does. He or she flies high to get the big picture but can quickly zoom down into a specific trouble spot and attend to minuscule details. To that concern we now turn.

Answers to Puzzles

1. Compress the two days into one. If two scouts go in opposite directions on the same day, it is obvious that they will indeed meet along the way. That is the place.
2. Yes. The "Fourth of July" is both an American holiday and a regular calendar date.
3. The bottle costs $1 and the wine is worth $11 ($10 more than the bottle).
4. Yes, as a five-pointed star.
5. By not playing each other.

Answers to SAT Questions

1. e
2. d
3. b
4. d

6

Reality: Having No Illusions

In this chapter, you strengthen the sense of reality, the contact with the facts, the feeling of sinking your teeth into something, an attitude that is, as it should be, intensely cultivated in business. Such is the meaning of reality as a dominant leadership dimension, or strategy. Each tactic contains many elements, some overlapping. Together, they should craft for you a comprehensive mosaic of what it means to be in touch with the real world.

Elements of the Tactics

Meticulous Attention to Practical Details; Attending to the Precise Needs of Your Immediate and End Customers (Use High Technology). Visionaries often have difficulties with practical details. They do not comprehend that the forest is made of trees. Meticulous attention to detail is critical to the success of any enterprise. The owner of an international resort chain may have superb visions of expansion, a comprehensive understanding of the world tourist trade and of international financial markets, but if that person cannot be effective and get results in seeing that maintenance and service are impeccable in every detail— that there are no cigarette butts in the ashtrays and no leaks in the faucets— then a vast investment will sink as it crashes against the rocks of the more professional competition. Quality often can be reduced mostly to attention to detail. Attention to detail means methodical preparation and thorough planning. It

136

means installing the necessary controls. It means dividing up tasks efficiently. It means using resources well and being economical with time.

Another aspect of reality, which lies on the border between the objective assessment of reality and the ability to survive in it, is the bureaucracy that surrounds us. Balzac said that bureaucracy is a giant mechanism operated by pygmies. Concern with details is bureaucratic, but it is precisely such attention to meticulous preparation that ensures quality, and thus success.

The governmental environment is bureaucratic. International relations are bureaucratic. Your own organization, no matter how small, will have its own bureaucracy. Credit cards, insurance, loans, billing, taxes, employment regulations, corporate law, rules governing the use of financial instruments, stocks and bonds, futures, real-estate transactions, and so on, forever, engulf us in inextricable webs of bureaucratic red tape. Bureaucracy is depersonalizing, alienating. It entails treating human beings without feeling, without compassion, without forgiveness, without consideration for their uniqueness or their special personal circumstances. It entails not touching their center. Bureaucracy means elevating rules so high that they became more real than living persons. Surely, the following is bureaucracy uplifted to its pinnacle of glory:

> It will take something more than a nuclear attack to wipe out taxpayers' obligations to the Internal Revenue Service. . . . The new section—titled "National Emergency Operations"—had been added to the manual. . . . Within 30 days of an attack emergency, the agency would expect to resume assessing and collecting taxes. /At that time, the manual states, many employees might find themselves reassigned. . . . "On the premise that the collection of delinquent accounts would be most adversely affected, and in many cases would be impossible in a disaster area, the service will concentrate on the collection of current taxes," the manual says ["Nuclear War Plan by I.R.S.," 1989, p. D16].

Bureaucracy is nevertheless necessary for efficiency's sake. Bureaucracy gets you to work in the morning, provides your lunch, sends your paycheck, pays your medical bills, and sustains your job. Bureaucracy protects the nation from total chaos. It is a reality that you must confront, accept, conquer, understand, appreciate. But it is also a reality that you must never allow to destroy you as a human being, as a soul embodied in flesh and blood.

Extensive Information and Objectivity. Leaders who are realistic are well informed. They thoroughly understand the company, the business, the industry, and the national and international political, social, and economic realities that their organizations confront. Leaders with a highly developed sense of reality keep up with their professions, continuously updating their skills. A leader is intelligently and continuously apprised of the innovations, trends, news, interpretations, and context of all that is germane to his or her executive responsibilities.

Survival clearly requires awareness of the world in which you live and in which you must manifest your leadership effectiveness. You must, therefore, understand the organizational structure—the lines of authority, the demarcations of responsibility, the sense of turf—in your business or professional community.

One particularly important part of the current business bureaucracy is the matrix organization. It is an organization with crisscrossing (intersecting) lines of authority, creating confusion, double loyalties, contradictions, and intense frustration. The matrix organization is often perceived as accountability without authority. It is nevertheless necessary in order to meet the economic realities of today's increasingly competitive world. To cope with the human side of project management requires *matrix intelligence*—a special way of perceiving the contemporary workplace. It requires inordinate patience, diplomacy, endurance, credibility, initiative, and persuasiveness. To succeed in such objective situations is to have a mind that is results-oriented.

Survival (Take Care of Yourself); Relentless Results Orientation and Market Orientation. Realism in business means first and fore-most a market orientation. It is a form of perception, a pervasive attitude toward life itself. Peter Drucker has said that marketing is everything. Business is an attitude — the attitude to be totally and fully in touch with the reality of the market and respond to it effectively and successfully. Business, like science, is a language, one constructed to cope with recalcitrant reality. But the princi-ples of the language of business extend far beyond commerce; they reach into all aspects of life. *Results* are the only language that makes sense to the business mind. *Results* and *reality* are the same word. Unfortunately, large businesses, like governmental institutions, surround their employees and middle managers with a protective wall that blurs their perception of the market and other economic forces. The market is real, and every em-ployee must feel it. As a rule, only owners of small businesses feel, directly and daily, the impact of the marketplace, but only in such realistic circumstances can authentic leadership be exercised.

Two rules of market orientation define the well-led com-pany: every employee must be close to the customer, and every employee must be close to the company's total business plan and understand the reasons for it. This kind of realistic contact is not a matter of mere words or instruction or communication; it must result from the structure of the organization itself. Intel-ligent decentralization can put every employee face to face with the customer. Rotation, for example, as well as participative management taken seriously, can put every employee in contact with the strategic needs of the organization.

Specifically, market orientation means to know precisely who your immediate customer is and to be aware at the same time of who your end customer is. In a sales organization, for example, the salesperson's immediate customer may not be the prospect but rather his or her sales supervisor. Understanding what the prospect perceives as value may be far less important for the career of the salesperson, and even for the effectiveness of the organization, than accepting what, for the supervisor (who makes commission and promotion decisions), is the perceived value.

Market orientation is close to results orientation. Some management, however, focuses on process instead of results. It demands continuous improvement, constant analysis, and modification to enhance the quality of the work performed. That is good. That is the pragmatic level of leadership. But there is also results orientation, which comes closer to the breakthrough level of leadership. Results are category leaps, quantum transformations. They require the genius mindset, the thirst for transformation.

In Japan, continuous improvement is the management rule. In the United States, many companies still adhere to the uncompromising, hard, militaristic attitude that only results matter, an attitude well illustrated by *Fortune*'s yearly compendium of "America's toughest bosses." Such bosses say, for instance, the following things:

> "Good operations succeed with a minimum of foolishness and glitter." (Carl E. Reichart, Chairman, Wells Fargo & Co.)
>
> "I am demanding, not mean. Forgiveness is out of style, shoulder shrugs are out of fashion. Hit the targets on time, without excuses." (Richard J. Mahoney, Monsanto)
>
> "I expect the Herculean. There's no golf in the middle of the day, no coasting to retirement. If you're not leading, you're out of here." (Hugh L. McColl, Jr., Chairman, NCNB Corporation)
>
> "You don't build a company like this with lace on your underwear. There is no room for error." (Harry E. Figgie, Jr., Chairman, Figgie International) ["America's Toughest Bosses," 1989, pp. 40–50].

These exalted views of toughness are not necessarily shared by subordinates, and *Fortune* quotes them. Of the Wells Fargo chairman, someone says that "his narrow focus may be

limiting middle management; a lot are leaving." Of Monsanto's
chairman, others say, "He has a big ego . . . subordinates have to
stroke him a lot . . . listens to others but doesn't understand . . .
little empathy with subordinates . . . can't believe he's wrong."
"We sit on the edge of our chairs," say others of ex-Marine Hugh
L. McColl, Jr. "The fastest way to get to see Hugh," says a subordinate, "is to close your door. He hates that." Says another, "Hugh's
always breathing down your neck. He's such a forceful person
that it's hard to be who you are." Harry E. Figgie, Jr., others say,
ranges "from horrendous to delightful, from idiotic to brilliant . . . working with him was a nightmare . . . really abusive . . .
the Steinbrenner of industry."

These examples illustrate situations in which the survival
tactic either constitutes the entire personality or is so overbear-
ing that the other strategies and tactics pale by comparison. It is
demonic in the sense that one trait takes possession of the entire
personality. What is recommended is integration. Survival is a
leadership trait, but if it exists in isolation, we have the phenomenon of the collapsed leadership mind.

On a fundamental level, results and marketing orienta-
tions are strictly tied to survival. But the mind obsessed with
survival, and with survival only, is more like a predatory animal
than a balanced human being: survival is all that matters. Soldiers
understand that. Civilians in war-torn cities know that. Impover-
ished immigrants know that. Wild animals—from deer to rab-
bits, from foxes to hyenas, from birds to fish—all understand
that. Success in leadership depends heavily on how task-obsessed
and survival-focused the leader is. A mouse, when threatened,
zips to a shelter. It will also eat anything edible, and then some.
That is its life. Its little mind is conscious of but two things: safety
and food. It does nothing but pursue those two goals, as if nothing
else in this world existed. That encapsulates the results-oriented
tactic of the leadership mind. It is the survival tactic, the results-
and market-oriented tactic, in the reality strategy of the leadership mind. It is unpleasant and mean but effective.

A realistic leader who is obsessed with survival always
asks, "What specific things can you do?" and "What specific
results can you achieve?" If the answers can be quantified, so

much the better. A realistic executive has an iron grip on the core of the business, on what is needed for survival. That is what, in business, is meant by content, as opposed to process.

For you to survive, in business and professionally, you must also recognize the realities of the political process. Company politics are inevitable. Company politics are apparent and implied, manifest and tacit. You can try to avoid the negatives in company politics and use organizational politics positively (see Block, 1987). Do not fail because you do not know how to work the process, how to survive the culture. That is part of the reality you must confront when working in organizations. That is realism. That is survival.

A final example of the survival tactic comes from another executive who at one time was named by *Fortune* as America's toughest boss: Jack Welsh, chairman and chief executive of Westinghouse. His leadership philosophy is well summed up in these hard-hitting principles:

- Face reality as it is, not as it was or as you wish it were.
- Be candid with everyone.
- Don't manage; lead.
- Change before you have to.
- If you don't have the competitive advantage, don't compete.
- Control your own destiny, or someone else will.

Looking beyond mere survival, we know that the surest way to pragmatic executive success is to train the mind, principally in two separate tactics. The first is systemic and strategic thinking, which is part of the strategy of vision. The second is survival (discussed here), which is part of the strategy of reality. If you make yourself like that, people may not like you, and you may not be happy — but you will surely be financially successful. You can add the critical success factors from the strategy of ethics (teamwork) and from the strategy of courage (will power). In this way, you will have fashioned for yourself a complete profile for executive success, going beyond the limits of the tactic of survival in the strategy of realism.

The realistic leader always has his or her mind sharply

Figure 6.1. Outcomes.

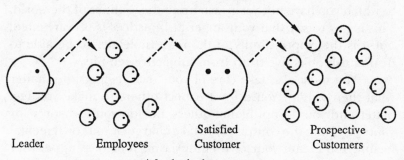

Leader   Employees   Satisfied   Prospective
                                   Customer   Customers

A leader in the company
looks at the prospects in the market

ends: ———— means: - - - -

focused on outcomes. That requires vision, in addition to realism. The means are always secondary. The results are where vision is focused. Getting into that habit of thought toughens the mind to realistic performance. Even a satisfied customer is not enough; what you need is to excite the general public to want to purchase the product or service (see Figure 6.1).

"Take care of yourself" is a not infrequent admonition of psychotherapeutic treatment. In this view, a person's first obligation is to survive, especially emotionally. Authentic people take care of their emotions. They do not allow others to manipulate their feelings. Realism, conceived in this fashion, describes a reasonably detached and independent human being who is, as it were, systematically selfish. "Do not become too attached to others" is the prescription: do not allow your children to control you; have a life of your own; do not fall hopelessly in love; be ready for "tough love"; always look out for yourself; do not sacrifice yourself for others; and so forth. We are dealing here with a very pragmatic, unromantic, and unsentimental approach to life. That, too, is realism.

But there is a less cynical, more positive way of taking care of yourself, of managing survival. It can be stated as follows: *the realistic leader takes care of his or her own feelings.* If you are depressed or disappointed or feel unfairly treated, then you, as a realistic leader, must recognize, first of all, the degree to which you are being childish, infantilistic, or even neurotic—the extent to which you have not yet grown up to the realities of the world. This is not to say that your anger at injustices is unwarranted; but it is the responsibility of the realistic leader to be able to distinguish objective truth from subjective self-pity.

You must also take care of your own feelings, no matter what their origin. You do not expect others to make you feel better and you do not blame others, nor do you feel sorry for yourself. Quite the contrary: you take charge of your own mental health. You create your own enthusiasm, your own hope, your own solutions. You meditate on the symbol that has been made of Churchill during the most desperate days of World War II. To go beyond self-pity and take charge of your own emotions is the height of realism. But this is more than the strategy of realism. It is also the strategy of courage, with a strong dose of the tactics of isolation and free will thrown in.

Although leadership is about yourself, it is not only about yourself. What do you do when your colleagues—subordinates, superiors, or peers, or even your customers, for that matter— deny their responsibility for themselves and instead wallow in self-pity? As the leader, you need to manage that, with realism. Be understanding, be compassionate, be sensitive; give comfort, provide help and support. But also expect healthy behavior, adult comportment, grown-up demeanor. Demand the governance of reason. You must also be prepared to confront people with the truth that reality has limits. Above all, you must communicate. You must engage in dialogue. Always offer dialogue. Never give up on dialogue. Always communicate with candor. Beyond that, you yourself must be the model, the sterling example of adult behavior, of taking care of your feelings. And you, as leader, must always give hope to others by generating your own energy, your own vigor, your own resourcefulness, showing effective responsibility for your own sustained enthusiasm. Remember that the personal side of leadership is what, in the end, supports the strategic business needs of the organization. That will always remain the secret of a well-managed and profitable company.

***Direct Contact and Embodiment—with Yourself, with Other Selves,
and with How Others Perceive You (Bonding and Definitions of
Mental Health).*** This tactic deals with reality at its deepest: the
philosophic level. Some points are difficult and may even appear esoteric; nor do they necessarily form a cohesive argument,
being more like a collection of images and insights.

Realism as *direct contact* is a fundamental metaphysical
category. It means to be in touch with what is real, to be connected—either as a unit (like a bond) or in dialogue (like a
dance). Contact represents an overall orientation toward life
and is a key to emotional health. Full contact means presence,
being fully present in the world. In the authentic leadership life,
you are fully present to yourself, recognizing that all the world
exists *now*, only at this precise moment. All of the past exists now,
closed, as memory; all of the future exists now, open, as anticipation and freedom of action. The entire universe is related to you,
and you to it. You are truly a child of the universe. All your
unconscious also exists now, but hidden. To be fully present is to
have all that material available to you now, each aspect in its
unique way. (Many of these themes, touched on before, are
intimately connected to physical health and longevity. They are
the themes in psychotherapy where philosophy and psychiatry
intersect.)

Direct contact occurs in the three "worlds" described by
the German psychoanalyst and philosopher Ludwig Binswan-
ger. They are the *Eigenwelt*, our private world, in which we
struggle with our existential boundary situations (God, death,
immortality, guilt, anxiety, isolation, freedom, and so forth); the
Mitwelt, the world of intimacy (what the philosopher Martin
Buber called the "I-Thou connection"); and the *Umwelt*, society
and nature around us. In each of these worlds, the orientation of
consciousness is radically different.

Reality is a philosophical concept under the scholarly
rubric of metaphysics. The question is always "What is the
nature of reality?" Much pain and conflict stem from discrepancies between different senses of reality. Islamic fundamentalists
and free-thinking, libertarian atheists see different realities in

one and the same world. Culture clashes and culture shock are part of the reality you must acknowledge if you are to be truly pragmatic.

There are many levels of reality and many different types of things that are real. You must acknowledge each of them and make your peace with them, for, being real, they are often stronger than you. The many phenomena that are real fit into the following categories or types: nature; society; your business or profession; other selves, who can validate you, open themselves up to you, or deny you; your body; your own inner self; and the realm of values (which, according to Plato and others, exists independently of you but nevertheless makes a claim on you). Each of these classes of events or entities has its own unique reality, and you must cope with all of them. In their own way, they are immovable.

A word about other selves: realism means to be aware of how the other person thinks, how you are perceived by others. That is often much more difficult to bring about than it may appear to be. It is important, for example, to understand how others are affected by the very system in which we live.

A further point about the reality in which we find ourselves: there is the not uncommon theory, which has serious political ramifications, that poverty is a metaphysical category. This is the belief that individuals are not personally responsible for being poor but are oppressed, specifically by Western ideologies, which, these theorists maintain, necessitate the permanent existence of an underclass in order for capitalist economies to be successful. This point is then carried farther: at an even deeper level, there is the theory that, in order for one thing to *be*, another thing must *not* be; that for the class of A to *exist*, there must also be members of a class called "non-A," who, as it were, *do not exist*. In other words, definitions involve affirming one thing by denying or negating another. This is known as the rule that "determination is negation." Even the word *de-fine* implies setting limits. This kind of philosophy, right or wrong, finds considerable resonance in the Third World. It speaks to nations that feel they are permanently oppressed—by the *thinking* of the rest of the world, not by the *actions* that they themselves (or even others) either take or do not take. In fact, it is likely that over two-thirds of the world's population has, at one time or another, responded favorably to such ideology. Whatever action they do take will be futile in their eyes, because the world system will neutralize their efforts. To understand and assimilate this point is another proof of realism. Greatness in realism is to understand how such a "necessary and inevitable outsider" feels, and to know what to do about it. Frantz Fanon's classic book *The Wretched of the Earth* (1965) exemplifies the political power of this way of thinking.

Many people are or have been outsiders: lepers, Jews, AIDS victims, homosexuals, criminals, prostitutes, the mentally ill, blacks, foreigners, Catholics, the Irish, the Italians, the Puritans, socialists, and so forth. Systems (in order to exist), the mind (in order to think), the senses (in order to perceive) may require the metaphysical structure of "contaminated" outsiders, of an outside that must be rejected so as to establish the insiders' sense of identity. It may matter little whether such a theory accurately reflects reality. What matters more is that people feel discriminated against on this basis; they feel it is no fault of their own that causes their excruciating pain. To know that such a situation exists, one that is both unfair and explosive, and to be prepared to deal with it effectively and sensitively — these are the marks of the realistic leader. We may call this condition "the syndrome of the necessary outsider." Realism is to understand how an outsider perceives you, the insider.

A word about the body: contact must occur with each one of the three worlds. Thus, contact means to be in touch with your body, to know that you live in your body and that you *are* a body (or, better still, a bodymind), that you contact the world through your bodymind. This concept is useful therapeutically, for this kind of felt contact with your body can be a path to higher emotional and physical health.

Direct contact, then, implies that you share your full presence with another person. You are fully present to another person because you are fully present to yourself. This is the meaning of human contact.

Contact means that you are fully conscious of your personal situation. In a leader's life, involvement with one's family and one's personal relationships play a critical role in one's contact with the real world, for these are an important part of the real world. They may offer support and solace or may present obstacles and interferences. They may be sources of great joy or occasions for bitter conflict. But whatever they are, they are realities with which leaders must cope and on whose influence they depend.

You must understand your organizational culture. It takes time to experience it, and it requires interpreters to explain it. It frequently takes stamina to survive in it.

Other fundamental aspects of the strategy of realism in the leadership mind are contact with life's boundary situations, or limits. These refer to the human condition. Merely by virtue of being human, you are immersed in anxiety and guilt, surrounded with death and isolation, condemned to be free and to make choices. Self-doubt is a natural human state, and all of us have exalted as well as despised self-images. How in touch are you with these realities as you go through your daily leadership challenges?

There is also contact with ethnic boundary situations: characteristics of your deeper cultural heritage, not necessarily part of the human condition in general. Most people in the West have roots in Greek civilization and in the Judeo-Christian religious traditions. Others, whose origins may be in the Third World, may have Buddhist, Hindu, Moslem, and other identifications. But everyone is in contact with his or her own local history. You may be Irish or Egyptian, Scottish or Nigerian, French or Mexican, Australian or Navajo. All these factors are part of your reality. They help fashion you, organize your world view for you, set your values, define your view of human nature, and determine your views of life after death.

The most obvious limit with which you are in contact is the hard and impenetrable barrier that is reality, a wall that confronts every executive daily: frustration. It could be the weather, like a drought to a farmer; it could be politics, like a lost election to a candidate; it could be the obstinacy of a willful boss or employee. And it is uncontrollable market forces and demographic movements. There is also lack of clarity and absence of precision. Directives are unclear or irrelevant; instructions are imprecise and confusing.

What is more real than money, especially when you don't have any, when you can't eat, can't make it to the end of the month, when your car or house is repossessed? What about credit? You can't get a loan; then you know that money is the ultimate reality, the ultimate limit to your freedom of operation. At least it is in a free-market economy. The leadership mind understands these boundaries and is always prepared, always acts accordingly, always is conscious of these impenetrable barriers. These are not only personal matters but also corporate and national realities. Nations have debts, and these limitations can crush them.

These frustrations and ambiguities are not temporary conditions but eternal verities, nor are they unhealthy, for the human organism thrives under a robust struggle with reality. To complain or be depressed is an inappropriate response. The leader exists in a realm beyond frustration, where reality is transformed from adversary to ally, where mistakes are simply ways of learning—as long as the same ones are not repeated. Leadership always exists in conditions of ambiguity and polarization. In a sense, conflicts are never settled, for the resolution of one makes room for the appearance of others. As Tom Peters has put it, to be a leader is to thrive on chaos.

In brief, realism means to be in contact, not only with economic and organizational matters, which are relatively easy to assess, but also with oneself and others. Here is where realism and ethics overlap, for to be realistic about oneself and others is also to be sensitive to people—to be ethical.

How well do you know yourself? How objective, really, are you about yourself? How rational is your assessment of yourself? How well do you understand what others think of you, how they perceive you, how you come across to them, what emotions and thoughts you trigger in them, what they say behind your back? The reality a leader confronts is his or her personality structure. Would it be of value to learn to assess yourself with psychological or psychiatric professionalism? How does your stress compare to that of others? Your compulsiveness? Your self-respect? Your rigidity? Your fear of authority? Your ability to deal with sexual matters? Are you a workaholic? How well do you assess others? Are you seduced by their words? Are you deceived by their manipulations of their own images? Do you think of them what they tell you to think? Do you accept their explanations of themselves? Do you think of them what they want you to think? Or do you have the skill to see them as they really are? Can you predict their behavior under stress, or in very private circumstances? Can you fathom their true intentions, even those unknown to them? Can you plumb their secret thoughts? Do you see others with compassion? With detachment? With projections of your own issues? Which is it? Which should it be? In short, how in touch are you with your own reality as a human being and with the human reality of others?

You must understand the statements that people make with their bodies—not only in how they act (walk, sit, hold themselves) or in their general health but also in the kind of care they have taken of their bodies. There are no hard-and-fast rules, and it is important never to be unfair to any person. Nevertheless, every human being makes a statement with his or her body. A body is a text that can be deciphered. One's body holds the record of a lifetime of decisions. That body statement must be read, even though the analysis may be tentative, in order to help one know the truth about people. But such an examination must be undertaken in an atmosphere of great caution, flexibility, and openness, of deep helpfulness and compassion, never with a view to manipulation or exploitation.

Are your hopes and dreams merely illusions? Not if you see them as heuristic—that is, as guides, directions, tendencies, trends. What matters is that they should have a direct line of connection with the reality of your here-and-now. We all have myths we live by. When you are in trouble (have symptoms), your myth is no longer serviceable. You then need a new myth.

The ultimate courageous leadership life is free of all myths. Leadership Diamond theory calls that phenomenon *contact* and *presence*. Contact means to experience the reality of intimate others, of society, and of nature. Presence means to be in touch with one's feelings, hopes, and fears. That is to be in touch, and that is the philosophic level of reality as a leadership strategy.

Typical leaders in business, government, and the professions are strongest in the reality strategy. Here, they tend to be
more powerful than in the others. Also expanding their minds
in the other three strategic directions can promote new heights
for them in leadership breakthroughs.

Realism means to avoid self-deception. Freud discovered
that human beings operate from unconscious motives. We deny
what we think and feel. We tell ourselves stories to cover up what
is real. We use numerous techniques of self-deception: denial,
displacement, projection, dissociation, doubling, and numbing.
Psychoanalysis is the art of living a life without illusions. In fact,
a typical definition of psychiatric morbidity, fully supporting
the equivalence of health with realism (for mental illness is lack
of contact with the real world), is as follows: psychiatric illness
consists of behaviors, emotions, and cognitions that are mal-
adaptive to reality and disruptive of interpersonal bonds and
that derive from and result in the creation of an alternative
reality, pathologically characterized by isolation or withdrawal,
identity disruptions, functional impairment, loss of meaning,
hopelessness, and helplessness. This definition states clearly
that mental health is a function of how well one is connected
with reality.

The leader resorts to continuous reality testing, and that
means to adopt an experimental attitude. It means to see failure
as the best teacher, the necessary learning tool.

In sum, realism is a generic approach to life. The key
words for describing it are *direct contact*. The ability for direct
contact is an unfailing sign of mental health. The question is,
contact with what? Of course, the true answer is "everything."
From a practical point of view, however, direct contact means
contact with consensual reality—the social world. To understand what the culture demands is realism. It is important to
function effectively among the cultures and subcultures within
which one finds oneself. Direct contact also means to be in
touch with one's body, to be aware of the effects of proper
exercise and nutrition, to be conscious of one's physical health
and sensuality. Direct contact with intimate others, with values,
with nature, and so forth, is also included in the other strategies.

The key to living without illusions is to see yourself and your culture through the eyes of other people and other cultures. That skill, and your unwavering dedication to it, is the final realism.

The authentic leadership mind is intimately in touch with all these elements of the tactics of reality. Two reality issues, entirely different from each other, are sales and the career-home conflict. They are practical applications of the tactics support- ing the dominant leadership strategy of reality. To these we now turn.

Leadership and Sales

You do not sell leadership to people. You help them buy it. People want to be leaders; they need to have leadership minds. Any major purchase requires vision and courage, to say the least; and leadership—perhaps the greatest purchase of all—is certainly no exception. Helping people buy leadership in their affairs is what authentic business is all about.

Since, on the basis of the theory presented here, all busi- ness transactions include the teaching of leadership, you can help people buy leadership by recognizing one simple fact: many, perhaps all, products contain a certain amount of infor- mation. Many products are specifically knowledge products. A newspaper contains information, a book contains information, a videotape contains information. A medical examination con- tains and yields information, and so does a dental procedure. Some other products, upon analysis, also show themselves to contain what can legitimately be called information. For exam- ple, information about comfortable sitting is built into a rocking chair, and, using it, one receives that information. One's enjoy- ment of the chair is in the transmittal of information (or knowl- edge) to you from both designer and carpenter. A product has information built in, and that information can also be extracted or retrieved. One country seizes a missile or a fighter airplane from another in order to abstract from it the information built by the engineers of their potential adversary. A typewriter con- tains information on how to print letters. An automobile contains information on combustion, braking, reading speeds, making turns. Clever technicians, by carefully studying a product, can winnow that information from it. The information that matters to us here is information about leadership.

The ground rule is that all authentic products (including services) must contain within them at least one element or module of leadership information. Thus, whatever else you sell, you are also selling leadership help to your customers. This is a fundamental principle of ethical and successful business transactions. To sell real estate is to teach leadership in owning a home and in investing. To offer banking services is to teach leadership in money management. To sell a car is to teach leadership in transportation management.

In short, authentic selling means to help people, through the products you offer, learn (or be helped to buy) leadership greatness. A salesperson must always be conscious of one fact: he or she is helping the customer develop leadership in the one particular area covered by the product. The transaction is successful to the extent that the parties are conscious of the basic strategies of leadership involved, from the commitment to greatness to the elements of vision, realism, ethics, and courage. A salesperson must always ask, "How can the product help my customer or client think big, increase contact with reality, be more sensitive to people, and stimulate the courage for initiative? How are these virtues related to the general effectiveness, the greatness, of my customer?" These views may seem contrived, but they introduce both authenticity and success into the fundamental business transactions of buying and selling.

Good salespersons sell only authentic products, at fair prices, and they familiarize themselves with all the types of leadership information implicit in them. How will your customer be helped toward a personal vision of *greatness*? How will the product help your customer think big? How will the product help your customer see things in perspective? How will the product help him or her cope with the tough *realities* of life? How will the product assist the customer in *serving* others and expressing care for people? Finally, do you challenge your customer to the *courage* for greatness that this product makes possible? Does your customer have the capacity to initiate action, so that his or her life will indeed be more worthy through this product? All selling or buying involves an *action* (known as the *close*), and that is always an act of courage. To lead is to help others be courageous in their own lives. These may be extraordinary demands and excessive claims; but, adapted to the circumstances of your product and to the level of development of your customers, these considerations can be effective and serviceable approaches to one of the most difficult tasks faced in business.

Remember: to sell authentically is to challenge customers to their own sense of greatness. In the end, all people want to challenge themselves and need not be challenged by others, for the customer wants to buy. The customer wants to buy leadership. The customer neither wants nor needs to be sold anything. What makes a transaction successful, in all the senses of that word, is that it is a realistic, meaningful, imaginative, and ethical *transfer and assumption of leadership*.

Love Versus Work

One of the most painful realities facing executives is the conflict among work, home, and self. It is reflected mostly in the balance between love and work. The Oracle exercise has yielded many questions on this issue:

How can professional and domestic life be unified?

How do I know the proper balance of my responsibilities as a husband, parent, and professional?

Work has been the most influential controller of my life for over twenty years, sometimes at a cost to my individual and home life. How can I achieve a holistic balance on self, home, and work while concurrently improving my leadership and effectiveness at work?

Very early in my business career, before starting to work for this company, I went to a retreat for re-newal, both spiritually and materially. At the com-pletion of the retreat, I established my life's pri-orities as (1) my God, (2) my family, and (3) my job. Every decision made since that time has been based on these priorities. Lately, with the downsizing of the company and the increasing work load, my job has required more and more of my time. It is be-coming more difficult to meet the obligations of my number two priority, my family, and this creates conflict within me. Further, I have become more aware of my age and, therefore, more concerned about job security, which results in my becoming more of a risk averter than a risk taker. I must resolve this conflict within me because the conflict takes energy away from both my family and my job—I always find time for priority number one, my God. This conflict reduces my effectiveness in handling family-related affairs and job-related af-fairs. What advice do you offer that would help me reduce or eliminate this daily conflict?

My early life was cataclysmic in many ways. Trag-edies occurred. Out of this, I became "successful" in my social community, my family, my job environ-ment, and personally (individually and financially rewarding, plus promotions). However, I yearn for a better way to live. This is because I do not feel that I am dedicating myself adequately to my three pri-mary engagements: (1) my family, (2) my work (job), and (3) me. Since there are only twenty-four hours in a day, I cannot spend more time with one engagement without reducing time with the other two. My question is: Shall I live with a "balanced" life, dedicating myself to all *three* engagements (and probably not being *really* successful in any of the three in terms of greatness, even with a transforma-

tional "snap"), or shall I pick one or two of the three
and dedicate myself to them, abandoning the
other? It seems strange to me that I could be greatest by abandoning one or two engagements, but I
would be sad and heartbroken, perhaps. I struggle
with this every day of my life.

Many people have worked this issue out, and they feel little
conflict. But for many others, it is the central problem of their
personal reality. The needs of one's personal life are intensely
important. Most people with families would say that their families are the most important commitment in their lives. Nevertheless, their work will falter and the competition will prevail if
their work is neglected as a result of their living with an un-
cooperative family. Difficult as this is to say, from the point of
view of the organization, work must come first.

Farmers and immigrants appear to have no problem in
the area of the home-work conflict. Their work and home lives
seem to be integrated. Working fathers and mothers must not be
made to feel guilty through expectations that they will be able to
solve this problem better than they actually can. Most parents do
their very best, and they need to be given appropriate credit.
Moreover, children must learn that their parents have the work-
home problem, and children should be expected early to contribute to its solution, mostly by recognizing the importance of
good behavior. By participating in their parents' work, they can
point to it with pride.

Work is, for most people, the source of identity, not to
mention of financial security. Their self-respect and self-esteem,
their sense of honor and worth, depend on accomplishments in
their careers. Through their work, they become models to their
children, they reward their parents, and they earn the respect of
their spouses.

A career provides not only financial security but also
emotional security. Managed properly, it produces these values,
not only for the executive but for the entire family. A child's
illness or homework is a family concern. So is a woman's preg-

nancy. So is an executive's out-of-town conference, or a drop in the company's stock price.

Solutions include high-quality child-care centers. These must be sponsored jointly by parents, business, and government. Furthermore, maternity and paternity leaves are appropriate. Also, children, according to their ability to understand, must be expected to be as involved with their parents' work as the latter are in their children's lives. Both spouses should attend each other's management programs and otherwise promote the sharing of work pressures and responsibilities. We see another angle of this problem in the following news item:

Daddies, Too, Have Needs That Companies Fail to Answer, Researchers Say

With more dual-career families, men's roles are changing just as much as women's roles, contend Douglas Hall and Kathy Kram, professors of organizational behavior at Boston University School of Management. As a result, they say, many male executives — even some on a recognized fast track — are trying to establish a balance in their lives: leaving work earlier, shunning travel and spurning promotions that make unacceptable demands on family time.

Felice Schwartz, president of Catalyst, which seeks to foster careers for women, stirred up a storm recently by suggesting that companies recognize separate career paths for women who want to combine motherhood with work. But men, too, hanker for "multiple choices," Mrs. Kram maintains. And companies have generally failed to recognize this need because, says Mr. Hall, "it isn't considered legitimate for men to talk about family concerns."

A corporate culture that says executives

must give their all or nothing "is ridiculous," Mr.
Hall insists ["Daddies...," 1989, p. 1].

The home culture must clearly understand the importance of work for the business's competitive advantage (that is,
survival) as much as the corporate culture must understand the
importance of the family and of employees' private lives. The
answers to conflicts lie in dialogue and clarity more than they do
in rules or policies. Unless married partners can generously and
compassionately (that is, maturely) support each other in this
dilemma, there can be neither marriage nor career. Together,
companies and families must choose to assume full responsibility for managing—intelligently, sensitively, and, above all, realistically—the damaging family-career conflicts.

7

Ethics: Providing Service

The formula statement for ethics is "Be of service." Generosity as the best policy is a good summation of the meaning of ethics. In practice, this can mean, for example, the simple matter of willingly sharing the blame for failures—especially when coupled with the preeminence of team spirit. In one American firm, a creative scientist was punished for being oriented more toward product integrity than toward costs. True, as a result of his orientation, the company did experience a drop in its stock price. The blame was leveled firmly at the creative scientist, not at the CEO, even though the CEO is held accountable for the entire firm. In Japan, by contrast, it is customary for the president of a company to take the blame for errors clearly committed by subordinates. The *Wall Street Journal* took note of this difference in a recent article:

Why Do Japanese Bosses Share Blame While Americans Hang Tough?

Haruo Yamaguchi, president of Nippon Telegraph & Telephone Corp., typifies the Japanese response when companies are embarrassed by public scandals: He cut his own pay, even though he wasn't at fault. In the U.S., by contrast, collective guilt is an alien notion, declares Joe O'Donnell, chairman of Campbell-Mithune-Esty Advertising, Inc. "Our culture is based on the acts of individuals," he says. Management's role "is to explain what is acceptable

159

and what is not," he asserts; "when someone strays, only the guilty pays."

Bruce Wilkinson, president of CRS Sirine, Inc., thinks we're actually tougher here; "we tend to throw them out." But John Peterson of recruiter Russel Reynolds Associates says "it's unfortunate" but Americans don't believe in sharing blame. "People here don't have that kind of commitment to an employer," he states.

Some executives deride corporate guilt. Will "the paper atone for every typo?" a Chevron spokesman sniffs ["Why Do Japanese Share Blame...," 1989, p. 1].

Being of service also means seeing things from another person's point of view. It means having the ability to put yourself into the mind of another person. It is also to have the desire to do so, to find meaning and value in your interest and concern for another human being. Such is the definition of *care*.

From the level of a deeper philosophical point of view, we must be aware that a human being, until witnessed by another person, does not know he or she exists. This phenomenon is known as *validation*. You do not know that you exist until you are reflected in a mirror, and the only mirror to a soul is another soul.

In some organizations, there is fear that recognition will cause employees to stop working. The motto in such industries is "More is not enough." The pressure is fit for mechanical devices, not for human beings, and there is no redemption for such insensitivity.

Ethics in leadership means mentoring. Rather than developing people for the sake of jobs, it is wiser to develop jobs for the sake of people. This statement may seem excessive, for companies must make a profit; but profit comes when people find meaning in their work. One famous computer company used to hire outstanding people, not because there were jobs for them but because they were excellent resources. Only when they were already on board were they asked to find or create work for themselves. The assumption was that good leaders would take personal responsibility to be good for a company, no matter what circumstances prevailed in the business at the time. That may be difficult (and is certainly not management by objectives), but it can elicit the best from employees and managers, to the eventual benefit of the entire organization.

Mentoring means that a leader is a teacher. A leader's obligation is to develop the people for whom he or she is responsible—to help them become more marketable, more qualified professionals, to further their careers, to help them feel better about themselves, to equip them to confront the toughest vicissitudes of life. Mentors are like loving parents who feel fully responsible for developing the independence of their children. This kind of teaching is based on a high degree of loyalty and commitment to the individual employee and on the recognition that human beings are not expendable. Employees can also be expected to adopt a similar attitude of dedication to the organizations for which they work.

Elements of the Tactics

Teamwork and Loyalty to Task Forces. The professional tactic of ethics is teamwork. That is a critical success factor. It is discussed in detail at the end of this chapter.

Meaning. Each human being needs a vocation, a calling. Ethics in leadership means having a passion for meanings. To be ethical is to understand that a life not devoted to superordinate goals is of little value. It is to understand our need to make a commitment to people, organizations, meanings, and ideals that survive us. It is to have feelings, as well as obligations to establish a moral world order. As Dostoevsky said, neither man nor nation can exist without a sublime idea. Every person needs something to which he or she can make a commitment. That is part of meaning. A life not devoted to a cause that extends beyond its own narrow limits will end in depression.

Companies often look for ways to stimulate their employees to meaning. Sometimes these efforts are profound, when the meaning issues are matters of high integrity, including the commitments to quality and customer focus. Sometimes they are superficial, more like a circus or a sports event, such as a sales contest in which the reward for selling life insurance is not to gain the satisfaction of helping a family in its quest for security but rather to win a trip to Hawaii. Like sports, these meaning-creating episodes may be quite ephemeral. Sales spurt as a result, but the effects often do not last. Nevertheless, such efforts touch our ancient need to belong to something larger and more worthy than we ourselves are — something, like a noble river, that flows from a distant past and will endure far into the future. Here is an example of connecting productivity with meaning:

Top Quality Is Behind the Comeback

Five years ago, Motorola had a nasty problem with its cellular telephones — some died in customers' cars. Higher-quality Japanese models began to steal Motorola's customers.

Motorola had two choices: settle for second-best, or retaliate with products so superb that nobody could challenge them. Motorola surrendered to the Japanese in TVs (1974), stereos (1980) and computer memory chips (1985). It didn't want to raise the white flag again.

Instead, Motorola engineered one of the most dramatic comebacks of this decade. Now, says Ralph Rosati, quality director at Eastman Kodak, "Motorola is simply the best this country has to offer. . . ."

The quality effort has turned into an international crusade. On Jan. 30, 98,000 Motorolans celebrated Quality Day at 23 plants. In Tempe, Ariz., 650 employees formed a "Q" for an aerial photo. In Tokyo, 800 Motorolans marked the eyes of a "daruma" doll in a ritualistic dedication to quality. . . .

On Jan. 15, 1987, [Chairman Robert W. Gal-

vin] wrote a letter to employees, challenging them
with new goals: a 10-fold quality improvement by
1989, 100-fold by 1991 and Six Sigma quality (3.4
defects per million) by 1992. Wallet-size cards stat-
ing those goals in 11 languages were given to all
employees. At officers' meetings, quality reports
were shifted from last to first on the agenda. Executives began to wear pagers so customers could
reach them anywhere in the USA, day or night.
Other departments began to compare themselves
to top-notch outside firms. Finance studied Chicago's First National Bank. Distribution examined
Spiegel. Delivery and warehousing looked to L.L.
Bean. . . .

In 1988, 66 U.S. companies — including divisions of Kodak, Hewlett-Packard and IBM — sought
[the annual Baldridge National Quality Award, won
by Motorola]. Now dozens of those same companies are beating a path to Motorola to learn its
quality secrets ["Top Quality. . .," 1989, pp. 1B–2B].

It is amazing how many successful executives yearn for
meaning. They have solved the problem of existence for themselves by following the rules of society (education, career, marriage, children, home, recreation, summer home, church, health
insurance, children's education, retirement) and are greatly to
be complimented for that. But, by their own admission, this is
not enough. Life is an insatiable passion for aliveness, and that is
not to be satisfied with the conservative search for security, even
though security is an authentic value.

Many people have been touched by the following poem,
written by a much admired top executive, an attorney with a
large midwestern chemical company. He opened a locked
drawer to take out his poetry. He explained that if his colleagues
and subordinates were to discover that he wrote poetry, he
would lose credibility in this tough-minded and hierarchical
organization:

Where are the friends I knew in Youth? Where are they now that I have
time to talk, and joke, and "run around," as they once did in those days
long ago when I was busy growing up and had not time for such
foolishness?

Where is the love once offered me? Where is it now that I have time to
stroll in breaking surf on moonlit nights or through quiet woods,
as they were wont to do in those days, now gone, when I was
young and working hard to earn a name and some small
measure of security?

Where is the prize once promised me for years of self-denial in the cause
of building for a future when I could share such hard-won spoils with
those I love? Where are they now that I am ready to open my arms?
I see them not. Is it because my eye has grown too weak to see?
Or could it be that, like the Friends of Youth or the
Days of Spring, they could not
wait for me?

Where is the hope I once did know? The hope for a better tomorrow that
has now dissolved into regrets for wasted yesterdays full of
unshared dreams, and unfulfilled passions deferred to
another day—which, when it came, was itself
postponed for unknown cause?

So I, absent friends, love, rewards, and hopes am left with habit. To

try to go on when my heart is full of the pain of my own making.

I know of no other course but to stay with a life-long

pattern of "plowing on," carrying whatever load

Fate may assign in the ever-shrinking

belief that somehow it will all

work out satisfactorily

in the end.

But where are my dreams?

This executive is not atypical. Among the most common questions found in the Oracle exercise are problems with meaning. Here are several examples:

In many ways, I have led a life that supported the needs of others: parents, spouse, children, relatives, friends, and colleagues—and that has given me very profound fulfillment. It has also motivated me in achieving a degree of material success that has reasonably satisfied my need for self-respect.

Now, as I enter what is, at best, the last quarter of my life, I feel these things as generally accomplished and it seems as if I desire something different (what?) to satisfy—and yet I feel guilt because those things that satisfied me up to now are good and meritorious. How do I find my way?

I am pleased with my career to date and I have a *very* happy marriage, with children who are easy to be proud of. Yet I have not made a mark on the world. I have a deep need to accomplish greater goals, both in career and personal life. I feel capable of progress in both but feel blocked for some reason. What can I do to remove the block to greater satisfaction?

I am fortunate to have achieved business success and family strength. Despite my success, I find myself inwardly doubting the strength and quality of business and family relations, and I regularly seek and require positive feedback and reinforcement from business colleagues and family members. How can I overcome these self-doubts and need for reinforcement so that I can achieve my full leadership potential in both the business and family environment?

All my life, I have driven myself to do my best to achieve goals. Now that I am near retirement, my family is grown, materialistic goals near achievement, and so on. How can the wife and I find fulfillment in the remaining years of our lives?

Ultimately, ethics in leadership means having a sense of destiny—the desire for a legacy, interest in an immortality project. It is also important to take seriously the issue of deathlessness or immortality. This is where greatness comes in, for one of its definitions is to stand up to death and evil. To find the meaning of life, of which meaningful work is but a derivative, can also be to have an answer to the anxiety of death.

Questions of meaning are difficult to answer. In fact, to seek solutions may be to bark up the wrong tree. In philosophy, asking the right questions is often what matters. Answers can stop questions, and it is the latter that stimulate the mind to grow. But when such concerns are ventilated in a group (or in any other type of human relationship) and then connected with the stream of human history, an atmosphere of profound validation is created that, for many executives, is a brand-new and exhilarating experience. To know that my questions are also yours and that, throughout the ages, other human beings have struggled with the same concerns—that is support, confirmation, the euphoria of resolution, the peace of fulfillment.

Communication, Caring, Love; Commitment, Loyalty. Do not underestimate the power of love, perhaps the greatest known energy. We all recognize the importance of love in life—how we need it to be happy, to grow, even to be healthy. But, regrettably, many people feel it has no place in business. Love means that you really care about people, whether you are a mother or a general. To love is to communicate intimately in the sense of establishing an intersubjective field, a joint ego or communal self. Love establishes a higher unity, a spiritual connection, an emotional bond.

Even in business, people need to be heard; they need to be understood. We all hunger for emotional safety; for example, we appreciate the value of a support group. Some leaders fear that asking for support may tarnish their executive self-images. Seek out friends and allies. Recognize that there are people who want to support you and can do it well. Ask freely.

Love means making contact, contact with another person or a group; that is closeness, intimacy. It is a special feeling, a special truth not necessarily tied to the revelation of personal secrets. Contact is, in essence, a reality tactic. But here, in the strategy of ethics, contact is with the heart and soul of another person.

The formula for effective leadership through love is presence and contact. This means that you must first develop your heart, and then show your heart to your people. Many CEOs are high-quality individuals but have never shown that adequately to themselves or to their people. They may engage management-consulting firms or public relations specialists while they shy away from visibly leading the charge. But leaders' ultimate influence, their leadership clout, their credibility, lies in revealing themselves as they are. Certain requirements, of course, must first be met. Leaders must understand the business and have the skill, knowledge, and experience to manage, but they must also have a high level of personal maturity and, as Plato insisted, they must possess wisdom. That means depth. Without it, they do not deserve the responsibility and trust invested in them. Further, they must be prepared to reveal that depth. Executives who do not heed these words often live to regret it, and so do their companies.

A well-known and large international company went through the paroxysms of a violent reorganization. Divisions were closed, functions were eliminated, and people were fired. The CEO, although he made the decision, nevertheless found it deeply painful. He bit the bullet. He showed no mercy, although in his heart he bled. Then, with the new fiscal year, he hired a consulting firm to build up the sagging morale of those who were left. What he failed to do was appreciate his own sense of morality, his own deep feelings, his own genuine emotions—and then show this best part of him to his people, let them know how he felt, share his inner conflicts, be human. The result was heaping alienation upon alienation. The company was sold, and the CEO was fired.

The solution to many a CEO's concern with credibility and influence—the need to reach his or her people—lies right here. Establish contact. Connect who you are with who they are. This cannot be done without a clear understanding of the philosophical level of the reality strategy, which is the so-called level of direct contact. But when contact is with a soul, rather than with the jungle (and we are in the strategy of ethics, not realism), we call it an *encounter*. This is a special and different kind of contact. It goes beyond the mechanical and the material. It involves heart and soul. It relates subjectivity to subjectivity. It is a hard fact that effective management must understand the soft center in every person. The true leader cares hard. Challenging this expanded and humanized leadership consciousness into being—among all concerned, from CEOs to new hires—is the foundation of modern business thinking.

Integrity, Morality, and Principle. The deepest tactic of the dominant leadership strategy of ethics is principle, the integrity of your value system. Ethics means that your organization is differentiated by its values. It is your serious commitment to them that makes you and your organization strong. You and your organization need to have ideals, a sense of destiny, to know the value of greatness. It is their undeviating commitment to values that makes companies great.

What, precisely, *is* ethics at this, its deepest level? It is integrity, morality, and principle. In business, unlike in academic philosophy, this is the common meaning of the term *ethics*. Ethics, as integrity, morality, and principle, can be defined by reference to the concepts of equality, dignity, truthfulness, and liberty. Ethics and integrity mean a free commitment to justice and equality, to fairness. This aspect of being ethical often requires one to choose self-sacrifice willingly. Ethics and integrity mean a commitment to the preservation of human dignity. All human beings are created equal and should be guaranteed equal opportunity; that is justice. Yet each individual is nevertheless the center of his or her universe; that is dignity. If the lights go out for the center, they also go out for the rest of creation. All the world relates to one individual; and, correlatively, that one individual relates to all the world. As far as you are concerned, my world is part of your world; you will never know anything but your world. This sense of specialness, which exists for every person, must be respected and preserved. Because you experience yourself to be the center, not only of your world but, from the point of view of direct experience, also of the whole world, you are indeed something unique and very special. From this hard-to-describe fact of universal human experience follows the concept of human dignity, of the infinite value of a single human being.

Integrity means a commitment to openness, truthfulness, transparency, which leads to trust. An open life is a simple life — you never need to remember the lies you have told, or bother to hide. Being open may be difficult at times, but overall it is the easiest life of all. It is the most effective life, the life with the most warmly developed human connections. To be human is to need intimacy, bondedness, connectedness. None of that can be achieved without openness. Two hearts must be revealed to each other, and so must two minds. That transparency is brought about by directness, clarity — in short, openness.

Finally, integrity means valuing and preserving liberty.

Civilization journeys toward individualism, valuing the individual, which requires respect for liberty as the supreme virtue. Business, like all other social institutions, must reflect this historical leadership imperative. Happy persons are those who manage to live their lives in their own way. They think for themselves and are in charge of their own existence.

There is a conflict between individualism and teamwork, but conflict is in the nature of existence. One characteristic of the Leadership Diamond, which gives it its shape, is the spaciousness of the leadership mind: the ability, as in an orchestra or a jazz band, to incorporate in one totality a variety of conflicting feelings and ideas. To be a contributing member of a team is to manage this ambiguity, to take full personal responsibility for the successful performance of the team as a whole. That is indeed difficult, but who said leadership was easy? Freedom is one of the great values of civilization. It is institutionalized in democratic political systems. Business must reflect freedom, not only because it is right but also because any valued executive will demand it for his or her personal life.

Why be ethical? People feel more comfortable with each other when they are ethical in the four senses just described. It is a subjectively felt, fulfilling way of being with others. Being ethical encourages the two touchstones of mental health, presence and contact—being fully present to yourself and to others, and being fully in contact with your feelings and those of other persons. It simplifies life. It makes life clean.

In short, to have integrity and principles means to have made a choice: to be civilized. Civilized behavior exists only because free men and women have defined the nature of authentic human relationship by choosing ethical behavior, as defined here. You and I, with our free choices for equality, dignity, truthfulness, and liberty, maintain civilized behavior in existence. Through ethical behavior, we define the meaning of a civilized existence, and no one else will do that for us. If you and I neglect it, civilized behavior disappears.

Further, in business, integrity means integrity in products and services. A material product that is technologically rich is also knowledge-rich or information-rich. In addition, it must be ethics-rich. It must not only satisfy material needs but also address the needs of the inner side, the feelings, the attitudes — the subjective side. It must not only have material content and knowledge content but also have ethics content. That is the deeper meaning of quality.

Integrity also means nobility. Nobility of character, part of greatness in general, is also an ethical theme. Individual nobility may well be at the human core of all four Leadership Diamond corners. In business, that is all expressed in the commitment to quality: being of service to another human being.

There are additional matters to consider within the tactic of integrity and morality. Ethics is a matter of principle. All members of an organization must understand the larger context, the implications and consequences, of what they do. There is no moral protection behind the walls of large companies. Consider the following example:

Random Boeing Flaws Raise Safety
Question on Workhorse Planes

Leroy A. Keith began worrying about Boeing's entire design and production system more than a year ago, when Japan Air Lines and British Airways sent the Seattle-based manufacturer letters criticizing the quality of new planes they were receiving. As manager of the airliner certification for the FAA's Northwest Mountain Region office, Mr. Keith was already studying reports of miswired fire-control systems when a new British Midland 767 crashed Jan. 8, triggering a series of inspections that extended to Boeing 747s, 757s and 767s. . . .

"The critical aspects of this are that Boeing is trying to keep its costs at a minimum and is trying to meet production deadlines," says John B. Gallipault of the Aviation Safety Institute, an independent air-safety watchdog group in Worthington, Ohio. "Morale is terrible. And that all adds up to an inability to get a quality job done. . . ."

adership

Further, the British Airways letter to Boeing reports faults "on every aircraft" in the airline's 757 and 767 fleet. An "underlying reason" for the wide variety of problems, the letter said, was that Boeing workers "are in general inadequately trained, possess a low level of basic working skills, and of paramount concern, *seem oblivious that they are building aircraft where any mistake not properly corrected, or hidden, represents a direct compromise with safety* [italics added]. . . .

[An inspector on the line] says engineers often fail to eyeball equipment before writing their reports. It happens so often, in fact, that mechanics have a name for it: "thousand-yard trouble-shooting" ["Random Boeing Flaws . . .," 1989, p. 1, 5].

"Boeing workers seem oblivious that they are building aircraft where any mistake not properly corrected, or hidden, represents a direct compromise with safety." What an understatement! A mere "compromise with safety" means the horrible deaths of hundreds of people, perhaps including your own child or mother.

The issues here, of course, concern both ethics and business. Safety is a moral issue. No human being has the right to promise safety to another and deliver danger. Workers and managers have no right to be ignorant of the larger implications of their work. Such ignorance is proof of lack of leadership in all ranks, from individual workers to union leaders, from managers and executives to planners who devise manufacturing and installation systems, from customers who pressure manufacturers for on-time and at-price delivery to stockholders who demand highest profits. As far as business is concerned, an article such as the one just cited, which appeared on the front page of the *Wall Street Journal*, can be a damning indictment, an image-shattering blow to any major company, neutralizing years of advertising and millions of dollars spent on goodwill.

Ambiguity is a pervasive concern, in leadership as in business ethics. Part of that ambiguity arises from your commitment to customer focus. What may seem ethical to the stock-holders may not be so for the employees. What appears right for your customer may not be right for your supplier. If you decide that your principal ethical obligation is to your customer, then you must know who your customer is. If you are a salesperson, the question becomes whether your customer is your sales manager or your end customer, the wholesaler to whom you sell or the wholesaler's retail customer.

Ethics, or wisdom, seen as a dominant leadership strategy, is the commitment to be of service. In Agra, India, near the Taj Mahal, there is a hotel where guests find posted the following quotation from the greatest servant to humanity of this century, Mohandas Gandhi:

Gandhiji said,

A customer is the most important
Visitor on our premises.
He is not dependent on us,
We are dependent on him.
He is not an interruption of our work,
He is the purpose of it.
He is not an outsider to our business,
He is a part of it.
We are not doing him a favor by
Serving him,
He is doing us a favor by giving us
An opportunity to do so.

While ethics, in the long run, may be good business, to be ethical is to be motivated in a unique way — not by pleasure, fear, inclination, habit, approval, social pressure, or what is prudent; the source of your action is instead the rational fact that it is *right*. You do what you do because it is right. This is not to endorse either dogmatism or fanaticism; it is simply to say that to have character and integrity is to act on the basis of what is morally right (upon which there is often far less dispute than generally thought), a position called *deontology*. The greatest ethicists have taught us that: Socrates, Plato, the Stoics, Spinoza, Kant.

Ethics in leadership, as is true in greatness generally, means that your values give you character. Socrates' many celebrated statements speak to this point: "The only way to harm a man is to make him a worse man." "Virtue is knowledge." "No harm can come to a good man." The final strength of every human being is to preserve his or her dignity, integrity, values — to protect the solid core. Your identity is your integrity, not your wealth or your skills, and only that which tarnishes your integrity does any significant harm to you. Your integrity is your decision to abide by the principles of equality, your decision to respect the dignity of all human beings (yours included), your decision to be transparent in your relationships, your decision to respect the liberty of others and of yourself. As long as you live by these decisions, you have integrity. To do harm means to choose no longer to live by these decisions. That is up to you and no one else. No clearer definition of the ethical life than this Socratic one has ever been given.

To try to destroy a person's character is the ultimate evil. Torturing prisoners, to make them confess to lies or betray their comrades, is a perfidious case in point. "If Mr. Edison had known how his light bulb would be used, he would never have invented it," goes an Amnesty International advertisement displaying a naked light bulb. To rob a person of sleep is to invade his or her soul. That is brainwashing — a brutal crime, condemned by the United Nations as the rape of the mind. That is one of the few ways to corrupt the spirit of a human being. Breaking a person's soul is the final evil.

Besides deontology, there is another definition of ethics. What makes you an ethical person is your worrying about ethical issues — struggling with them, losing sleep over them. That is how we teach young children ethics: not by pontificating to them about what is right and wrong, rewarding them for one and punishing them for the other, but by allowing them to experience the difference between civilized and uncivilized behavior. If Johnny cheats on an examination and no one else does, then that is not an occasion for punishment but rather for class discussion of how all the children feel about the event and what its implications are for themselves and for successful group life.

The Oracle exercise in which executives are asked to formulate anonymously their one deepest leadership concern brings out profound ethical struggles, struggles with integrity. Here are a few examples:

How can I effectively demonstrate leadership in a system that perpetuates human injustices through planning decisions and budget-reduction constraints?

I believe that I've been betrayed by the very system that I've supported, with great personal and professional dedication, for my entire career. How do I (or *should* I) resolve the deepening conflict between my strong inner desires to *contribute*, to *achieve*, to *teach*, to *develop*, and the growing realization that my career will likely fall short of my expectations, due primarily to basic flaws in the system I've helped create, and not in me?

If you know you have been dishonest in your life, how do you restore your integrity?

I believe I have caused a life to be taken. How do I reconcile myself to move on, to have hope, to lead others, with this issue constantly before me?

In many private sessions with executives, one hears statements like these:

Philosophy does not interest me.

I never took philosophy in college, mostly business courses.

I don't know anything about philosophy, and I don't even care to know.

Yet these statements are made in the context of extraordinary ethical searching, exemplified by the following Oracle question:

> I am the top executive in a very large organization. And I live with a deep conflict. There is a fundamental "bad" in business, a pervasive cancer. Business lives in a cutthroat, ruthless, dishonest atmosphere. You do what it takes and care nothing about morality. You are not true to your word. In the end, you cheat, deceive, and lie. Eventually, even the most determined among us must contract this disease. This presents me with a fundamental dilemma: Can you win being "good"? I do not want to take on the characteristics that disturb me in some of my colleagues. I have announced to my board that I will quit if I'm cornered — which means I sense danger to one of two basic things: my family or my values. But the very thought of the dilemma itself upsets me!

Is this true of business alone? Is this conflict not also found in the professions, the arts, education, politics, the military? Would it not be good for this man to add to his ultimatum "I want you to join me in creating a company where I will never need to make such a decision"? Is this man's concern with integrity different from that of Socrates, the first ethicist? If not, then how can this executive say that he is not a philosopher? To be a leader is to be condemned to philosophy.

The bottom line, when it comes to principle, is the willingness to die. Sometimes this harsh ethical reality is literally true, but most often it is a powerful metaphor for loss of ego, loss of position, loss of friends or colleagues, loss of money, loss of opportunity. To risk death is to risk oneself, even sacrifice oneself, for the sake of the company or the customer, the partnership or the client — for what is right.

The example of Socrates serves as a fitting conclusion to this discussion. In Plato's dialogue *Crito* (Jowett and Allen, 1986),

Socrates is in jail, having been condemned to death. The laws are just, but the judges (of whom, according to Athenian constitutional procedures, there were about five hundred) are not. Crito, his friend, has arranged for Socrates to escape. But Socrates refuses because he thinks escape unethical. Socrates' actions are guided by ethical considerations alone, not by such emotions as fear.

The following quotation is an excellent example of integrity—that is, the need to be ethical for ethics' sake, and not for an ulterior purpose. In this passage, Socrates is describing the laws of Athens as they concern him (Benjamin Jowett's translation, from Jowett and Allen, 1986):

> All patriotic citizens will cast an evil eye upon you as a subverter of the laws, and you will confirm in the minds of the judges the justice of their own condemnation of you. For he who is a corrupter of the laws is more than likely to be a corrupter of the young and foolish portion of mankind. Will you then flee from well-ordered cities and virtuous men? And is existence worth having on these terms? Or will you go to them without shame, and talk to them, Socrates? And what will you say to them? What will you say here about virtue and justice and institutions and laws being the best things among men? Would that be decent of you? Surely not. But if you go away from well-governed states to Crito's friends in Thessaly, where there is great disorder and license, they will be charmed to hear the tale of your escape from prison, set off with ludicrous particulars of the manner in which you were wrapped in a goat skin or some other disguise, and metamorphosed as the manner is of runaways; but will there be no one to remind you that in your old age you were not ashamed to violate the most sacred laws from a miserable desire of a little more life?
>
> Listen, then, Socrates, to us who have

brought you up. Think not of life and children first, and of justice afterwards, but of justice first, that you may be justified before the princes of the world below. For neither will you nor any that belong to you be happier or holier or juster in this life, or happier in another, if you do as Crito bids. Now you depart in innocence, a sufferer and not a doer of evil; a victim, not of the laws but of men. But if you go forth, returning evil for evil, and injury for injury, breaking the covenants and agreements which you have made with us, and wronging those whom you ought least of all to wrong, that is to say, yourself, your friends, your country, and us, we shall be angry with you while you live, and our brethren, the laws in the world below, will receive you as an enemy; for they will know that you have done your best to destroy us. Listen, then, to us and not to Crito.

The Teamwork Basics

Ethics in leadership is the commitment to make others suc-cessful—your boss, your employee, your partner, your colleague, your client, your shareholders. Therefore, ethics means to work as a team. It is to place the needs of the team at the top of the list of your priorities. It is the responsibility of each team member to work for the success of the team, which includes making his or her best personal contribution. The contract with your company is that, in return for pay, you commit yourself, in what is to become your foremost ethical obligation, to meet the needs of the organization. Correlatively, the company has equal responsi-bilities to its employees or partners. The organization and you have an ethical obligation to each other.

The team satisfies ancient yearnings for community and belonging. The team concept has developed from the tribe, where the individual is submerged, to selfish individualism, where the individual is indulged and unconstrained, to the authentic team, where the individual counts and is respected but is at the same time responsible for the success of the total venture. Such *individual* accountability for *team* accomplishment requires mature sensitivity and imagination, as well as courage. Teamwork is thus an art, not a science.

The teamwork basics are the conditions that determine whether a team, rather than an individual, thinks and acts with leadership. Each member of the team, as well as the team as a whole, must demonstrate acceptance of these twenty-one principles:

1. Understand that, to be effective, organizations need teamwork.
2. Do not dominate the team. Do not use the team for an "ego trip."
3. Do not sabotage the team. Intelligent people can be very subtle in how they sabotage. Slavish adherence to *Robert's Rules of Order*, distracting suggestions, vapid criticism, and a generally negative, unsupportive, unconstructive, self-centered attitude can be enough to make even the most determined team ineffective. Do not use the team to serve your own neurotic purposes. Make the commitment to serve the rational and legitimate purposes of the organization, with which you have, in effect, a reciprocal, businesslike, contractual agreement.
4. Do not hide behind team decisions. That is neither responsible nor courageous.
5. Make your own independent and creative contribution to the team.
6. You must feel that you alone are personally responsible for the success of the entire team. Do not wait for the team to be a team before you join in. Such an attitude is the kiss of death for any team. You do not say to your marriage partner, "I'll stick around. I'll wait and see. If the marriage works, I'll join in. If not, I'll leave." That statement itself is the end, and you have caused it. *Ownership* is the key word. Each team member must have a sense of owning the work of the whole team. One measure of ownership may be the number of suggestions made. It demonstrates the respon-

Table 7.1. "Ownership" in the United States and Japan.

	U.S.	Japan
Percentage of employees making suggestions	8	67
Number of suggestions per 100 eligible employees	13	2,472
Average award per suggestion	$604.72	$3.23
Suggestions' net savings per 100 employees	$24,891	$274,475

Source: Adapted from the National Association of Suggestion Systems and Japan Human Relations Association, *Wall Street Journal, Europe,* Oct. 24, 1989, p. 1.

sibility that employees feel for the firm's success. Compare the statistics in Table 7.1. Those figures suggest that Japanese workers feel much greater ownership of and personal involvement with their companies than Americans do with theirs.

7.   Understand that teamwork does not succeed unless you clearly make a personal and independent decision to *want* teamwork.

8.   Know that your job as team member is to empower your colleagues, to make them successful, to make them powerful—for ethics is service.

9.   You must understand the systemic rules that govern group behavior. Group behavior is often not the result of individual decisions but rather of group dynamics, of the group's behaving similarly with different players. To improve a team, you change the system rather than the participants. There are cultural differences, different expectations of efficiency and speed, or of reflection and the mature seasoning of decisions. What is normal for one team is aberrant for another; the rules applying to one team are violated by the rules of another. The sense of time, responsibility, risk, efficiency, politeness, outspokenness—all these vary from culture to culture.

10. As a team leader, you must know how to guide a team, a knowledge acquired partially through learned skills, partially through experience, and partially through the quality human being who you are. If you are the team leader,

then that is your responsibility. If you are not, then it is your responsibility to expect guidance of your leader, to challenge that individual, to teach him or her, and to enlist your colleagues to do the same.

11.   Remember that teams are important but not absolute. People with leadership minds do not do well under regimentation. Some of the greatest achievements of civilization have been accomplished by individuals. Individualism is the great ideal of Western civilization. The emphasis on teamwork promoted by business needs must not blind us to the American Bill of Rights, which protects individuals. And the individual, not the team, is the final unit, the cell, of the social organism. Just because people sit together at a table does not mean that they automatically form a team.

12.   Remember that teamwork can be very satisfying emotionally, for it responds to an ancient desire: to participate in something bigger than each of us is individually. We want to belong to something that existed before us and that will continue after us. We join teams to reawaken this ancient hunger.

13.   Understand that most of the time when people think they are a team, they are not. Only when people understand that they are far from being a team do they have a reasonable chance to become a team. Always be alert to the possibility of self-deception.

14.   As team members, you must think as one team. Team members feel the cohesion of the group. They do not think that they are doing their work alone. They think, always, that the work is being done communally. "*We* are doing the work." It is not sufficient to say that *I* contribute to the group. *We* are working. *We* are accomplishing. And it is *our* work, *our* task, that we are accomplishing. Team members literally adhere to an extension of the motto of the Three Musketeers: all for one and one for all.

15.   Understand that teamwork means that the group works on *one* single concept, one shared vision. Team members have, collectively, one answer to the question "What is our task,

our function, our job, our business?" One concept, one idea, a single goal, one vision activates them. For example, restaurants do not serve food. They serve customers, give them an experience. And if the restaurant is part of a hotel, then the staff is responsible for coordinating the customer's total experience. Similarly, teachers will say, not that they teach one subject matter to many students, but that they teach many subjects to one student.

16.   As a team member, everyone must understand that the perfection of the team is not the same as the perfection of each individual. Perfection in the system and perfection of its parts may be contradictory propositions. This is an axiom in systems theory. Each member adjusts to the needs of the team. In an individualistic society, to carry out teamwork successfully is extraordinarily difficult and commonly unsatisfactory. The converse is equally important to point out: every member of a team suffers if the team itself is dysfunctional. Thus, there is ample individual motivation for cooperating in making teams effective. In short, individuals should be willing to sacrifice their own interests and the interests of their units for what they view as the needs of the whole.

17.   It is the responsibility of each authentic team member–teacher–leader to use the Leadership Diamond model to establish successful teamwork. Do it in a great way, and take personal responsibility for approaching the problem of teamwork with vision, with realism—ethically and courageously.

18.   Assess the productivity of your teamwork. One way is through the number and quality of decisions made during your work or meetings (see the sample scale for scoring in Figure 7.1). *Importance* means that some decisions are insignificant, whereas others are exceedingly important. And leaders know the difference. *Acceptability* refers to how palatable a decision is to those affected by it. *Follow-up guarantee* refers to provisions made for implementing and monitoring a decision. Every one decision creates a basketful of many new decisions to be made. *Quality* refers to the

Figure 7.1. Sample Scale for Scoring Productivity.

Productivity Measure

Productivity $= (I + A + F) \times Q$

Decision made	Importance	Acceptability	Follow-up guarantee	Quality	Total
#	0 – trivial 1 – average 2 – superior	0 – poor 1 – average 2 – superior	0 – poor 1 – average 2 – superior	0 – poor 1 – average 2 – superior	

amount of thought, information, experience, maturity, and consideration of contingencies that goes into the making of a decision.

19. Ensure that meetings end with energy, hope, and good feelings, not with bitterness, depression, and exhaustion.

20. Remember that effective group work depends on honest, deep communication among the participants. That demands solid human understanding and considerable personal maturity.

21. Never allow teamwork to lead to mediocrity. It must always be carried out in the spirit of greatness.

In terms of these twenty-one principles, how does your team measure up?

Using the Leadership Diamond Model to Analyze Teamwork

In Chapters Ten and Eleven, we will use the Leadership Diamond model explicitly as a grid for analyzing leadership situations. Here, the issue of teamwork provides a first example of this use of the model. A few amplifying thoughts about teamwork analysis are now in order.

The Leadership Diamond model consists not only of one central diamond but also of four additional diamonds, one on

Figure 7.2. Teamwork.

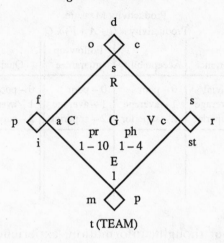

t (TEAM)

each corner (see Figure 7.2). Thus, *ethics* (E) is not a single point but rather a diamond itself, consisting of the resources of the leadership mind — the tactics, which are team (t), meaning (m), love (l), and principle or integrity (p). Similarly, *reality* (R) is not a simple diamond corner but consists of detail (d), objectivity (o), survival (s), and contact (c). *Vision* (V) is not merely one point but is supported by the tactics of reason (r), systems (s), creativity (c), and space-time (st). Finally, *courage* (C) is upheld by the tactics of product advocacy (p), isolation (i), anxiety (a), and free will (f). Further, we must be sensitive to the two dimensions of greatness (G), the pragmatic (pr) and the philosophical (ph). Strictly speaking, we must also make allowances for each one of the subdivisions of these two approaches to greatness. If, for example, the issue is denial of reality, we invoke at least two elements from the toolbox: R (reality in general) is dealt with negatively, and G_{ph3} (resistances to authenticity, self-deception) is invoked.

In diagnosing a particular leadership situation (such as, in this case, teamwork), we set the Leadership Diamond on its relevant dynamic corner and dynamic subcorner. In the case of teamwork, we place the Diamond on its ethical corner (which is now the dynamic one) and within it we place the subdiamond on the team corner. We then understand that every corner and

subcorner of the Diamond, every strategy and tactic, is a resource that must be enlisted in support of the one leadership
situation at hand—in this instance, teamwork. This method
mobilizes the full power of the entire Leadership Diamond—
and, with it, the full armamentarium of the human mind—to the
benefit of the one leadership issue we are managing.

Each tactic and strategy, as well as greatness in general,
can now be correlated with teamwork (which rests at the base).
Each capital letter represents a strategy, and each lowercase
letter represents one tactic (for example, reasoning, systems,
creativity, and space-time under *vision*; and product, isolation,
anxiety, and freedom under *courage*).

Each of the twenty-one principles of teamwork is supported by one or more resources (tactics) and dimensions (strategies) from the Leadership Diamond model, as follows:

1. R,s	8. E,l	15. V,s
2. E,p	9. R,o	16. V,s
3. E,p	10. R,o	17. G
4. C,f	11. C,i E,p	18. C,f
5. C,p	12. R,c	19. C,f
6. C,f	13. R,o	20. E,l
7. R,o	14. V,s	21. G

In this way, we see how the full powers of the Leadership Diamond model—that is, the full range of the resources of the
leadership mind—can be mobilized in the service of teamwork.
That is effective leadership.

8

Courage:
Acting with Sustained Initiative

We now explore in greater detail the supporting tactics of the strategy of courage. The goal is to challenge you to connect ever more deeply with the very source of your power.

Elements of the Tactics

Aggressive Education and Management of Markets, Product Advocacy. Let us first consider aggressive marketing. There are many types of products and many types of customers. Anything that you create and offer to others is a product. Your service to your superiors is a product; your service to your subordinates is a product. You have external and internal customers; you have immediate and distant customers. Whatever you offer to them, from paintings or education to health or food, from ball bearings to stock market information, is your product.

Even as an independent individual, whether you work for a large organization or are a private entrepreneur, a retired golfer or a student embarking on a college career, you will benefit by conceptualizing yourself as a business. *Business is the language of effectiveness.* Its categories help you tune up your mind for the race toward success, no matter what your enterprise. Ask yourself Peter Drucker's questions, "What is my business? What is my product? Who are my customers? What do they perceive as value?" These questions force you to rethink what, in a larger sense, you are doing. Systems thinking and strategic intelligence are required to answer them. And remember Peter Drucker's ukase: The only reason for the existence of a business is creating satisfied customers. Your business may be to write a poem or to find a lover, to accumulate wealth, promote justice, fight crime, eliminate poverty, build a legacy, create an estate, start a dynasty, own a ranch. Give your "company" a name, such as "Unlimited Potential," "The Happiness Conspiracy," "Meanings for Everyone," "Transportation Solutions," "Nutrition Intelligence," "The Truth Initiative," "The Knowledge Cooperative," "Action, Inc.," "Earth Love," "Anima," "Terra Firma," "Omnia," "Eartheart," or be like the veterinarian who calls his hospital "Aardvark, etc."

Be original. By thinking of yourself as a business, you formulate your thoughts and focus your mind, with the best chance for achieving your goals. That is the generic meaning of being a product advocate: you have something to create, something to market, something to sell, because you *are* something. You stand for something. Now promote it.

Markets must be integrated and managed, not merely accepted for what they are. The aggressive management of markets is not a matter of vision alone but also of courage. Neither the automobile nor the computer was merchandised in response to a need. Marketing analysis could not have discovered customers for recombinant-DNA products. The market must be educated, and the visionary, courageous leader does precisely that.

Let's say that a customer is difficult—unpleasant, even unethical. You are angry, irritated, even disgusted. What is a courageous response? Remember three things. First, the customer treats you the way he or she has been treated by the world. "It's a jungle out there," and not only for you. You market your product by putting yourself in your customers' shoes. You are therefore qualified to deal with the customer. You have courage, and you are effective in advocating your product.

Second, your job is to teach your customer leadership, whatever else may be your product or services. You do that by modeling how you respond to the frustrating encounter: not with anger or depression, but cheerfully, with resourcefulness, enthusiasm, and positive energy.

Third, your customer wants to buy what you have to offer. It is unlikely that you would be in a business relationship if that were not true. You must therefore help your customer find ways to use your product.

By teaching leadership, you can serve your customers twice. You show them how to cope with their general frustrations by showing them how, in this situation, you cope with yours. It is a bonus for your customers. This guarantees you an attitude of genuine tolerance and compassion. You are teaching how one stands up to defeat. That is not only a business virtue but also a human virtue. You also look for ways to make it possible for them to obtain and use your product, by fully putting yourself in their shoes. The relationship is one in which you help them. It is neither argument nor confrontation. It is this total customer focus, an act of generosity of spirit and personal loyalty, that can make business successful to the precise degree that it is ethical.

You are successful in product advocacy because you can handle frustration better than the next guy. And never forget that your frustration is the same as your customer's. If your customer can handle frustration better than you can, then the roles are reversed, and you are the customer, and he or she is selling you something.

What do you sell? If you are a physician or a psychotherapist, you sell health; if a lawyer, protection; if a priest, religion; if a teacher, knowledge and self-development; if an artist, experiences. And if you court someone, you are trying to sell love—or yourself. The principles of successful product advocacy apply everywhere.

Innovations in companies—new products, new processes, new organizational ideas—often meet bureaucratic resistances. Organizations may claim that they want innovation and that they promote creativity, but when you propose it, you meet sluggishness, inertia, and stultifying organizational rigidity. The cause is not so much individual managerial malevolence as systemic inevitability. To move an organization can feel like eating your way through a gigantic marshmallow mountain:

it absorbs all assaults, its demands are endless, and it envelops all efforts to move it in an amorphous mass, bland and sticky. It is at such moments that product advocates are welcome and needed. Do not give up. Persist. Have faith. Today's heresy is tomorrow's dogma. It is just such kind of people that have become history's heroes.

Aloneness, Autonomy, and Independence of Thought. To be courageous is to be prepared for the isolation of leadership. Thus, to be a self-starter is to be autonomous, to have given up the helplessness and dependency that are often fostered by the presumptive security of larger organizations. Autonomy is the ability to live in isolation and be comfortable with the feeling of aloneness. For the person who cherishes intimacy, isolation is as painful as it is fundamental to integrity, since intimacy without the courage to stand up for one's rights is empty servitude. Intimacy is a virtue when it is given freely by an autonomous soul. Autonomy is not an infrequent concern in Oracle questions. How does one develop into being one's own person after a lifetime of being totally compliant, just wanting to be loved, concerned with what others think?

To have courage is to think for yourself. It is to reason independently when assaulted with conflicting opinions. It is to have clear and firm values, of which you are proud, and which support you under stress. It is to have faith—in yourself, your family, your organization, your religion, your country, your ideals, your profession, your friends. Each person has faith in different arenas. What matters is that you be capable of faith, which makes you independent of the winds of doctrine that blow around you. You have the power to generate inner data that exert more influence than external data.

To think for yourself means that you are steadfast in turmoil, in chaos, under stress, in doubt, in anxiety and guilt, in depression and anger, under assault and abandonment, in change, in ambiguity, in uncertainty. You are a fortress under siege, a ship in a storm, with experienced and calm commanders.

Here, visioning leadership intelligence overlaps with the

strategy of courage. The visioning mind must be prepared for the loneliness of leadership, for holding on faithfully to a vision frequently derided by others helps you remember that persistence wins. Steadfastness is the courage strategy applied to vision.

Be prepared for the loneliness of leadership. It is worse and more difficult than you may have thought it would be, for it is not a thought; it is real. Are you adequately prepared for loneliness? Do you face it or repress it? A leader is not a lonely person, nor is a leader necessarily an introvert, but a leader can withdraw into total isolation, from within which he or she can then make difficult and painful decisions—often unrecognized for their high ethics and noble courage. A leader can be a very private person. If circumstances warrant it, he or she can suffer in silence.

Anxiety. The most difficult aspect of courage is its psychological dimension. It is therefore critical to understand that anxiety is the *key* to courage, for courage is the decision to tolerate maximum amounts of anxiety. You should face your anxiety, you should stay with your anxiety, and you should explore your anxiety. The same is true of the decision to tolerate guilt. In general, management techniques, useful as they may be, are often more escapes from courage than effective tools to harness courage.

Leadership means presence, contact, and credibility, and these come only with character. Character is developed by going through the existential crisis, which means to allow anxiety to come to full flowering. Do not fear anxiety. Instead, allow yourself to feel it fully. You come out at the other end of the process strong and resilient, wise and mature. You prize the value of integrity. No significant decision, personal or corporate, professional or military, has been undertaken without its own existential crisis, the leader choosing to wade through rapids of anxiety, uncertainty, and guilt. It is such crises of the soul that give leaders their character and their potency. Dostoevsky wrote, "Taking a new step, uttering a new word, is what people fear most."

Figure 8.1. The Existential Crisis.

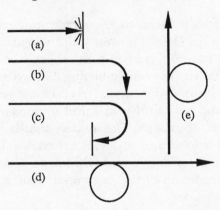

Anxiety is a cognitive emotion, which means that it can reveal the truth about the human condition and, in its special way, provide answers to the eternal questions.

Anxiety can usefully be understood to repeat the trauma of birth, which is the most dramatic change a human being will ever experience. This metaphor dramatically reveals that pain can be the door to a new life, since in birth there is pain for both mother and child. The word *anxiety* itself comes from the Latin words *angustus* and *angere*, which point to the pain of going through a narrow passage. Leaders choose to be born; non-leaders choose to avoid birth. What admits you to life is the choice never to avoid the anxiety of death.

You meet the existential crisis (see Figure 8.1) whenever you confront any crisis, when you hit a wall of frustration [(a)]. On the present view of anxiety and its relation to authenticity, you are then encouraged to pursue that which produces anxiety, only to find yourself in a downward loop [(b)] and eventually also a backward loop [(c)] in the journey of life. (You may say, "Thanks a lot!" to the person who gave you this advice.) Carried to its full conclusion, you will eventually move forward and continue on your journey of life, now strengthened and renewed [(d)]. You will have character and hope, power and effectiveness. Turned vertically, it becomes a primitive drawing of a pregnancy [(e)]—a fitting symbol. And the process of building leadership character will never reach its apotheosis if, midway, cowardice stops you.

What does it mean to encourage your anxiety? Do not hide your feelings. Do not repress your thoughts. Do not ignore the pain; feel free to discuss it with others. Know that there is more pain, that you are only touching the surface. As you talk, think, feel, write, question, and read about the issue that causes you anxiety, you may find your mind flooded with emotions. These are part of growth. The anxiety that is buried in you, properly understood and properly experienced, can translate itself into growth, strength, and fulfillment. That would be the successful completion of the existential crisis, and such is the pattern of the leader's life.

In sum, anxiety is how it feels to grow. One becomes an adult by learning to move through anxiety, to stay with and not avoid it. Leadership, therefore, means to face anxiety, not fear it, to make it your constant companion. We are here at the very nerve center of courage.

Theories of anxiety have had a curious history. Medical science, beginning with Freud, has viewed it as an illness, and there is much merit in this position; that is a healthy and intelligent attitude toward one of the grave problems of humanity. But there also exists an entirely different position regarding anxiety, a position that promises to be the axiom of leadership. That view is the contribution of contemporary philosophy, especially of Kierkegaard, to the understanding of anxiety and its relation to your personal authenticity. Anxiety is the natural condition of human beings. Anxiety reveals truths that we wish to hide but in fact need for our greater health. Anxiety is the experience of growth itself. How does it feel to proceed to the next stage of growth? The answer is, be anxious. Anxiety must, therefore, be valued, not denied.

Anxiety is the revelation that there is death, and that we must face it. Anxiety is the revelation that we are surrounded by an emptiness, an abyss best described as nothingness, and that life's projects are defenses against this dismal but ineluctable truth. Therefore, the healthy person is the courageous one, the person unafraid of anxiety, who says yes to life in spite of the overwhelming omnipresence of this abyss of death. In fact, courage means to know a secret: *anxiety is pure energy*. It can go in either destructive or constructive directions; you make the choice. To be is to say yes to anxiety. That is the meaning of courage.

Anxiety has many additional sources besides the fear of death. Anxiety derives from the fear of abandonment as much as from the fear of assault. Anxiety results from the fear of ridicule as much as from the fear of insanity, for all human beings are easily ridiculed; many people feel ridiculous without anyone's having said anything to trigger it. And many healthy people worry about whether they are normal. But what is normality but the consensual, what society has agreed to accept? And doesn't that change from age to age and from civilization to civilization? Isn't that the lesson that history teaches us? Knowledge of history liberates us from the tyranny of the culture into which we were thrown quite accidentally. But history, while it emancipates the spirit, also throws it into a vortex of anxiety.

Anxiety also results from the knowledge of our freedom, for the inherent freedom of being human often precludes a clear right or wrong answer. Frequently, right and wrong are created by our choices—an insight as painful as it is profound. Again, the result is anxiety. The authentic leadership solution is not to deny this anxiety of freedom but to live through it, to face it, to go "cold turkey," to sweat it out. To give up something, without frills, gimmicks, or support, is to face your naked anxiety. That is the true meaning of courage—to choose freely to tolerate anxiety. That is how we grow; that is how we exhibit character.

Freedom also leads to the anxiety of guilt, for whenever you choose freely, you also deny freely, and whatever value you deny by your choice can lead to guilt. In fact, the existence of guilt is proof of the existence of freedom, for guilt is what you feel when you have made a deeply personal and very difficult choice. To face the anxiety of guilt is to move forward with courage.

Change, too, is a source for anxiety. Change disorganizes stability. It creates confusion, which is experienced as anxiety.

In real-world situations, the practical formula with respect to anxiety is this: *go where the pain is.* In other words, be ready to talk with evil. That is a technique for achieving leadership courage. Explore your moments of anxiety. Examine your nightmares. Do not fear them, and do not deny them. They hold the answers to otherwise unanswerable questions. The passport to authentic life is to integrate and transcend both pain and evil. The soul that can absorb its opposite, the enemy, is on its way to power and character.

If a friend dies, don't pass it off as something you must overcome and say that you must get on with your life and be practical. In the end, that *is* what you will do, but from the point of view of leadership potential, it is best for you to feel your pain. Give yourself permission to grieve, and pour out all the grief that is in you — not only the grief about your friend's death but also the grief that has accumulated over decades.

Anxiety is "where the rubber hits the road"; many a novice pilot will tell you that upon a first landing. Anxiety is the experience of thought becoming action. What do you feel when reflection becomes behavior, when strategy becomes implementation? Anxiety is the feeling of leadership in action, of theory being transformed into practice.

Free Will and Responsibility, Energy and Power, Centeredness. The very heart of courage, the philosophic core, is our human freedom. That is the fourth tactic or resource, the critical success factor. Freedom is a fact inside your heart. It is your most precious possession. It gives you power over your life. It gives you the benefits of being responsible for your existence and accountable for your life. Free will cannot be explained scientifically — only philosophically, poetically, religiously, or mythologically. Claiming your freedom is the ultimate secret for mastering your life. To discover your freedom inside your heart is an exuberant experience of both exhilaration and hope, and that freedom can never be extinguished. Heroes have exercised this freedom at the risk of life itself. True love means to surrender that freedom to another. The greatest gift you can ever give is the surrender of your freedom. That is the ultimate act of love — toward a spouse, a child, a boss, a friend, a nation, a leader, a cause, an ideal, or God.

Irvin Yalom (1980) writes about "leverage-producing insights," insights that stimulate you to claim your freedom. They are called *insights* because they are truths. Once we recognize them as such, we are, as it were, provoked to courage. Remember these affirmations:

- Only I can change the world I have created.
- There is no danger in change.
- To get what I really want, I must change.
- I have the power to change.

This is how a person feels who has discovered freedom. That discovery can make the individual into a leader.

From your freedom follows the power for initiative. The leader is a self-starter. Leaders energize themselves; they do not require external sources of enthusiasm. They know that to be human is to be a creator, to have the ability to start something from nothing. The creation of the world, a theme in all of the world's mythologies, is the cosmic image of our subjective initiative—a cosmic metaphor for our innermost truth.

Energy, as it is subjectively experienced, is not derived from the chemical properties of food but is the decision to be, the courage to be, the commitment to exist. Energy is self-chosen, self-started, self-initiated. Its source is not visible to us, for we *are* it. Further, the energy we can summon—from sheer free will, self-discipline, determination, resoluteness, or guts—appears to be inexhaustible.

It is psychologically true that our environment can either energize or deenergize us, motivate or demotivate us. But it is also true, at a deeper level (that is to say, it is philosophically true), that we have the power to choose to energize ourselves (and, of course, to deenergize ourselves). At the seat of the soul resides the power of spontaneous free will, which can choose to motivate or demotivate, to create enthusiasm or decide for depression.

Through their behavior, executives are expected to demonstrate redoubtable action and inspiring initiative. In practice,
however, it appears that they often are conservative, cautious,
and protective. That may make good common sense. Nevertheless, when questioned, many executives insist that their biggest
failing has been not to seize the initiative, needlessly to postpone action, and that applies as much to their business lives as
to their private lives. Furthermore, for initiative to make a difference, it must be sustained. It must be persistent, continuous,
unbroken. Everyone can exercise his or her freedom once in a
while. What is rare is the ongoing, ceaseless, unfailing manifestation of the power of freedom—which means to act with
sustained initiative. That is indeed the mark of authentic
leadership.

Leaders must make good decisions, fast. Good decisions
now are mostly participatory decisions, team decisions, but the
requirements of today's organizations are so stiff that good team
decisions must be accelerated. And they can be, for an authentic
leader knows how to get to the point, the real point, quickly. Real
philosophic wisdom, not technique, makes that possible.

Initiative, freedom, and energy are intertwined. You have
the power to start your own energy, but you also have the power
to create energy for your organization. Some people take energy
away. You feel it when you are in their presence. Some give
energy to you. It is an exhilarating experience. A "manager"
takes energy away from the organization, drains energy from his
or her people. A leader gives energy to the organization, infuses
energy into his or her people. What kind of executive are you?

Freedom, as the heart of courage, as the critical success
factor of this strategy, is related to one of the fundamental points
of contemporary philosophy: that truth is action. Truth is not
what you say but what you do (with the understanding that
saying is frequently doing, as when we promise, love, or insult).
This truth is unsafe—a risk, a commitment. You may be terribly
wrong but also profoundly right; perhaps "right" is what you
make it. A fully human life is not a reflective existence but an
acting one. The reason for resistance to courage (fear of courage)
is that a transformation occurs, a conversion, from reflection to

action, from thought to implementation. The mind that acts is different from the mind that reflects. Both are important, but the translation from one to the other is an act of will that is the special prerogative of human beings. It is as important as it is difficult to explain the mystery of action from the point of view of the reflective consciousness. In fact, it is equally difficult to define the reflective consciousness from the point of view of action. It is almost as if, by some magical process, we think that we can bring a dream image into the real world.

The tradition of Athens is that value, reality, and knowledge (which is truth) — the three primary fields of philosophy (ethics, metaphysics, and epistemology) — are given by an impersonal general theory, a dehumanized abstraction of universal validity. The tradition of Jerusalem, by contrast, defines truth, value, and reality in terms of a fully personal decision, an individual commitment, an act of great risk. As an example of the tradition of Athens we have Plato, who, with his theory of ideas, defines truth as eternal forms that the soul perceives both before birth and after death. These forms represent verities that hold for all time. The tradition of Jerusalem is exemplified by the crucified Jesus, who made his statement, at one time in history and at one point in space, by surrendering his life. The first kind of truth is what you produce in the safety of your study or laboratory. The second kind is what you find in the danger of the barricades.

To gain your freedom, you must be prepared to be anxious. The result is centeredness, which returns us to the philosophic level of tactics. To be centered is to have the feeling that you touch the ground of your being, the seat of the self, which leads to the miracle of self-validation or self-authentication. This deep faith, springing genuinely from the center, that you are basically right, legitimate — that you, as a child of the universe, belong here — is the true foundation of character, maturity, and emotional stability. The effect of claiming one's freedom and the choice of energy (that is, to choose to be an energetic person) is centeredness, the peaceful feeling that one is living from the inside out. It results from choosing freely to withstand anxiety, the anxiety that follows when we overcome resistance to the truth.

Everyone, in his or her heart, is isolated. That is the human condition. Friendship and love are the communion of two isolated selves sharing their sense of isolation. As we penetrate our isolation more deeply, we also discover that the center we reach connects us with the entire universe. To reach that innermost still point is the goal of many religions and philosophies. Once we have found it, we do not feel lonely at all. We feel rich and peaceful. It is the discovery of maturity. The end of courage is to reach that center of our inner earth. There is no greater depth than that; moving on, beyond, is to go back to the surface. That center is the point of ultimate stability. To have courage is to operate from within that still point.

The philosophies of the East have as their primary objective the recovery of this center—reminiscent also of the philosophic tactic under the strategy of vision. But so likewise have many philosophers of the West. It is all splendidly captured in these lines from T. S. Eliot's "Burnt Norton."

> At the still point of the turning world. Neither
> flesh nor fleshless;
> Neither from nor towards; at the still point, there
> the dance is,
> But neither arrest nor movement. And do not call
> it fixity,
> Where past and future are gathered. Neither
> movement from nor towards,
> Neither ascent nor decline. Except for the point,
> the still point,
> There would be no dance, and there is only the
> dance.

We can summarize all these truths about the depth of the human soul with a single phrase: *the anxiety of freedom*. Anxiety about freedom is a central aspect of the human condition. Deny it, and you are stultified. Acknowledge your anxiety, let it go where it wants to go, and you understand that a human being is meant to tolerate anxiety. And you are equipped to do so—

physically, morally, mentally, and emotionally. Surrender to your anxiety will make you free. Here is the secret of courage. It can be yours. It can change your life. It is your key to leadership.

Courage: Summation

It is time to weave together all the tactics of courage. For this purpose, let us turn to another Oracle question:

> I have high-level project-management responsibilities. I have serious problems with a key subordinate. He, in turn, manages a team of twelve persons, who fan out to the full organization to effectuate the strategic messages from senior management. He and I together make bad chemistry. I believe his capacity as leader is limited. He is entrenched in his position and cannot easily be replaced. Anyway, it is company policy to challenge and train managers, not to replace them. He lacks control over his organization, and I seem to have no control over him. I do not want to go over his head and manage his organization directly. Morale, of course, is low. The work is not getting accomplished. It is a hopeless situation. I think I do not have the courage to face this problem. My anxiety level is too high. Is there anything I can do? Although I am embarrassed to admit it, I'm rather desperate! I feel anxious every day I go to work.

Here is a clear case of the need for courage. And here is a message to that question: As a leader, in this situation, you must have a strategy—a point-by-point management plan—to deal with your problem. But the strategy, which is the systematic approach expected of managers, accomplishes little if it is not also buttressed by a strongly developed personal side of leadership. You yourself must develop that inner side, and you must challenge it in your subordinate. To marshal your courage, you will find it useful to adopt three attitudes: objectivity, credibility, and effectiveness.

These points are about the inner side of leadership. They are states of mind. *Objectivity* means understanding the objective facts and the objective responsibilities in your work situation. One objective fact about business in general is that people must do good work. This is a nonnegotiable proposition. It is not a rule but a reality. There can exist no business where people do poor work. This is a fact, and it must be clear to all. It is not a decision, not a human creation. It is not an opinion. It is the truth. You cannot compromise over good work. If you are tempted to do so out of fear, then the reality is that you are not a manager. This is also part of objectivity.

To see reality as it is is not the same as to take personal responsibility for it; the weather is what it is, and the meteorologist has no responsibility for it. The habit of differentiating between fact and freedom must be ingrained in everyone (you and your subordinate) who wishes to manage. We are responsible for actions, but not for natural facts.

Often this limitation is not clear to managers, nor is it apparent to subordinates. Managers are not omnipotent; reality is. We can protect no one, not even our children, from what is. It is an objective fact that people are responsible for their own actions and for the consequences; no one else is. Human beings are but the consequences of their actions. (The philosopher Gabriel Marcel used the phrase *homo faber* to refer to this concept.) You are what you do.

Remember always, however, that people are extremely sensitive to their sense of self-worth, self-respect, and dignity. Do not make them wrong. Never diminish a person's self-esteem. People of all cultures must save face. Do not moralize. Do not tell people what they must do. Draw attention strictly to the facts, but know exactly what the facts are. There are social facts, emotional facts, moral facts, and material facts. That people are responsible for their actions is one of these facts. Stick to reality, but never forget that people panic when their self-respect is threatened. Do not humiliate them. Humiliation is unethical and unpragmatic. These are facts—interpersonal, relational facts. To balance standards and respect is the art of leadership.

Credibility means that you are believable. To get through to your subordinate, you must first be credible. You cannot afford to appear the fool. Credibility is a function of your personality. It is not what you do but how you do it, who you are when you do it. People must learn to respect what you say. You must be heard when you speak. People must learn to trust you. This means that you must be open to feedback. It means you will have the inner strength to ask for genuine feedback and assimilate it well. You will have the courage to ask, "What, in my behavior, would you like to see different?" And you will possess the fortitude to elicit honest answers and have the good sense to give satisfaction. That requires extraordinary centeredness, a strong sense of inner security, which you can achieve through a solid philosophy of life. (The Leadership Diamond model is intended, in part, to facilitate that for you.) Only in this way will you gain or regain control over your organization.

Effectiveness means that you get results. They, and only they, count. Why? Because executives are mean? No. Because nature is that way. Who says so? The market speaks. The supremacy of results is not an opinion but a natural law. Results are translated into survival. Never let go of this insight. No matter what you feel, you are obligated to achieve results with your organization.

On the softer side, you must have an emotional alliance with your subordinates. You must feel connected, even close. That demands cooperation, considerable maturity, and mental health. People often choose not to cooperate. That is partly their fault and partly yours. But without that conscious connection, a common intersubjective space, there is little hope for effective management, and it is time for the parties to separate. You need to be compassionate, but you must also know the limits.

Effectiveness requires consistency and perseverance. The soul grows slowly, but it does grow. It wants to grow. You must have the power that comes from being comfortable with isolation, so that you will be centered enough to wait patiently for results.

The manager who posed this Oracle question resists confronting his subordinate. His fear is understandable. With his mind focused on objectivity, credibility, and effectiveness, however, his courage can be strengthened.

Courage is the foundation of leadership. All other leadership values are brittle unless reinforced with the steel of courage. Some executives choose security over courage and are not proud of it. Security is indeed a value, but the only real security lies in your leadership courage. There can be nothing more dangerous than being lulled into security by avoiding anxiety. The sole security lies in confronting and living through the necessary anxiety to act with courage. Aristotle understood correctly that courage is the first of the human qualities because it guarantees the others.

Imagine a young and highly ambitious midwestern oil-company executive who has everything going for him: a promising career, a charming wife, a new child. He and his wife have just made the down payment on their first house, and now they also have a home. The boss calls him in and gives him the good news: "We have a promotion for you. We have a demanding and challenging position for you in Egypt. The position requires that we advance you, simultaneously, *two* levels of management. It will also ensure for you a virtually unlimited career in the company. The committee selected you from among a large pool of promising candidates. Congratulations!"

Overjoyed, the man returns home to inform his wife. She, however, far from applauding his success, packs up the baby and, drowning in tears, yells at him, "I'm going home to mother. Call me when you get back — that is, if you care!" And she slams the door.

Nonplussed, he knows that reality has hit him. Courage, here, is not in compromise. The company cannot make adjustments, for the world oil crises are not sensitive to a young couple's immaturity. He cannot relinquish his promotion, for he will resent his wife's ruining his career. Nor can she herself compromise, because she will only hate him for squashing her ideals for the baby and herself. Moreover, the young couple will be tempted to believe that maturity means denying their archetypal feelings (on the contrary, doing so leads to illness, depression, lack of affection, and the end of sex). Where is the solution?

Courage means going back to fundamentals. Are we a family or not? Are we individual prima donnas, or do we operate as a team? This choice requires a root decision about the values to which we make a commitment. That is the courage of taking a stand. Right and wrong are not decided by society or by absolutes, but by individuals resolutely determining what they believe in as their fundamental value commitments to life. That stance means access to one's freedom. It means risking guilt, anxiety, and anger in the journey toward authenticity. It means knowing what it is to make a decision and flesh it out by the way one lives. Such is the metaphysics of courage.

Whose job is it? It is the family's job: the husband's, the wife's, even the child's. The correct and mature response is "I want you to have it your way because I love you and because I live for you. That is the meaning of our marriage." The husband, then, wants to stay, and the wife now wants to go, and the child will adapt. Finally, each partner can venture to disclose his or her true feelings: "I love you, but I want to stay home," says the young wife. "I love you, but I want a rising career," says the young husband. A loving family decision emerges.

This may be the couple's first real-life challenge to serious maturity, to real-world ethical decision making, and to the serious assumption of personal responsibility—accountability that rises from the depth of their souls' freedom. The solution, whatever they choose in the end (and we must not exclude even divorce as an option), will be their first act of courage, for courage, you will recall, is not to conquer others but to conquer oneself.

Courage does not mean to boss others around, but to choose from the inside out who we truly are, to define who we are and prove that we mean business about our values. What matters is not the *what* (that is why advice and logic are of little importance); what matters is the *how*. How does the couple choose? The *how* gives them character. It solidifies their individuality. It is the fire that tempers their freedom. The *what*, which at first appears paramount, is in the end of no emotional significance. Authenticity develops from how one chooses, not from what one does. When it comes to courage, results are in the process, not in the product. The Danish philosopher Kierkegaard said it well: joy is "to will to be that self which one truly is."

How to acquire courage is a frequent Oracle question:

How can I overcome my lack of courage?

How can I beat complacency and maintain the will power for the rest of my life, to keep focused on leadership intelligence?

There are many things I feel I need to change in my life. I procrastinate because they are difficult decisions about work, family life, and so on. How do I force myself to accept the fact that I control my own destiny and therefore must stop procrastinating and take action?

My self-diagnosis confirmed that my most serious weakness in the path of achieving greatness is the lack of courage. This has overwhelmingly prevented progress. The thinking process we have been through has further highlighted the issue— lack of courage to speak up on issues, follow convictions, and motivate people to follow my way. How can I, by myself, overcome the fundamental lack of courage?

And here is a person who does not yet accept the fact that courage is acquired only by going through some very difficult periods of anxiety, and that these steps are not taken through techniques but involve the raw freedom of our elemental decision-making powers. There is no escape from freedom:

Life is an array of compromises for most of us, and achieving a balance that we can live with is a goal, but one balance eludes me. In the area of courage, I agree that the decision to deal with anxiety is a measure of courage. But where do you draw the line with a leader who needlessly belittles people for sport, or out of his own lack of ability to deal with his own anxiety? If you allow yourself to be trampled, you won't feel good, but if you are not tolerant at all, you will be downrated.

To have courage means to claim your freedom, to reconnect with your will power, to reach the source of your resoluteness and determination as a person:

My taken-for-granted, high-potential, fast-track career unexpectedly stalled. I am emotionally in a rut, although considered successful by family and friends. My ego is seriously wounded, and the myth that I am living is no longer tolerable (alienation). How do I get to again be a leader of sterling character, when I have great difficulty concentrating on the reality?

Many courage questions have to do with marriage-career conflicts:

As my children are reaching their critical, formative years, I see a real need to provide more leadership and guidance at home, to truly fulfill my responsibilities as a father and achieve personal satisfaction. Yet the requirements of my job are expanding dramatically as demands to participate and assume leadership roles in more and more teams, task forces, process improvement groups, and so on compound my existing work load. The days regularly expand to the late evening hours and to weekends and often end in personal frustration and adversely affect my loved ones. It seems to be a vicious cycle, with no near-term prospect for improvement. In fact, conditions could deteriorate as business activity slows. How can I slow or halt this pattern, to achieve better balance between my career and family and gain the inner peace so necessary to be productive?

In my drive for success, I have failed in my obligations to my family. Do I stop now and try and reconstruct those relationships, or do I continue to drive forward on my present course?

What might be a response? In this situation, the decision is not between the two alternatives of continuing as you have been or reconstructing your family. Probably neither alternative would work or please you. Confronted by an insoluble dilemma, the leadership mind rises to the next level of reflection (vision, nonattachment). Thus, the solution is to make a commitment to values clarification. You are in a midlife crisis, which is when you ask yourself, "What is the meaning of life? Am I living the life I want, or must? What are my deepest values? What must I accomplish before I die?" Then—summoning the courage, freedom, and willing resoluteness to go through anxiety—you are on the way to choosing a new level of authenticity.

What kind of general answer can one give to all of these Oracle questions? While simply airing them may be more than enough, they are still on the threshold of some of the deepest insights into human existence. They lead to the realization that, for example, an understanding of death may be the key to an understanding of life. They are the secret of understanding, for instance, that at the core of the person is the nonbiological, nonscientific sense of free will—the ability to choose, the miracle that can create meaning out of nothing. Seizing that freedom, claiming that truth, actually living out our lives in the experience of our freedom, means being willing to face grave anxiety, uncertainty, and doubt. It means facing guilt, anger, and depression—what Saint John of the Cross called "the dark night of the soul" and Jonas called "the belly of the whale." It means that we accept pain as natural to growth, as the actual feeling of maturation. We recognize that the meaning of life is to be deep, rather than to have fun, to understand rather than be entertained, to see rather than be blind. We come face to face with our self-deception, with how we deny our true nature. We discover the perniciousness of ignorance and the worthlessness of superficiality. And these become emotional insights and experienced confirmations.

The meaning of freedom—the heart of courage and, at the same time, the philosophic tactic in this strategy—is by far the most difficult idea to communicate. It is the point where thought and action meet. Properly understood, this insight can be the answer to all leadership questions.

The Fundamental Business Issue

I am often asked this question: "What is the most important issue that you find in your consulting experience?" And here is my answer: getting people to understand, viscerally and not only intellectually, the rich experiential meaning of their free will—specifically, the meaning of four concepts.

1. The ultimate unit of society is the individual. Everything starts with the individual. "Subjectivity," the Danish philosopher Kierkegaard told us, "is the starting point." True, we must work in teams, for teamwork is the essence of business success. True, managers and employees are expected to be loyal to their companies, and vice versa; companies need it, and so do employees. But teams are made up of individuals, and individuals make or break teams. The individual commitment to successful teamwork is what makes individuals choose to study team dynamics. Individuals make the decision to apply this knowledge. Only the individual can make this one unflagging decision: to commit himself or herself personally to contributing to the team's success.

2. You are fully and personally responsible for what happens in your sphere of influence. This attitude comes from a severe ethics, extending from the Stoic philosophers of ancient Greece to the post–World War II period of the European existentialists. Such a sense of total responsibility for events is a subjec-

tive truth—that is, it is true inwardly. Here, your responsibility is 100 percent. Understanding responsibility is a key to maturity. To be an adult is to understand that responsibility is a law of nature. Further, to be an adult means that you find responsibility desirable, attractive, something you want. To be an adult is to treasure your self-reliance. Objectively speaking, we may say different things, but leadership is a subjective phenomenon, a subjective attitude, an inward transformation. We must use a language appropriate to its subject matter.

The real world seems to have been created precisely for people whose personal growth conforms to this fundamental principle of freedom. This is a philosophic insight. It makes sense in theology, in literature and the other arts, but not in the behavioral sciences, for we are speaking here of the truth of subjectivity, not of something measurable and objective. Not to be sensitive to this key insight is to miss the center of gravity of the leadership challenge. Leadership is a personal phenomenon, intelligible only in the tradition of Jerusalem, not in that of Athens. This is true of the leadership that works *in fact*, not of the leadership that looks good on paper. To be riveted to this deep point is the reality connection, the results focus, the passion for effectiveness.

3. You must understand the meaning of initiative and its source in your innermost freedom. You are responsible, fully and alone, for taking the initiative—in understanding problems, coping with them, in managing people (some of whom will help, some of whom will trouble you with their indifference, and some of whom will interfere). You, at all times and in all circumstances, must take the initiative to achieve results.

4. This truth of your freedom is not limited to your work life, which would merely trivialize it, but covers the full spectrum of the human condition. Only when you grasp your freedom in its wholeness are you the effective leader that you can be.

The essence of a human being is this nonmaterial, nonbiological core of freedom, this divine sliver of light inside your body. It is an authentic splinter of God the Creator. To be human is to harbor that freedom within, but to be a leader is to have chosen, with that very same freedom, to claim the power of freedom, to own it, to consciously and deliberately activate it in everything you do.

Nothing happens unless you make it happen. Your responsibility is wide-ranging. Wherever you find yourself, your sphere of influence, your capacity to affect events, to make things happen, reaches well beyond the sound of your voice and the reach of your eyes.

These are facts—philosophic facts, if you will, but facts nevertheless. These are realities of the world in which we find ourselves functioning and alive. These are not matters of opinion, of variable value systems, or changeable belief structures. These are truths of our human condition. We must live consistently with them, lest we become "unnatural."

Freedom

You look at the Leadership Diamond and you say to yourself, how do we translate these noble thoughts into action? Here are typical comments:

> We have an excellent leadership program. It is democratic and compassionate. It is based on a few simple principles: People are different. The leader must develop sensitivity to this diversity and must learn how to approach employees in accordance with their individual and separate needs, and in synchrony with their expectations. These needs and expectations are based on upbringing, social forces, and other personal experiences. We have superior trainers, but after spending large sums, we discover that employees simply do not make use of what they have learned; they do not apply it. A major reason they cite is that they do not see these practices exemplified by upper management. The expression is that they do not "walk their talk." What can we do? We do not want theory, but we want action. We need to know what to do to over-

come this problem. Is it all up to top management?
Or have I met the enemy, and it is me?

We are the management team of this company. We
are a young organization. Our acknowledged problem, recognized as such by us and by our employees, is that we are *not* a team. We do not cooperate.
We are not unified in our vision. We do not adequately respect each other. As a result the entire
company suffers. It is our company. We own it, and
we cannot afford to lose it.

I understand all about empowerment. But how do I
make it happen? What do I do? How do we change
this situation, how do we solve this problem? How
do we make the answers work? We do not wish to
waste our time once more on touchy-feely stuff or
mindpoking or even team building. We demand
results.

These are legitimate questions. They deserve answers, and they
have been given answers. But those answers, as the questions
themselves insist over and over, simply do not work.

A team of twelve engineers, in charge of about a thousand
technicians, could not get along; they were prima donnas. After
struggling for almost a year, they reached the following insights:

As engineers, we viewed our lack of teamwork and
cooperation as a problem, and engineers are
taught that problems have solutions. In the world of
construction, they do have solutions: here is the
formula, and the structure either stands or falls.
But we now understand that thinking of people as
if they were objects is fundamentally wrong. We
knew that in theory, but we did not understand it in
practice. It leads to distortions and ends in failure.
  Instead of attempting to go from problem to
solution, and then failing, we changed our lan-

guage. Now we say we have pain, not a problem, and then we talk about the pain. The problem was not the disagreement but how we handled it, how we spoke to each other, and the emotions we allowed to rise within us as a result of improper communication. Now we say, "I feel, I understand," rather than "You are" and "You believe." We communicate, we speak, we listen; we try to see the other person's point of view. We establish relations. We accept that we feel good or bad about each other. We learn, and the result is that our perception of the problem shifts: the energy has left the problem; the pain has diminished. We cannot explain it, but we like it.

We call that *growth*. Rather than going from problem to solution, we go from pain through dialogue to growth. We grow as persons, as managers, as executives, as human beings. We treat each other better. We are more willing to make compromises. It is not how we behave that matters, it is the character and the maturity of our souls — the heart behind those actions — that come through and are convincing. The bottom line is that productivity has increased significantly, not to speak of the healthier atmosphere around the workplace.

Why does growth occur at some times and not at others? What are the precise differences among improving, remaining the same, and getting worse? We train managers. They learn skills, are knowledgeable and polished. They know the answers. But only when they become leaders do actions follow and do we see results. Where is the difference?

No words on paper can answer that question; actions alone can. And actions spring from a transformed vision. The transformed vision (which itself represents an action) means seeing the truth of your freedom, having direct access to the brilliance of your free will. Freedom is a reality within your heart. Know it, acknowledge it, claim it, use it. The key to leadership effectiveness lies in this clear understanding of personal responsibility. What we forget is that, although we already have the world's best techniques, they do not work, because people make the decision *not* to make decisions. They decide to postpone decisions, to look for experts who can help them avoid decisions. How lovely, if this were possible; but it is not. Once we accept that, we rise to a new level of health, to a new joy, a new vibrancy of being alive. When we see that abdicating responsibility is wrong, our reward is a better world.

People choose to rely on manipulating behavior, not on managing the will. Behavior is visible, measurable, trainable, and even mechanical; the will is not. We are not conceptually equipped, in our society, to deal with the fundamentals of the soul: death, guilt, anxiety, love, commitment, hope, joy, and freedom — our free will. We have lost our sense of myth, the readiness to view the universe as our partner. Therefore, we cannot lead.

It is not that we do not understand or cannot understand; it is that we do not *want* to understand, that we choose *not* to understand. It is not that we lack the inner experience of our freedom but that, when we are face to face with it, we call it trivial, or common sense, or simply ignore or deny it; we mistake its poetry for platitudes. The best road to freedom is through an analysis of the resistances to freedom — fear of the new, terror of the unknown, the pleasures of passivity, the delights of dependency, the cultural hypnosis of clinging to society's directives. The root fact of human existence is that we choose to deny our nature. We choose to avoid self-disclosure. It is the surrender to eternal ignorance about what we can be, what we could be, what it means to be created in the image of God: a freedom, a creator, a free creator. That profound betrayal of our nature is the fall of man, the expulsion from Eden, original sin.

Once we understand this point, the search for correct techniques becomes less important. Techniques will still be recognized as the products of genius, but we can create our own, find our own; and many different ones will do. Once we have the *will*, once we have the connection to the engine of our decision making, once we claim the power of our freedom, once we are prepared to see the world and ourselves in a different light, we have what we used to call *the solution* but now call growth.

Motivation

The strategy of courage is closely connected with motivation. The most powerful sources of motivation are not money or fear of punishment but rather pride, honor, self-respect, self-development, and the sense of accomplishment. Recognition and acknowledgment, as well as their symbols, also matter greatly. Other sources of motivation, of course, are sheer will power and uncompromising self-discipline. Ultimately, only you can motivate yourself. Others can make it easy or difficult, but motivated people come just as often from sabotaging backgrounds as from supportive ones.

It is relatively easy to inspire organizational members to leadership. They are then ready to tackle any task. But management often fails to take advantage of the culture's readiness. Enthusiasm is like a jet aircraft—it must maintain speed to stay in flight. Once airborne, it cannot slow down without crashing. Once leadership energy has been released in an organization, its momentum must be sustained. Leaders cannot afford to lose precious time. In managing the "turned on" organization, there must be a management strategy that can be grafted onto the enthusiasm. The organization must know what to do. It must know how to channel the newly mobilized leadership energy. Furthermore, employees and managers must understand the full and real meaning of responsibility, initiative, and empowerment. Enthusiasm is preserved only in the psychological autonomy and emotional maturity of individual employees and managers.

How does one put teeth into newly released leadership energy? Through a contract and a public commitment. A contract means that an employee makes a riskier commitment to a manager and colleagues ("I'll resign if we fail"), and, as a result, the employee feels entitled to make much more severe demands on the dedication, caring, and competence of the manager and colleagues. This tightening of relationships is excellent for the well-being and effectiveness of the organization. It is the secret of building powerful teams. The contract must be made publicly, for that is how words become transformed into living commitments.

The question of leadership effectiveness is really the question of motivation. How does one motivate others? How does one motivate oneself? To motivate is to win the hearts of your people. How is it done? There are certain basic principles of motivation:

1. People can motivate only themselves. The best a leader can do is to serve as an example and present a challenge. Motivation is a personal responsibility.

2. True motivation arises from a sense of pride, honor, self-esteem, and self-worth. People will do good work because their joy lies in accomplishment, in the fulfillment of their potential, and because their self-respect demands it.

3. The sense of pride can be enhanced through love. We must add, as a source of motivation, recognition, acknowledgment, and confirmation of a person's value.

4. People are motivated when they are noticed and heard. People want to feel that their bosses care enough to open their hearts and minds to them. A person needs attention, a human openness to what he or she is doing. Employees must know that the boss is fully conscious of how hard they are trying. It is the attention and the care that motivate.

5. Acknowledgment must truly mean something. It must be earned, so that it is the truth and not a lie. Support must also be given — not as a technique, but with heart.

6. Compensation, in the business culture, is a sign of realistic acknowledgment.

7. A powerful motivational tool is faith in one's subordinates. The highest motivator is belief in another human being.

8. You must develop your people, give them added value, make them better human beings, and make them more marketable.

9. You must model, in every way, the authentic leader and worker in yourself. Your example is still the most potent motivator of your people.

10. There is a hard side to motivation: limits and expectations are (and should be) inflexible. Only by experiencing the impenetrability of reality is the soul motivated to mature. Reality has two hands: the soul (or ego) has its own inner need to grow, but it must equally acknowledge the tough demands for maturity of the world around it.

11. Greed is never an authentic source of motivation. In the end it will not work, for it contradicts itself: if greed succeeds for everyone, then no one will be left to manufacture the products and perform the services that greed was meant to buy.

12. Security is not a legitimate motivator, for it diminishes life.

13. Growth is a legitimate source of motivation, for growth is the nature of life itself. Growth means experiences. Growth makes employees and managers more marketable.

14. You must announce that you will always distinguish clearly and sharply between good work and bad, and you must not be afraid to make decisions accordingly.

The good leader is the leader who sets the example: the general who shows up on the front line, the manager who visits an employee in the hospital, the cost-cutting CEO who cuts his or her own salary. The inadequate leader is the one who delegates the personal contact, the one who sends memos instead of appearing in person, the one who sacrifices an employee to avoid personal embarrassment to himself or herself.

There is a simple formula for understanding motivation: *leadership effectiveness* equals *power* (charisma, credibility, achievement) plus *acknowledgment* (recognition, "making the little guy feel important"). Part of this formula represents technique; part represents character. Power results from both personality and accomplishment. A person with an authentic presence (one who has personality) is so credible that validation from that person means something.

Democracy

In the political struggles of this world, totalitarian societies are
founded on highly developed and widely disseminated ideologies. An ideology is a complete, quasi-scientific world view
that explains, accounts for, and justifies (in terms of a philosophic theory of human nature) a particular social and political
order. (In post–Tiananmen Square China, for example, severe
indoctrination is forced on all students—hard labor and military service, as well as the intensive study of communist
speeches—so that state officials feel secure enough to consider
students' minds ready for physics and chemistry.) Nazis, fascists,
Maoists, religious fanatics, racists, all autocratic and elitist societies require (and have as their foundation) a clear, simple,
extensively propagated ideology—that is, a system of thought, a
metaphysics—that justifies their view of human nature and the
subservient role of the person within the state.

Democracies lack this commitment to such a widely disseminated ideology. This means that—in the struggle for the
minds of men and women, in conceptual argumentation, in
schools, and in the political arena—democracy is far too frequently put on the defensive, and this is a monumental tragedy.
Business, like politics, requires a solid philosophic base in support of freedom.

At the risk of vast oversimplification, one can usefully
argue that totalitarianism tends toward a materialistic and ob-
jectivistic world view, toward philosophic positions based on the
denial of subjectivity. Totalitarianism is rooted in a metaphysics
that posits reality as exclusively material or objective, so that the
animal kingdom and the realm of the physical sciences are,
theoretically, enough to explain human behavior, drives, and
aspirations.

Democracy does have an ideology, but to understand it
requires a more developed mind. The ideology of democracy is
founded on the primacy of subjectivity, on the sanctity of the
center, on an understanding of the reality of consciousness and
inwardness, and on the ability and the willingness to explore
that realm, the seat of the soul. Ethics is a phenomenon of

consciousness. It is a law of subjective mind, not of the objective cosmos. The tactic, or resource, of freedom under the strategy of courage—the last item in the Leadership Diamond Toolbox—exists to defend and propagate this view.

Business requires a solid philosophical base in support of freedom, but the argument for democracy cannot be only an economic one: that a free economy produces more wealth than a planned economy; that may not even be true, and in any case it is logically irrelevant. When we talk of democracy, we talk of ultimate values, and these are not money but human dignity. They are not in the economic realm alone but cover the full spectrum of human existence, in all its freedom and consciousness.

Freedom is the heart of consciousness. The sense of being free, of spontaneous creation, of true initiative, of starting an action and of generating a thought, is the very source of consciousness. Inner exploration, exploration by an eye turned inward, leads to what can justifiably be called scientific or empirical (that is, factual) discoveries about that consciousness. Among these discoveries is the dual fact of freedom and responsibility: *I am* the consequences of my actions.

That is the meaning of responsibility. My actions grow straight out of my consciousness. My actions *are* my consciousness, my freedom made visible, made into an object. Accountability must be reckoned to be a philosophic fact of human nature and of how human nature fits into the world. That is why we can say that it is natural to be responsible and unnatural not to be. That is why we can say that accountability is healthy and irresponsibility is unhealthy—not because of utilitarian considerations, not because business needs it, but because the facts of autonomy, responsibility, and accountability rest on the very nature of human existence. To be human is to be responsible. It is also to *know* that we are responsible.

These are key insights into the foundations of democracy, and the necessity for these philosophic truths is patently obvious in the current crisis of business management, which turns on whether managers and employees will assume full personal responsibility for the success of their organizations. Only this level of emotional ownership can make a business competitive.

Thus, business exigencies have forced us to recover a fundamental philosophic truth: human freedom. The need for autonomy among employees and managers is deepened into the recovery of democracy. Business and democracy are inextricably interdependent.

These are difficult concepts because they represent areas of experience that the social consensus teaches us to ignore. It is difficult to explain subjectivity to a materialistic world, a world obsessed with objectivity; those who can see find it difficult to explain color to the blind, and those who can hear cannot fully explain sound to the deaf. It is difficult (but, we hope, not impossible) for a mature adult to explain the sense of justice to an infant.

Business, the active core of today's world community and even of world history, depends, for its authentic existence, on the ideology of democracy. Successful business requires masses of people who understand that to be human is to be *autonomous*, to choose *commitment*, and to choose to work through *teams*. They must not only understand but also live by this understanding. The key is always "choice," and one's ability to make basic choices rests on the knowledge of one's freedom. The knowledge of subjective freedom — the fundamental philosophic category of existence — makes sense only to those whose minds are open to the vast regions of their inwardness, to subjectivity, to the realm of the center.

Business — to the degree that it endorses freedom, to the extent that it knows it needs freedom as a philosophical category — is at the center of the deepest and most important struggle in the world today. Freedom is important — and not because business needs it. Business itself is important because it provides an opportunity for the expression of freedom. Freedom is human nature, and organizations that do not reflect that freedom are unnatural. It behooves business to place at the heart of its training programs a simple but mature, understandable but sophisticated, analysis of freedom. That is good for democracy; it also happens to be good for business. A philosophy of freedom, an ideology that says democracy is natural to the human condition, provides sound credibility for the current business demands of autonomy.

9

Implementing the Leadership Diamond

Having covered in detail the four dominant leadership strategies, let us now turn to the question of how to implement the Leadership Diamond model. We consider first the operational rules for using the Leadership Diamond, then the individual's own use and development of leadership thinking and tools, and finally the application of the model to organizations.

Operational Rules for Using the Leadership Diamond

Once you have diagnosed your leadership style, you have the opportunity to reorganize all of the resources or tools in the model to create an ideal profile for your future development as a leader. We must therefore now consider the important technique of Diamond reconstruction.

The operational rules for using the Leadership Diamond include, first, commitment—the resolute, inside-out decision to think and behave as a leader. Second, they include imagination—maintaining permanently before you a lucid and living image of the structure of leadership intelligence. Third, they include leverage—knowing your leadership deficits. Do not intensify what you already know how to do. Find the lost parts of your personality, and develop these. Then, reconstruct the Diamond by mobilizing the remaining strategies to support leadership healing and growth.

In Part Three, we will consider in detail how to use the Leadership Diamond as a grid for diagnosing individual and or-

219

ganizational leadership situations. At this point, it suffices to see a few illustrations of how the model becomes operationalized.

One executive wrote the following self-diagnosis:

> *Reality* is lowest. I must therefore first review each reality tactic. Am I paying enough attention to *details*? Do I see myself *objectively*? Do I really put *survival* first? Am I in *contact* with what is real, or do I live a life of fantasy? Then, I must in general be *more realistic*, which means to focus my *visionary* capabilities on creating better strategies, to know how the *people* in my leadership situation sabotage or support me or are indifferent, and to try to understand why I lack the *courage* to do something about it. What might be the secondary gains?

Another wrote:

> Our foreign partner's weak point is ethics. He talks ethics beautifully, but when it comes to money, he turns into a savage. He doesn't really understand that one must *mean* ethics and not just speak it. My temptation is to give up on the soft side and play hardball, as he does. Authenticity, however, demands that I use my *courage* to insist on ethics as the foundation of business and human relationships — even if, in the process, I risk touching on matters that are culturally sensitive. I must then use my creative and innovative *vision* to build a business relationship truly sensitive to feelings and generously oriented toward service. But I must not be a fool, either. I cannot do bad business or lose my dignity. I must bring in bottom-line results. I must be *realistic*.
>
> Thinking further, it occurs to me that I must remind our partner that we are not only in business but that we are human as well, that principles matter: *integrity* counts; morality is important to us all.

Also, we are a *team*. I cannot impose my world view
on him, but I can try to see things his way, give him
the benefit of the doubt. I must not dismiss him but
must make my own commitment to his success—
include him on my team, and ask him to admit me
to his team. Unless I reach this deeper understanding with him or at least attempt to do so, my own
job is bereft of *meaning*. I am then a materialist and a
manipulator, a Machiavellian person, connivingly
exploiting other people. The real meaning of life
lies in good human relationships, and business
must be, at minimum, a good human relationship.
Finally, I must conduct myself and my business at a
higher level of maturity and civilized behavior, and
I must raise him to my level, not go down to his. We
are not only in business, we must also *communicate*
in depth and speak with compassion—at least
make the effort, no matter how different our backgrounds and our views of the world may be. In this
way, my thinking covers all the *tactics* in ethics, since
it is in ethics that I feel our partnership is weak.

     In short, I must take personal responsibility
to initiate reconstructing my partnership to restore
to it full ethical respectability.

It is in ways such as these that the Leadership Diamond can
strengthen your leadership thinking and acting. Let us now
examine more closely how you can develop your Leadership
Diamond tools so that you can use them to fullest effect.

Sharpening Your Leadership Diamond Tools

Successful application of the Leadership Diamond model requires succinct images of the leadership mind and practical
recommendations on how to develop leadership intelligence.
The following steps show what you must consider and the
choices you must make to cope with the demands of your leadership life—not in a good way, but in a great way.

Preparation

Selecting a Target. There are various possibilities. You can examine your own leadership style (recommended as a starting place) or that of your boss, subordinate, colleague, customer, team, division, company, and so on. Or you can consider a specific leadership problem or situation, such as one project or a specific crisis. There may also be other targets that you wish to examine in Leadership Diamond fashion.

Exercising Caution. Use many or all of the tools, not just one or two. Pay special attention to the critical success factors discussed here and summarized in the Toolbox (see Chapter Two). You must also know the Leadership Diamond model.

Foundations. For the development of a leadership mind, each of the following points must be remembered and requires careful attention:

1. The Leadership Diamond model must be actualized in all of the five "Olympic rings" of life.
2. Leadership intelligence is spacious. It is open to the fact that a leader's life is paradoxical.
3. The dominant leadership strategies are all contraries of one another. To combine them is an art form.
4. The more difficult the times, the more leadership is needed.
5. The transformation to the leadership mind is radical and likely to be permanent.
6. To think and act as a leader is to be always aware and alert, not asleep or in a trance. There is no routine, no security, no safety.

Greatness. In general, greatness matters. Executives who cannot relate to this concept will simply not be comfortable in today's demanding leadership climate. Stand up and be counted. Affirm the value of life against the forces of destruction, degradation, and depression. Acknowledge how much we human beings deceive ourselves. We may be conscious, but rarely are we adequately self-conscious. Create solid reasons to be dignified and proud. Encourage religious and esthetic feelings. Discover the sense of the oceanic.

Strategies and Tactics

Vision (V), or visioning, in general, requires the development of a sense of history. It encompasses the study of futurism, and it demands an ongoing search for innovation. Visioning can be stimulated by reading good science fiction, high-quality utopian works, and all types of history.

Reason (r), or reasoning, can be fostered by the study of mathematics, geometry, and theoretical physics; through fun with riddles; and through practice with college-entrance examinations.

Systems (s) can be understood through such esoteric subjects as the study of logic, the philosophy of science, the philosophy of language, the theory of numbers, and epistemology (the theory of knowledge), as well as through such pleasures as chess, bridge, and related games. Systems thinking is further helped by familiarity with the philosophy of history and the examination of historical trends, study of political theory, and the study of macroeconomics. Systems thinking can also be encouraged by tracing the development of the great paradigm shifts in science and philosophy, such as Descartes's universal and systematic doubt, Copernicus's denial of geocentrism, Newton's theory of gravitation, Einstein's relativity, Freud's unconscious motivation, and Jung's analyses of dreams.

Another way to develop systems and strategic thinking is to concentrate on overarching questions: Name the three most fundamental political issues of the day. What is the basic economic issue in today's world? What have been the four most important events in human history? Which two scientific developments in history have had the most pronounced impact on future events? What was the most fateful decision you ever made? What was, in your life, the most interesting opportunity that you let go by? On what core myth has your life been constructed? What would be a better myth? If you were married to yourself, how would you describe life with you? Can you imagine what it would feel like to be a dog? An elephant? Life on a planet in another solar system would be totally different from ours. Can you imagine and describe what life forms could be found there? You probably can take a meaningless pattern, like a cloud or the shadow of a tree, and see pictures in it. Can you do the reverse — take a representational painting or a familiar scene and disorganize it into mere lines, shapes, and colors, and see it with no meaning at all? The effect of this kind of thinking is to shake your mind loose to experiment with new patterns of organization. It stimulates systems and strategic thinking.

Creativity (cr) is fostered by dream incubation and analysis, by artistic pursuits, and by adopting a positive attitude toward spontaneity and intuition.

Subjective space-time (st) can be facilitated by meditation practices, both Eastern and Western, and by making the examination of consciousness a separate and distinct subject of study.

Reality (R), or realism, in general, involves making up your mind that you will always be conscious of the market and will know what other people truly think about you. Realism represents the fundamental category of psychiatric health. You must make the constant and deliberate effort to be in touch with consensual reality and be on guard against the subtleties of self-deception.

Detail (d) can be brought about by your insisting on being well organized, making ample use of the latest communications and office technologies, and taking advantage of time-saving systems.

Objectivity (o) is promoted if you read daily the newspapers and periodicals that inform you about your business and its world. If you can afford one, hire a briefing officer. You must make the unwavering commitment to keep up-to-date and continually gather wide-ranging information.

Survival (s) means that you willingly take the risk to think the way a predatory animal does, a wild animal cornered and fighting for its life. Only then can you fully understand the intensity of survival consciousness required in effective leadership. There is a danger that you will become unpleasant, but

don't forget that the authentic leader orchestrates all four dominant leadership strategies, including all the tactics of ethics, and
not just the realistic tactic of survival.

Direct contact (c) means that you continuously make the
effort to know your limits, the impenetrable constraints that
define the human condition. You open yourself up to your inner
voices, and you remind yourself that other people have absolute
power over you: to say yes to you (which is often precisely what
you want), to say no to you (which is often exactly what you do
not want). You always seek to know what others, through their
body language and their behavior, are expressing and feeling
about you. The leader is constantly on guard, to be sure of being
in touch with what is real. You can promote that contact by
constantly asking for feedback and then listening to what you
hear. Direct contact with reality means that you have made the
effort to see yourself through the eyes of your boss, your subordinate, your spouse, your child, your parent, your adversary, your
enemy — even through the eyes of a foreign culture. You have the
courage to consider the possibility that others are right and you
are wrong.

Ethics (E) means that your consciousness enters into the
mind of another, and that you perceive the world through those
new eyes. You see yourself, not from within yourself, but from
within the center of another person. The driving force is not self-
knowledge, not reality, but love; and your devotion is to that
person. You are motivated to help that person, to be happy for
that person, and to grieve if that person grieves. You desire to do
that. You get joy from such genuinely innocent commitment to
service. When you make up your mind that you are indeed such a
caring person, that you want to be such a person, you become
such a person. You are finally an ethical leader. Without ethics,
there can be no true leadership effectiveness.

Team (t) involves making up your mind always to remember what a good team is. In a good team, each person
knows the importance of teamwork, and each person takes
individual responsibility to bring about the effectiveness of the
team. No one excludes himself or herself from this integrated
responsibility. Always to think of this, always to remind your

colleagues of it, always to act in concert with these two fundamental principles—that is entirely your choice. Here, practice
clearly makes perfect.

Meaning (m) can be brought about by choosing to be a
joyous, energizing, happy, and fulfilled human being. This is a
matter of personal decision, deep in your soul; to make that
decision is your responsibility, and it is contagious. Meaning is
not only a function of your job, it is also a quality of your
personality. Make the decision not to be depressed. Resolve to
energize your colleagues. It is up to you. Make it happen. Create
meaning around you through the kind of person you have
chosen to be. Meaning, for yourself and for others, is in your
hands.

Love (l) is what you promote by making the distinct decision that support, intimacy, and understanding are nonnegotiable values *everywhere*, including the workplace. Your question is
not "Do they care about me?" but "Do I care about them?" In
cultivating this attitude, be alert to self-deception. People project their own hostile feelings onto others, and they disguise
their own anger as love. Don't you do it. Be sure that you are not
the cause of hostility in others. To have such deep resolve about
your commitment to understanding and compassion is a profound mark of leadership.

Integrity (i) is a very special virtue. It means that you are
motivated by a rational, ethical rule, not by feelings of pleasure
and pain or emotions of happiness and fear. To be effective in
this supporting leadership tactic, you must resolve to be a fundamentally different kind of person, an unorthodox individual. A
rule governs your life, not a feeling. Reason, not emotions,
dictates what you do. Justice, not happiness, is your guide. This
ethical act rests on a deep and completely voluntary decision,
which only you can make, and for which you may never be
rewarded except by the knowledge that you have become an
authentic leader—that, by your choice, you have helped create
and sustain civilization itself, joining the moral giants of history.

Reading basic texts on ethics (such at Plato's *Apology*, *Crito*,
and *Republic*, the Sermon on the Mount from the New Testament,
Epictetus's *Manual*, Marcus Aurelius's *Meditations*, John Stuart

Mill's *On Liberty* and *Utilitarianism,* Spinoza's *Ethics,* and Immanuel Kant's *Metaphysic of Morals*) can set clearly before you the significance of integrity and morality for the civilized consciousness of mankind.

Courage (C), in general, can be promoted by recognizing that it is the seat of action. To be courageous is to make the decision to enter your body, to enter the world. Courage means taking the leap, making the decision to commit yourself to this world, to choose your fate as a human being, to take your chances, to risk, to be prepared to die—and to start acting as a leader does, one who takes the gamble to be in charge. You relive the story of Faust, who risked being fully human, but endangered thereby the security of his soul. To be a leader is always dangerous. You always risk being wrong. To lead, in the end, is a choice, and you must make that choice alone; but you do have the power to make it.

Product advocacy (p) can be encouraged by asking Peter Drucker's questions: What is your business? What is your product? Who is your customer? What does your customer perceive as value? Repeated iterations of these questions, by yourself and in your teams, can help promote your business in exactly the way you want.

Leadership Diamond technology must be built into every product you produce and every service you offer. You do not sell leadership; you help people buy leadership. Therefore, Leadership Diamond technology must also be built into your marketing programs as well. Everyone wants to buy leadership. Because you are an authentic leader, you must benefit your customers. If you do not, drop your business.

Isolation (i) can be supported by reference to Biblical statements. We imitate God, in whose image we are made, by saying, "I am who I am." Your identity exists in isolation. Be prepared to be yourself, but accept the loneliness. This is an act. You can choose it, and it marks you as a leadership mind.

Anxiety (a), as a tactic, means that the authentic leader comes to terms with anxiety, for it is the key to courage. You cope with anxiety, inevitable in leadership, through a decision: you make up your mind to expect pain and value it.

Free will (fw) is the most fundamental element of human nature. This freedom is the core of leadership. God's creation of the world is the highest symbol for taking the initiative. We, who are made in God's image, are also like that. All tactics and strategies, in the end, are chosen. You are the chooser, the miracle who *can* choose, the mystery of the freedom that makes you great. Do you want to know the ultimate technique for being a great leader? Claim your freedom, make use of the secret miracle that you are — your capacity to choose, and to choose freely.

Critical Success Factors

The critical success factors are *systems* (Vs), *survival* (Rs), *team* (Et), and *will power* (Cfw). These supporting tactics, if interlaced, show the highest correlation with actual living, practicing, successful, admired, lionized, written-about, and imitated leaders. If you are more practical than idealistic, these are the tactics on which to concentrate. The more you think like them, and with all of them at once, the greater the probability that life will place you in a position of lucrative leadership. In philosophy, however, we want more than pure pragmatism; we want to fulfill the leadership ideals latent in the perfectibility of human nature.

Improving Your Leadership Thinking

How do you improve your leadership thinking? Such questioning must never end, for it is the task of a lifetime. Development can be stimulated in two dimensions: by strategy and by level.

One way to develop leadership intelligence by level, as opposed to by individual strategy, is to direct your energies toward socially accepted and institutionalized programs. For example, the professional level can be developed through traditional academic and intellectual pursuits. In fact, a good, balanced college career, at a minimum, enhances this professional level of the leadership mind. Figure 9.1 illustrates this point.

To take a second example (at the last level, the philosophic), one socially accepted institutionalized developmental program is the monastery, where life is devoted to the direct

Figure 9.1. Leadership Intelligence, Development by Level.

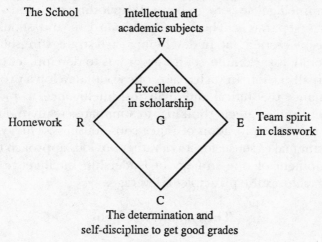

The School   Intellectual and
academic subjects

V

Excellence
in scholarship

Homework   R   G   E   Team spirit
in classwork

C

The determination and
self-discipline to get good grades

experience of the eternal truths (Figure 9.2). Of course, there are also many other paths to the level of philosophic depth. One accepted path is through depth psychotherapy. Others are through the study of philosophy, literature and the other arts, and meditation, or with the help of a good friend with whom one can discuss life's eternal questions.

Figure 9.2. The Religious Order.

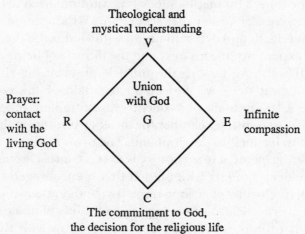

Theological and
mystical understanding

V

Union
with God

Prayer:
contact   R   G   E   Infinite
with the   compassion
living God

C

The commitment to God,
the decision for the religious life

The general principle invoked here for developing leadership intelligence is to go beyond expanding each individual
strategy separately. The latter program can and should, of
course, be carried out. In developing each strategy in isolation,
one could, for example, set up programs to develop, let us say,
principally vision. In such a case, one would develop a program
to enhance theoretical and analytical intelligence, to practice
systemic and strategic thinking, to stimulate creativity, and to
focus on the exploration of inner consciousness. This type of
program makes sense, for it is a rather obvious approach to the
development of one strategy of leadership intelligence. This
approach uses the principle of leverage.

The Atomic Metaphor

Perhaps a subtler approach is to view the Leadership Diamond as
an atom. The electrons orbit around the nucleus in rings that
form levels. There is a quantum leap from one electron ring to the
next. The outermost ring is the circle of tactics making up the
professional level: reasoning, detail, teamwork, and product advocacy. The corresponding proton cluster at the center is the
equivalent level of greatness — in this case, confronting death and
evil, which means to take a stand on the fundamental issues of
everyday life. One then develops the electrons of that ring, all at
the same time. This methodology is institutionalized in the concept of a school. Excellence in scholarship is the academic way to
confront death and evil, and union with God is the theological
way to experience the mystery and the miracle of being.

If we move now to the third level, orbit, or ring—the
psychological one—we end up in the field of the emotions
(Figure 9.3). These may be touched in a complete program of
intensive, in-depth psychotherapy, another institutionalized approach to leadership development. The proton cluster, the corresponding element in greatness, is to overcome self-deception.
It is the deep honesty with oneself that is encouraged through
the self-disclosure of a long-term psychotherapeutic process.
Such a process leads to creativity, the unfolding of new realms of
being. It promotes survival—coming to terms with the often

Figure 9.3. The Third (Psychological) Level.

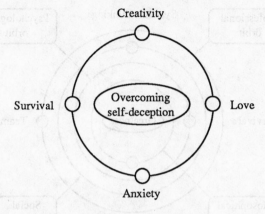

Creativity

Survival · Overcoming self-deception · Love

Anxiety

risky need to take care of oneself. It opens up the soul to love: how much we need it, how much of it we have missed, and how unconscionably we sabotage it. The entire process is fraught with anxiety, which is nevertheless the deepest source of insight about our true nature.

The second orbit, the social level, can be illustrated by an entrepreneur's establishment of a business (Figure 9.4). It requires strategy, data, facts, and information. It must have meaning and significance for all concerned, from the investors to the staff. The product, likewise, must have real meaning to attract

Figure 9.4. The Second (Social) Level.

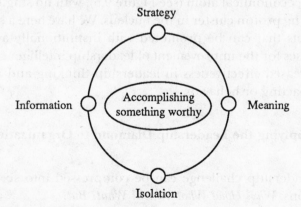

Strategy

Information · Accomplishing something worthy · Meaning

Isolation

Figure 9.5. Critical Success Factors.

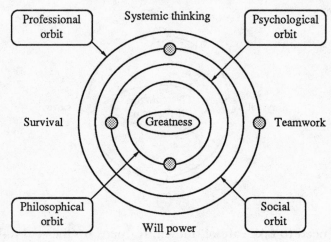

customers. This level requires that the leader be prepared to risk abandonment and isolation, for nothing is more lonely than the life of a dedicated entrepreneur. At the center of it all, like a cluster of protons, is the need to accomplish something dignified and worthy, something to which intelligent men and women can be loyal.

Finally, we come to the critical success factors. They create a "condensed" atom. In this minimalist approach, one electron is selected from each orbit, to form a highly effective, hard-hitting, economical atom (see Figure 9.5), with no single corresponding proton cluster in the nucleus. We have here a series of mindsets that can be promoted with institutionally available processes for the improvement of leadership intelligence—that is, increased effectiveness in leadership thinking and in leadership acting or behavior.

Applying the Leadership Diamond to Organizations

The leadership challenge can be compressed into six simple questions: *Why? How? Who? Which? What? But?*

Why?

Why leadership? A good executive can precisely diagnose the needs of an organization. Whatever the diagnosis, the solution universally requires leadership. It demands that a critical mass of the organization think and act as leaders do. Leadership is the principal action tool for implementing organizational objectives.

One can ask a company, "What is your problem?" One gets many answers, many different diagnoses, many different problems. Everyone, individuals as well as organizations, has reasons: the need for more decentralization, for flatter organizations, for more product and service quality, for higher productivity, for greater speed and quality in decision making; shifting markets, international competition; the need for continuous innovation, for more creativity, for more personal responsibility, for individual autonomy, for more teamwork, for better strategy; the wish to correct sluggish profits and planning errors and to temper excessive politics. The concerns are multiple, but the solution is always the same: release, among the members of your team, the power for leadership and creativity, for courage and character.

To teach leadership greatness is to help others learn how to think and act as leaders do. It means to challenge their will, to release people's latent greatness and to empower teams for extraordinary accomplishments. That is a service orientation, a commitment to caring, compassion, and love. It is also a challenge to courage and character.

How?

How is leadership to be instituted? By teaching, by placing the focus on "the other guy," the participant, the student, customer, or client.

Who?

Who needs the leadership challenge? Who needs it most? Who is
to be taught? Who wants it? Teaching is a form of marketing. You
must find your natural markets, and then you must reach them.
Who are your allies, and who are your opponents? Who is
indifferent? Who are the future leaders? Who are the culture
bearers? Make a list of those individuals and teams you decide
will be taught, and then outline the strategies you plan to use.

Which?

Which of the many leadership technologies will you adopt?
Philosophy is differentiated by depth, not by technology. Philosophy deals with access to the will required to understand and
use all technologies. Technologies are behaviors. They can be
imitated. Philosophy describes the universal human condition
behind them. That cannot be imitated; it must be understood.

What?

What, exactly, is leadership? What is to be taught? What will
release individuals' possibilities for power and creativity? One
answer is found in the Leadership Diamond model. Leaders
think differently, shifting into a gear that many people do not
use. They play a tape, insert a program, push a button, press a
key that is not available, is unknown, unrecognized, or simply
undeveloped in nonleaders. How, for instance, should a general's mindset be different from that of a nonleader? A general
thinks like the enemy, has a long time frame, cares deeply, and is
ready to die.

But?

But why doesn't leadership work? Why is skepticism inevitable?
What are the obstacles? What is in the way? Resistances to
leadership are internal (psychodynamic), external (systemic),
and philosophical (existential). Thus, there is unfinished child-

hood business, or plain immaturity. There is also the slowness to change of any system, no matter who the people are, and there is the radical chasm separating thought from action, idea from reality. This latter obstacle to leadership lies in not knowing, not having fully integrated, the categorical differences between theory and praxis, reflection and doing, planning and implementation. These pairs of concepts represent two different modes of being, two realms of existence, two poles of nature. One can never explain the other. Transformation comes, not through a theoretical insight, but through an individual act of courage.

Modern philosophy—influencing psychiatry, psychotherapy, theology, social action, and now business—has insisted that truth is in action (that is, in commitment, risk, and initiative, not in thought or reflection). This step is a transformation of, a conversion in, one's metaphysics. That truth is action has become a central theme in modern thought, expressed in contemporary literature, art, and politics, in liberation movements, in new theories of psychiatry and psychotherapy, and in religion and the social-action gospel. It is found in the popularization of such words as *autonomy* (as opposed to *dependency*), *choice* (as opposed to *fatalism* or *determinism*), *responsibility*, *accountability*, *effectiveness*, and *initiative*. We can, however, be more specific than this, for the challenge to leadership greatness goes through a series of predictable stages, some of which are resistances. Let us examine these stages.

Developmental Stages in the Challenge to Leadership Greatness: The Resistance

In a seminar for top management of a major oil company, the ranking member present, a vice-president, interrupted my very first words in a day-long seminar for executives with "Doc, I warn you, our minds are made of reinforced concrete!" In fact, as it turned out, nothing much happened all day to prove him wrong. Nevertheless, trying to save the day, I responded to his opening salvo: "Sometimes we must speak from the heart." The vice-president reflected a bit, and, in the spirit of a true oilman, retorted, "The heart . . . is a pump!" That was, in its finest form, the resistance to leadership depth.

We have said that leaders are prepared for every eventuality, and that must include the resistances to be expected when one challenges an organization to leadership greatness. Here are some of the developmental stages we can expect to encounter.

1. A need is felt—partly rationally, mostly intuitively. It is the pressing need to open the organization up to a whole new way of doing business.

2. The organization looks for help. Sometimes it searches for a consultant—perhaps an internal one, or even an external one. How the organization makes these requests can vary greatly. The manager may contract for one interview or one presentation or lecture, or the executive may extend the period of inquiry for a very long time, such as a year or even more. In that case, it may involve meetings, a series of fact-finding or even therapeutic interviews, and maybe a short introductory seminar. The general needs of executives can be expressed this way: "I want someone to interest my team in a challenge to leadership." Nevertheless, unless there is full and continuous support (or sponsorship) from the final organizational authority, such efforts are likely to lead to erratic results at best.

3. Organizational resistances are mobilized. That can happen instantaneously or very subtly and gradually. Executives attempting change in their organizations are likely to encounter several types of sensitive human issues:

- *Wounded pride:* A characteristic reaction is, in effect, "I (or we) must be the initiator, the author, the agent, the source—and not someone perceived as being an outsider." This is natural and understandable, but it also comes from a weak, closed, ungenerous mind. These are typical turf issues, concerns with territoriality.
- *Anxiety:* From the security of hard-won answers, organizations are challenged to move on to the insecurity of adventure. Employees experience this as a collision of cultures or of world views and as a violation of the psychological contract the company made with them when they were recruited.

- *Homeostasis:* This is preservation of the status quo, the tendency of a system to defend itself against attack by becoming rigid. It is no one's fault. Individuals give lip service to the leadership challenge and may even support it. But the collectivity of individuals, beyond logic, works its way through the system and brings change to a halt. The system's powerful resistance to change acts like a psychoneurosis: like a stupid rhinoceros, smashing endlessly against the iron bars of its cage, it bloodies itself out of antediluvian instinct, its behavior responding inappropriately to current needs. A system, like a prehistoric animal, does not adapt itself to new realities. Reason has never been tried.

- *Culture shock:* When individuals or organizations recognize that what modern business leadership demands is nothing short of a transformation, culture shock sets in. Leadership is not just more of the same. It is not, strictly speaking, building on what executives already know. It is not more mechanical thinking. It is not instituting new practices, adopting new behaviors, establishing new systems. It is, instead, changing the way we think, even the way we will. For example, it is transforming our perception from "confronting another person is too threatening" to "confronting another person is routine," from "taking a stand is embarrassing" to "taking a stand is natural," from "I cannot manage feeling guilty" to "guilt is the normal feeling following a tough decision." The reaction to culture shock is anger and hostility, expressed by rejecting either the new ideas or the bearer of these ideas.

4. The resistance is manifested by a wide range of clever defense strategies. The first step in managing them is to name them. Some typical defenses are silence, boredom, indifference, sleep, inaction, embarrassment at valuing personal support, always having something else to do that interferes, living in crisis rather than in a planned atmosphere, accusations of triviality, accusations of impracticality, lack of seriousness, no interest in thinking about leading, excessive expectations followed by predictable disappointment, indefinite postponements and

procrastinations, deliberate political sabotage, cynical manipulation and maneuvering, ignoring that solutions are in personal actions and not in abstract knowledge, and thinly dis-
guised hostility. All these strategies for resistance can always be
rationalized and legitimized by intellectual objectivity. A full
calendar gives the illusion of control. Reactive behavior is camouflaged as proactive leadership.

5. These strategies of resistance are verbalized in typical
ways:

> "This is dangerous, anarchist."
> "We don't need lectures, only discussions among our-
> selves."
> "This is superficial, obvious, trivial."
> "How do I apply it—*tomorrow*?"
> "I can't figure out how to make it operational."
> "You can't teach leadership."
> "The timing is not right."
> "Define your terms."
> "Too abstract."
> "How do you make these ideas work for one thousand
> people?"
> "I can't relate to it."
> "I'm on overload."
> "The language is too esoteric."
> "I'm a pragmatist."
> "Subsidized therapy!"
> "I'm here because my boss sent me."
> "I really can't see any particular use for this."
> "My customers won't buy it."
> "We have these types of meetings all the time, but nothing
> ever changes around here."
> "I must go back to work now."
> "How do you make these platitudes operational?"

Sometimes there is just a blank stare. Many of these statements
are simply the culture speaking through its willing, passive,
unconscious agents.

6. Resistance is a controllable interference with the growth process. Those issuing the challenge to leadership greatness must realize that resistance is normal, necessary, and understandable. The characteristic strategies used are projection, displacement (which can be somatic), denial, numbing, and sublimation. Resistances must be treated with patience and understanding, with compassion and humility, with respect but also with uncompromising realism. Sufficient ventilation of the resistances gets to root causes. Once we know what we are up against, we can begin to deal with it.

7. The demand that words become operational is thoroughly legitimate. In fact, taken at face value, it is the only legitimate demand. Leadership is nothing if it is not made real, nothing if not made concrete in the workings of a business. Leadership means nothing if it does not translate itself powerfully to the bottom line. But the demand to operationalize can also be narrow, hostile, and destructive, immobilizing necessary change. All relationships are dialogic, and if one party to a dialogue withdraws, progress stops. This is something for organizations to consider in engaging consultants. For organizations to get the most benefit from consulting, there must be an alliance between client and consultant. Both must be seen as working on the same project. Both must have an investment in identical goals, and there can be no hidden agendas. What bonds an organization with the consultant is the needs of the organization. What unifies them is whatever is the right thing to do for the success of the company. No one is selling, and no one is buying. The pair exists in an alliance and shares a single focus, one concern. The demand to make the leadership mind operational, to the degree that such a request is inauthentic, has many responses:

- One can respond to this demand by saying it is irrelevant: insight is enough; once you understand, you will act; what matters is your mental attitude; you are bright enough to figure out for yourself what you must do. No one else can or should do it for you. Your struggle was not in action but in understanding the workings of your mind. You do not need techniques to feel good physically; you need to have your body in good physical shape. So it goes with the leadership mind. What matters is that you be an authentic person. You will then automatically know what to do. In psychotherapy, insight heals. That is the theory.

- Others look for techniques and for skills of transition, for specific practical steps, things to do. In other words, what skills do you need in order to take the insights of the Leadership Diamond into the "real world"? The Leadership Diamond model provides a base from which derive specific actions and techniques. This is a constant effort; it should never slacken. And everyone needs to contribute. The results must be collective.

- Find the answers yourself. Peter Block, the outstanding consultant, had a sign on his door: "Superman doesn't live here anymore, go do it yourself!" Understand the leadership mind. Then revert to your center, consult your experience, and, being innovative, invent the actions that implement leadership intelligence.

- Question the question. Philosophers have spent most of this century trying to prove that profound questions—Does God exist? Is the world real? What can we know? Is consciousness different from matter? Is the soul immortal? Is there a right and a wrong in ethics?—are in fact meaningless. They are chains of words, grammatically correct but lacking meaning, like the Viennese philosopher Moritz Schlick's famous question: "Is blue more identical than music?" Sounds deep, means nothing. Nietzsche said that philosophers muddy the waters so that they may appear deep, and so it may be with the question of making the leadership mind operational. The question is wrong. It comes from a nonleadership mind. There are more answers to this puzzle. You can develop them yourself. Pick the one you like the most and discard the others.

8. The cost of the resistance, emotional and financial—ultimately, in terms of organizational survival—is clearly established.

9. The resistance gradually diminishes as trust is permitted to develop. New modes of leading, perceiving work, and thinking about life are then experimented with and tested in the real world of organizational objectives. This is what is meant by *reality testing*.

10. A critical mass is created within the organization. This requires unswerving commitment and undeviating perseverance by key decision makers, who must be the sponsors.

11. Gradual transformation of the organization occurs, like sunshine after the rain, daylight after a long night.

12. *Reinforcement:* The organization seeks ways to make the culture's new leadership consciousness permanent. There is constant danger of recidivism.

There are several underlying lessons to be learned from this predictable developmental sequence. You do not teach leadership to organizations. You help them learn it. Resistance is eventually overcome by a dedicated organizational sponsor who has the courage to be prescient, persistent, and patient. A developed, widespread leadership consciousness elevates the health, personal fulfillment, and productivity of employees more than any other single identifiable factor. The result is organizations that survive profitably, have high morale, and are respected.

The essential element of bringing about the challenge to leadership greatness in organizations is the leadership-greatness manager or educator, and that role requires three basic empowerment skills: teaching, psychotherapy, and modeling. *Teaching* involves what all of us have experienced ourselves: instruction or lectures, homework (consisting of reading and exercises, as well as other assignments), experiences (developing experiential knowledge), and a practicum (field work). The skill of teaching is taught in colleges and universities and has been developed into a fine art. It applies richly to the business world, as well as to government and the professions.

Similar thoughts apply to *psychotherapy*, which is merely another form of teaching, that is, teaching through experiencing, much of it based on the method invented by Socrates and exemplified in many of the dialogues of Plato. Psychotherapy is

likewise a highly developed skill, taught in schools and in-
stitutes. It has a few basic ingredients. Learn how to establish an
alliance with your client, which means trust. Learn active listening, which means that you reflect what the client says, instead of
interpreting; you are alert and supportive; you make clear to
your client that he or she is really being heard, at many levels of
depth. You must help your client ventilate — you encourage the
expression of the thoughts and feelings that were lost for decades. You must interpret your client's statements in a larger
perspective and with supreme realism so that unhealthy illusions and damaging "games" can be discarded. You must guide
the client to understand and to experience the strategies used to
hide the truth and the secondary gains that these "resistances"
achieve. You must also maintain the interaction at an optimum
level of anxiety: too much, and the relationship is over; not
enough, and there is no progress. Optimum anxiety means
growth. The anxiety must feel cleansing and invigorating.

　　Modeling is based on the theory that leadership is contagious. When you see it in operation, you recognize it as one of
your own possibilities. You imitate the actions of your model and
are inspired by that spirit. You have hope, which is still one of the
most beautiful of all the virtues. Aristotle tells us that children
learn by imitation; so it is that we learn leadership.

　　Leadership skills can be learned, but it is an illusion to
think that an undeveloped person can get away with techniques
alone. Underneath, there must be human authenticity. That will
always show through.

Gaining Support for Your Business Strategies

You have absorbed the Leadership Diamond model, and you have
used it to analyze your own leadership situation. You have committed yourself to using the model for challenging your organization to leadership greatness, in full recognition of the developmental course and resistances you can expect. Where, now, do
you begin? There are five basic steps in a complete leadership-
greatness challenge, to be correlated with the dominant leadership strategies.

Understand. Thoroughly understand Leadership Diamond theory (vision).

Do. Learn by doing. Own and experience the concepts. Attain facility in diagnosing a wide spectrum of leadership situations (reality).

Operationalize. Using the full power of Leadership Diamond theory, develop specific strategies, systems, and processes to manage your business objectives. This is your business plan: how you organize your company, your reporting chart, your rewards system, and so on (reality).

Implement. Use Leadership Diamond theory to implement these strategies (courage). This process requires, first, implementation strategies. One strategy is to develop, among your most promising employees, a cadre of leadership teachers, who then spread the leadership-challenge message throughout the organization. That creates a critical mass of leadership intelligence to support the organization's business objectives (vision). Second, implementation requires that you challenge people to greatness in leadership, empower them. That includes teaching leadership or teaching others how to teach leadership—to teach, as you work, the Leadership Diamond mindset. This is the real core of leadership (ethics). The first is conceptual, the second charismatic and inspirational. In fact, strategy is to leadership as a blueprint is to an actual house, as essence is to existence, as the mere thought of a thousand dollars is to actual cash in your pocket. The challenge to leadership greatness is not technique. It is personality. And philosophy is not simply another leadership technique. It is the trunk of which techniques are the branches. Philosophy supports and is integrated into all workable leadership techniques.

Measure. Use Leadership Diamond theory to measure and assess results. Ask subordinates how much leadership they are learning from their bosses (reality).

Key people, executives strategically located within their

own organizations, must be identified and trained in the inner-side-of-greatness leadership challenge. That is one approach to in-depth human quality. These people must be volunteers. They become the pioneers who train others in turn, until a critical mass is reached.

All training, recruiting, and promotion programs, as well as job descriptions, both technical and managerial, should contain a philosophic leadership challenge, an inner-side-of-greatness module. This fundamental step has rarely if ever been taken decisively, and it is long overdue. To establish inner-side-of-greatness modules that make a significant and measurable difference requires an internal elite of well-trained, well-educated teaching supervisors, managers, and executives who understand that teaching and leading are one activity, establish a leadership network with which they stay in touch, continuously refresh their leadership skills with new ideas and deepen their old ones, and have access to in-depth leadership teaching materials and effective follow-up leadership technologies and can therefore guarantee to provide, in a sustained fashion, a consistent, unified, and profound leadership message.

Large organizations may create their own sophisticated teaching materials, including surveys, interactive video, and computer learning. Television or videotaped programs, properly used, can bring individual depth and intimacy to very large numbers of people. These instructional aids are complex and expensive, although, if well made, they can also be highly effective.

Having now fully explored the theory of the Leadership Diamond model, we need practice in applying it. The next part of this book provides illustrative applications and examples, as well as a series of exercises that can be used in learning and in applying the model to specific circumstances. The first step is to learn diagnosis, which we will discuss in the next two chapters. We conclude this portion of our journey with a fable:

> A kindly and wise old man living in a small village
> is reputed to be able to answer all questions. Two
> young rascals want to trick him and prove him a

fool. They plan to catch a bird. One will hold it in his hands, behind his back. He will then test the old man: "What do I hold in my hand?" Should he answer correctly — that it is a bird — they will hurl at him the fatal trick question: "Is it alive, or is it dead?" Should he reply, "Dead," they will show him the living bird and prove him wrong. But should he say, "Alive," they will break its neck, show him the dead bird, and exclaim, "You see, you're wrong, the bird is dead! The villagers will laugh at you."

They catch a bird and approach the old man.

"Old man, we hear you can answer all questions," they say contemptuously. "We have one for you. Will you answer us?"

"If you insist," he responds.

"We do," replies one of the rascals, and he continues arrogantly: "I'll bet you can't tell what I have in my hands behind my back."

Gently, the old man asks, "Could it be something that flies?"

"Not bad, not bad," the rascals admit grudgingly. "You were right. It is a bird."

The one who holds the bird behind his back says, "But now, old man, comes the tough question: Is it alive, or is it dead?"

There is a pause. The rascals wait with devilish smirks on their faces. Finally, the old man, reflecting, answers, measuring his words.

"I think, young man, it is all in your hands!"

PART THREE

Leadership Strategies in Action

10

Building Individual Skills

In order to drive a car or play the piano, you require practice, and plenty of it. The same is true with Leadership Diamond methodology. In order to use it effectively, you need lots of practice, and that you gain through diagnoses. You must get into the habit of examining all life situations in Leadership Diamond terms. This and the following chapters will help you achieve this competence.

The Leadership Diamond is like a grid. Superimpose it on companies, on whole industries, on organizations within companies, or on individuals, and it will give you a quick and useful diagnosis. This chapter and the next illustrate the diagnostic utility of the Leadership Diamond.

Whatever you do, whether building your career and wishing to be more effective in your job, dealing with your relationships and your family, or focusing on your inwardness and your spiritual life, always ask the same questions, derived from the Leadership Diamond: Am I being visionary enough? Is this a breakthrough, in visionary terms? Or is the vision incremental? Am I displaying (or is the situation manifesting) the four tactics of this strategy? In other words, is the reasoning brilliant? Is there enough systemic and strategic visioning? Is this work based on an understanding of the infinity of inner space-time? Has the unconscious been properly enlisted for creativity? Continue this way with all the other strategies. In other words, whatever task you approach, small or large, whatever team or colleague you seek to inspire and motivate, always raise the same set of questions. Does the action conform to all the criteria

Figure 10.1. The Five "Olympic Rings of Life."

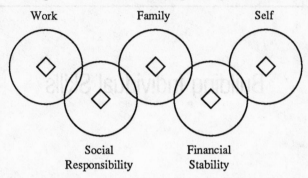

of the Leadership Diamond model? If not, what needs to be done to improve effectiveness? The diagram shown in Figure 2.1 may help remind you.

Marriage and Money

Let us examine the nature of each one of the five "Olympic rings" of life (see Figure 10.1). First, we will consider a checklist of what to look for in order to achieve a more successful leadership life. Then we will see how you can use Leadership Diamond methodology to understand better the leadership performance of one specific individual, and then we will see how it works for companies. In this way, you will get practice in making the Leadership Diamond model work to enhance your own leadership.

The Leadership Diamond model is perhaps most readily illustrated in its application to marriage and money. In the end, Leadership Diamond methodology is used to understand each of the "Olympic rings" of life: work, family, self, social responsibility, and financial stability.

Marriage. Let us start with marriage as an example of the family ring. We can examine the institution of marriage through the grid of the Leadership Diamond model. We check all aspects of an ideal marriage. In this way, we understand the nature of a marriage. We take a look at its full range of possibilities. We then compare, for example, our own marriage to that grid, and we uncover areas of strength and weakness, especially with a view to improvement. This profile is like a map that shows us, in the institution of marriage, where we are and where we may wish to go.

What is the meaning of greatness in marriage? Is your marriage a great one? What are the visionary elements of marriage? How are you doing with your vision of marriage? What are the realities of marriage, and how are you performing in that strategy? What is the meaning of ethics in marriage? How do you compare? What is courage in marriage? What does it profit you if you have it, and what are the losses if you lack it?

Vision asks whether the idealism of first love is still alive, the infatuation you felt when emotional attraction first seized you. Are you still fulfilling in your relationship the poetic possibilities of a great passion? Do you have the relationship you want? What are the implications? These questions about your marriage or relationship derive from examining vision as the dominant leadership strategy.

Are you in touch with reality? Marriage is a social institution and the foundation of human society. Marriage is practical. Do you cope well with the aspects of marriage that threaten its vision (such as money, children, the mortgage, housekeeping, chores, conflicting careers, ongoing stresses, pressures, frustrations, disillusionments)? Do you cope well with differences in upbringing, in expectations, different physical and emotional needs, different values, different intellectual standards, and with each other's unfinished childhood business (neurotic behavior, relics of infancy)?

Are you ethical in your relationship or your marriage? Are you loyal, in deed as well as in thought? Are you committed to each other? Are you truthful and honorable? Are you sensitive to each other's needs? Are you service-minded? Marriage is preeminently an ethical arrangement. It carries with it serious obligations and tough responsibilities, and these are sometimes difficult to bear. For instance, would you consider it a moral privilege to take loyal care of an invalid spouse?

Do you possess the courage to craft your marriage into

what it can be? To be honest? To hear the truth and tell the truth, even though that is painful? To be willing to grow? To allow your partner to grow? To take pleasure in your partner's growth? To change careers or jobs or residence, even friends, if the marriage requires it? Marriage is a condition of constant development, and authentic growth often produces anxiety. It takes courage to face that anguish and to develop through it and past it. Do you have the courage to move your marriage or relationship relentlessly in the direction of authenticity?

You need to understand two levels of diagnosis: the rings, and you. First, what are the strategies and tactics that characterize each ring of life? Second, how do you compare your own performance with what could be? Here, our concern is with the former. You should take care of understanding the latter.

How does one develop the structure of each "Olympic ring"? Some general principles may be useful. First, you must pick a target, a subject matter for analysis (such as marriage in general, a specific marriage that concerns you or that you use as paradigm, your own marriage, and so forth) and then select the point of view (the subjectivity) from whose perspective you perform the investigation. It could be from your own subjective point of view. It could be from the perspective of a disinterested observer or from that of a child of the marriage, a parent of one of the partners, a marriage counselor, and so on. Of course, the target could be entirely different (such as managing your physical health, performing your civic duties, or educating your children, not to speak of how you manage your job performance and your career).

Second, you ask yourself what specific living details need to be considered in each individual strategy. Who is responsible for the house or the apartment? Who is responsible for earning money? What are the emotional dimensions of the relationship? What are its difficult moments? What are its pleasures?

Third, you select your dynamic corner, the strategy with the most energy, and the tactic in which you are strongest. What are some of your victories in this strategy? How are you using the corresponding supporting tactics? How does it feel to be accomplished in this strategy? In this way, you get data. Your dynamic

Figure 10.2. Family.

The ideal for the marriage.
The ultimate romantic hope
for the relationship.

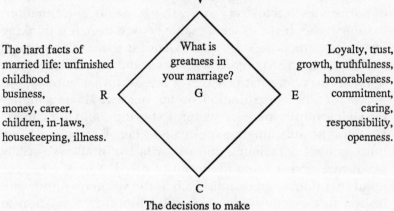

The hard facts of married life: unfinished childhood business, money, career, children, in-laws, housekeeping, illness.

R

What is greatness in your marriage?

G

E

Loyalty, trust, growth, truthfulness, honorableness, commitment, caring, responsibility, openness.

V

C

The decisions to make the changes and risk the maturity and openness to make the marriage grow.

corner gives you an above-average opportunity to describe one specific strategy in detail.

Fourth, you find your leverage corner, your weakest strategy. You fantasize what you would like it to be. You describe what it should be. In this way, you get additional data, and you enrich your paradigm with what is possible, what could be.

Fifth, you try to expand each of the remaining strategies in light of the insights you have derived from your dynamic and leverage corners.

In this way, you achieve as complete a picture as possible of what, for the authentic leader, one of the "Olympic rings" of life might look like. You can now use the results to check how you are doing in any one of the five rings. Your diagnosis becomes your guide for improving your leadership performance in all aspects of your life (see Figure 10.2).

Money. Let us now use the Leadership Diamond model to examine the meaning and function of money, in the ring of your
financial stability. In this ring, vision is the ability to recognize
value wherever it lies—in people, things, or situations. It is
making marketing intelligence work, having a nose for business
opportunities. It is always viewing things, events, and situations
in value terms. It is also seeing value beyond cash. It is thinking
like an investor, not a wage earner; like a speculator, not a saver.
It is always trying to predict what lies ahead, what future developments may be, what new trends are, and what implications
follow for one's organization or for oneself. Making money
through acquisitions, joint ventures, starting companies, mergers, buyouts, investments, speculation, tax shelters, stock op-
tions, golden parachutes, and so forth, is not always socially
productive and is often the result of greed. Nevertheless, the
mind that thinks opportunistically is the visionary mind, with
respect to the acquisition of wealth. Visioning, in relation to
money, is not merely having access to facts, data, but thinking
consistently in this unique way.

  Realism is seeing money for what, in an absolute sense, it
is—something *intangible*. It is not only cash, nor is it only property. It is a complex system of assets, all of which are calculated
into a comprehensive picture. Having realism about money is
always knowing exactly where you stand financially. It is possessing a clear picture of what your money is doing and of what it
could be doing. And realism is always maintaining that clear
picture before you, always being money-conscious.

  This realism does not apply only to your own finances.
You must also be aware of the financial relations among companies, industries, provinces, and nations. Financiers may not
perform a productive function, but their power is immense. The
world has constructed itself so that monetary maneuvers move
mountains.

  Realism is also knowing your products and skills. What do
you have to offer that the market wants? Your market value may
be higher than you think. You have untapped resources.

  There are some fundamental realities about money that
many people overlook. Many people are hurt by their lack of

"money literacy." For example, there is cash, and there is non-cash. Cash is like hard currency. It is "actual" money. Noncash is "funny money," potential money. Cash is what you find in checking accounts, money-market funds, certificates of deposit, and so forth. Cash is the most important form of money. That is reality. Noncash is borrowed money, taxable money, leveraged money, nonliquid assets, and so forth. It is money whose existence in your pocket is questionable. Leveraged money is probably the best source of wealth, however, at least in a capitalist economy. That is also reality.

There is the fact of inflation as well. Money kept in a vault erodes in value. That is reality. Money borrowed today is repaid later in cheaper dollars. That is also reality. Furthermore, tax money is soft money. It disappears, without careful planning, and that too is reality. Beyond that, the best source of income is not wages and salaries but speculation (with or without effort on your part) that what you own, whether precious metals or companies, will increase in value. These money manipulations may be questionable in the ethical sense of their not materially contributing to society, but they are still the result of the nature and flow of money in a free economy. In fact, if everyone were to be smart about noncash (potential money), many financial-planning and enrichment techniques would become null and void. Right or wrong, these are the realities of money, too often overlooked by too many people.

Money is about debt and about the uses and dangers of debt. Nationally, we have debts in the budget and in trade. We have federal, state, municipal, corporate, and personal debts. Debts can be purchased and sold. They can be refinanced or restructured. In short, money is a house of cards, held together mysteriously and by mutual consent, but always fragile. What are the implications for the global economy? For you?

What about ethics? Here, ethics means lawfully acquiring money and using it for meaningful things. The burden is on the owners to do useful things with their resources. Ethics, when it comes to money, is the clear understanding that the important things in life are not monetary. Money offers the opportunity for action—ethical action. Moreover, freedom and peace of mind,

time for reflection and opportunities for action, occasions for
compassion and chances for education can all be made real
because of money. Avarice is properly called a sin, and generosity is justly called a virtue.

Courage in relation to money is the willingness to take
risks. Investment means risk; changing jobs means risk. Entering
a new career means risk and requires courage. Betting on the
economy is a risk. We know a person's relation to being in general
by how that individual feels about money. Not risking with money
at all means not risking in life—in love, in one's career, in
creativity. Too much risking with money means irresponsibility
toward commitments, obligations, promises, and expectations.

But risk can also take the form of not making money a
central goal of life (consider a poet, for example). Commitment
to the life of the mind is similarly a risk: one risks one's soul.
Money is a barometer. How you relate to it defines how courageous you are.

At the level of business, it is also useful to examine attitudes toward money and financial policies in terms of the
strategies of the Leadership Diamond model. We look for the
"tilt" of the diamond—the point on which the company rests, the
dynamic corner. (This is the same diagnostic tool that is used in
the example of marriage.) Where is the emphasis? On realism
(making money at all costs)? Making profits the sole consideration? Making cost containment the principal policy? To be
ruthless in the worship of Mammon? Or is the compelling
energy tilted toward vision, toward money as the fuel of the
world economy, the means of supporting human destinies and
helping the fate of nations? Is money viewed as an instrument, as
a leveraging tool, as not a value in itself? Is money only a
metaphor? Is the real issue value? And doesn't value come in
infinite shapes? How can money best be used to reach the vision?

Is the prime motive for understanding money, for relating
the organization to money, an ethical one? Is the organization's
primary concern to improve the human lot? Is the meaning of
business, for example, principally to create jobs? Is there any
idealism? Is fueling the economy fundamentally a moral act, so
that survival and prosperity are not expressions of greed and

selfishness but of compassion and responsibility? Is the company being used clearly and principally to benefit the society in which it exists? Is it patriotic? Is it international? Is it socially conscious? Should investments be occasions for moral stands on political oppression or environmental pollution?

We can also analyze the courage with which money is viewed in a company. Inventiveness and entrepreneurialism are often associated with financial risk. How desirable is it to take risks? Is the decision to take risks a rational one, or is it unconscious, irrational, and more characterological (that is, more personality-dependent than analytical)? Which is the right way to make decisions about risk? Do we go into our individual depth? Do we meticulously analyze data? Can we do both? Do we do both? What is better—an individual, visceral risk from a transformational CEO, or a communal decision skillfully facilitated by a transactional CEO?

Having analyzed the question of the dynamic corner, we move on to the others to achieve our profile. If you review your organization's financial situation in terms of these strategies, what do you think will be the effect on its total health? Such examinations expand the mind and, like good warm-up exercises, loosen the muscles of the leadership mind for more nimble performance. A financial institution can build its marketing plan on a model like this. The product of a bank, for instance, would be helping customers buy leadership in their financial affairs, and that would be accomplished by using the Diamond checklist for structuring the organization in such a way that it marketed greatness for its customers and, specifically, greatness in financial visions, in understanding the market and fiduciary realities, in connecting money with values, and in risk management, financially (strategically) and emotionally (personally) (see Figure 10.3).

The "Olympic Rings." Each ring has its own profile. There exist many possibilities. The following are only examples, so that you yourself can create your own profiles to suit yourself and your life situation, to fit with your life-style and your values. Figures 10.4, 10.5, 10.6, and 10.7 depict, respectively, greatness in your

Figure 10.3. Financial Stability.

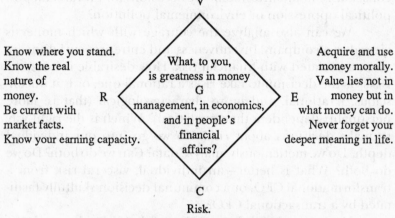

Recognize value, opportunity.
Create future scenarios.

V

Know where you stand.
Know the real
nature of
money.   R
Be current with
market facts.
Know your earning capacity.

What, to you,
is greatness in money
G
management, in economics,
and in people's
financial
affairs?

Acquire and use
money morally.
Value lies not in
E   money but in
what money can do.
Never forget your
deeper meaning in life.

C
Risk.
Financial management is risk management.
Are you emotionally equipped to
risk—neither too much nor too little
(Aristotle called it "The Golden Mean")?

work (both as an employee and as an owner), greatness in taking
care of yourself, and greatness in your social responsibility.

Analyzing Individual Leadership Styles

We have examined the structure, the components, of each of the
"Olympic rings" of life. Let us now apply the model to specific
cases—that is, use it diagnostically.

Understanding yourself in Leadership Diamond terms
can be one of the most successful ways to enhance your leadership effectiveness. First we analyze the leadership style of
individuals. Then we take a look at companies.

CEO-Owner. The basis of this diagnostic analysis is the Toolbox,
with special emphasis on the strategies for greatness and less
emphasis on its definitions: *effectiveness* and *character*. This partic-

Figure 10.4. Work (Employee).

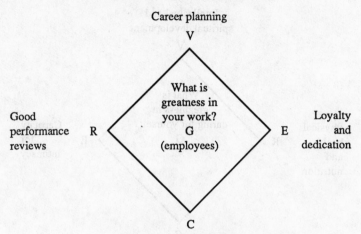

Career planning
V

What is
greatness in
your work?
G
(employees)

Good
performance   R
reviews

Loyalty
E   and
dedication

C
Priorities and decisions for individual and
organizational progress and growth

Figure 10.5. Work (Owner).

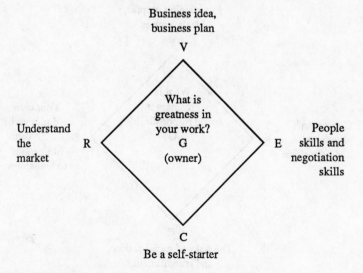

Business idea,
business plan
V

What is
greatness in
your work?
G
(owner)

Understand
the   R
market

People
E   skills and
negotiation
skills

C
Be a self-starter

Figure 10.6. Self.

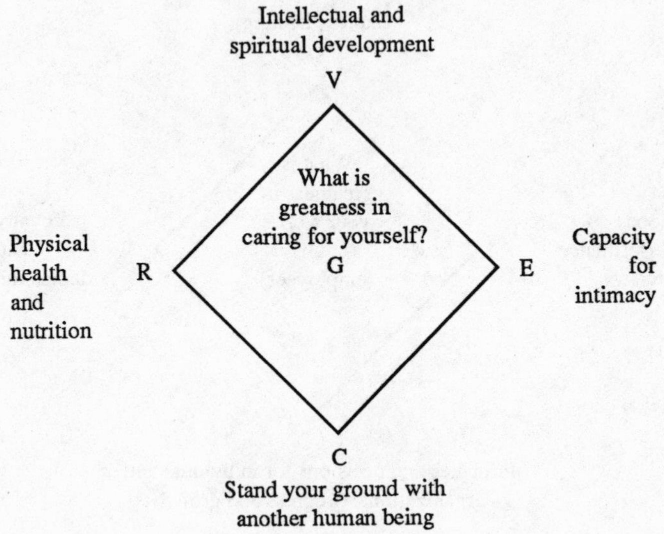

Intellectual and
spiritual development

V

What is
greatness in
caring for yourself?

Physical   Capacity
health   R   G   E   for
and   intimacy
nutrition

C

Stand your ground with
another human being

Figure 10.7. Social Responsibility.

Entertaining utopias,
ideals, causes

V

What is
greatness in
social responsibility?

Coping with   Your civic
pluralism   R   G   E   duties and
and opposition   your
                                                                           obligations
                                                                           to humanity

C

The risks of social action
and commitment

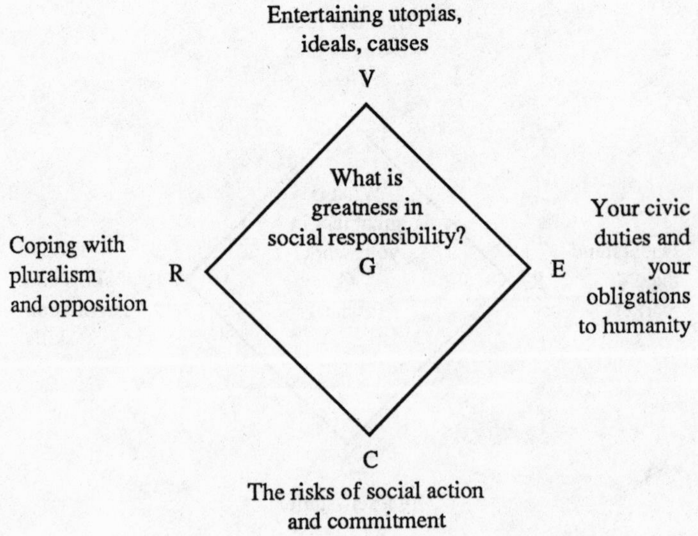

ular diagnosis is the result of a dialogue between client and consultant and was drawn up by the consultant. It is a diagnosis of the leadership style of Mr. X—an engineer and the founder, owner, and president of an international automobile-leasing chain. Mr. X is forty-five years old. The diagnosis is subject to change as further information becomes available.

In this as in other diagnoses, we begin at the center of the Leadership Diamond, with an evaluation of the individual with respect to greatness. We then assign evaluations to each strategy, its formula statement, and its supporting tactics. The result is a comprehensive picture of the individual's leadership style.

The following scale is based on what the observer believes is performance: how the subject is perceived by others. It is permissible to split the answers:

1. no performance
2. poor performance
3. fair performance
4. below-average performance
5. average performance
6. above-average performance
7. good performance
8. very good performance
9. excellent performance
NA. not applicable

> Greatness: 8/7. He is intensely committed to greatness, a commitment that is getting stronger daily. This attitude is the best hope for the company. If we consider the more sophisticated criteria for greatness, however, his final score might be lower at this time; nevertheless, he is fully prepared to deepen the person he is.
>
> *Strategy*—Vision: 8. He is an exceptionally visionary individual. He sees far into the distance, both geographically and historically, the significance of his enterprise.
>
> *Formula statement*—Think big and new: 8. There is no question that this person's mental ability is one of his greatest strengths. He will always surprise you with new plans and innovative ideas.

1.   Abstract reasoning and analysis: 7. Here he is rated "good," which is to be expected, partly because of this executive's strong engineering background.

2.   Systemic and strategic thinking: 8. This skill is highly developed in him, and it is to his credit, for he has learned it himself through years of hard work and business experience.

3.   Creativity and the unconscious: 5. This skill is highly developed in this manager, but, as is characteristic of many numbers-oriented people, it regrettably is not part of his daily business life. It easily could become that, however, probably with remarkable and highly visible results.

4.   Expanding and exploring inner or subjective space-time: 1. He is poor here because of his lack of knowledge of this dimension of human existence and the absence of serious development of the region of his inner consciousness. Work in this area, if he chooses to do it, can bring high-leverage results.

Strategy—Reality: 8/4. Highly realistic financially, but questionable realism when it comes to understanding himself and other people. Further personal growth can take care of this deficit.

Formula statement—Have no illusions: 8/4. No illusions in business realities, but significant illusions in people realities.

1.   Meticulous attention to practical details, attending to the precise needs of your immediate and end customers: 7/2. Uneven. Good detailed knowledge in the area of visionary projects, but poor attention to detail in the everyday maintenance and service areas.

2.   Extensive information and objectivity: 8. Uniformly well informed, from politics and world economics to operational details.

3. Survival—relentless results orientation and market orientation: 9/3. Uneven. Excellent in understanding and focusing on the external market, but weak in dealing effectively with the internal markets. More training of his personnel and better systems would be helpful. Better managers must be selected, trained, and supervised. When it comes to raw survival, however, this executive is undefeatable.

4. Direct contact and embodiment: with yourself, with other selves, and with how others perceive you (definition of mental health): 7/3. Uneven. Excellent in public, good public speaker. Evasive in private, especially in small groups of high-powered executives, where holding his ground may not be easy. Work for improvement in this area is crucial to increased leadership effectiveness and protection of investment. The problem with this tactic stems from issues buried deep inside his personality and is undoubtedly related to early family experiences, such as relation to parents and position among siblings.

Strategy—Ethics: 6. Appears to be very ethical but needs more maturity in human relations.

Formula statement—Be of service: 4. Needs to be more service-oriented when it comes to customers.

1. Teamwork, loyalty to task forces: 4. Is fearful of real and meaningful teamwork because it may mean loss of control.

2. Meaning: 9. Outstanding and exemplary. His work absorbs him totally, makes him happy, and leads to fulfillment and meaning in his life. His family fully supports him.

3. Communication, caring, love: 8. Outstanding and exemplary. A loving person, especially to his

family. A very loyal man to those with whom he has built a relationship of trust.

4.   Integrity, morality, and principle: 7. Observed as outstanding and exemplary. Insufficient data.

Strategy—Courage: 7. Does not lack courage in the business arena but hesitates to take the necessary courageous steps in personal growth and in the development of his company's culture.

Formula statement—Act with sustained initiative: 9. This man has no trouble taking the initiative and sustaining it. He may not always take the initiative in what one might call the "right" direction, but he knows how to act.

1.   Aggressive education and management of markets, product advocacy: 8/3. He is excellent in sales and promotion. He is superb in educating external markets but poor in mentoring some of his internal markets. He needs to educate and train all of his people extensively.

2.   Aloneness, autonomy, and independence of thought: 8. High in understanding of this strategy and in its implementation. Impressive. Here, necessity has been the mother of invention.

3.   Anxiety: 5. He does not consider enough the healing powers of anxiety (very few people do). He needs to work in this area for the sake of his personal growth and increased maturity. He is young (in fact, precocious), and for that he should be acknowledged, but facing more of his anxiety will help.

4.   Free will, energy, centeredness, and power: 7. High in understanding this tactic and implementing it. Impressive. He should concentrate more on using his power for the benefit of others. Other than that, this orientation will ensure his continuing success. His need to control his company testi-

fies to his strong will power, but it may also be a compensation for lack of centeredness and therefore may limit the growth of the business.

A more comprehensive analysis would also include the internal, external, psychodynamic, and systemic resistances; that was not done in this example.

What should the executive do with this evaluation? Here are a few suggestions:

- Reinforce strengths
- Work on weaknesses
- Ask colleagues and subordinates to produce a summary profile of his leadership style
- Compare the profile with other consultants' assessments and with the opinion he has of himself, and ask colleagues to discuss any discrepancies with him
- Cite examples for each of the diagnostic categories
- Analyze how this leadership profile affects his organization today, positively and negatively
- Discover the implications for the future and discuss how changes in his leadership style may influence his future and that of his company
- Trace, in detail, the nature of these leadership traits, and find the specific results that the business is achieving and is missing

The consultant reviewed all the tools with the client. Together, they decided that these were the areas where improvement would make a measurable bottom-line difference:

1. *Expanding and exploring inner or subjective space-time:* Extensive training, both on the personal level and for the team.
2. *Direct contact and embodiment with self, with other selves, and with how others perceive you:* First, seminar for management team;

then, private leadership coaching or CEO mentoring as follow-up processes, with a different consultant.

3.   *Meticulous attention to practical details, attending to the precise needs of your immediate and end customers:* Develop a massive strategy to create effective systems for his company, through one or more team sites, with special effort to get to root causes. This is a beginning. Concern here is with an action plan of the highest priority.

4.   *Relentless results orientation and market orientation:* Clarify the nature of the internal market. Management team develops and executes training program. This is a high-priority item.

5.   *Teamwork, loyalty to ad hoc teams:* Intense, consistent, quiet (behind-the-scenes), trusted, private leadership coaching or CEO mentoring, especially on the theory and practice of teamwork and group work.

6.   *Aggressive education and management of markets, product advocacy:* Educate internal markets with intensive training program.

7.   *Additional staffing or consultants:* Engage the services of a personal mentor, a strategy consultant, and a corporate training director.

Scientist. This is a diagnosis of the leadership style of Ms. Y, forty-two years old, chief research scientist and engineer in a major high-technology company. She was recently promoted to help steer the company's most important project to successful conclusion. The company's competitive position depends on the success of her work. This executive has a brilliant and creative mind. Innovative ideas come easily to her. She is a charming and gifted person. She has suddenly been propelled from scientist to leader of people, and she wants a diagnosis, performed by herself, together with an observer.

> *Greatness:* 4. She could be stimulated to greatness, but has not been, by the proper challenge. Her life is too comfortable to confront her with the need for greatness.

Strategy—Vision: 6.5. In general, she is an above-average visionary person.

Formula statement—Think big and new: 8. She is exceptionally good at new ideas, insights, inventions, and connections.

1. Abstract reasoning and analysis: 9. She has a brilliant scientific mind. One can ask for no more. For her own sake, she should systematically continue her theoretical training and lead the life worthy of her potential, that of a creative scientist.
2. Systemic and strategic thinking: 3. The lack of need to be a leader of people within an organization has atrophied this region of her mind. It could be stimulated into existence, but that would require a lot of pressure, many emergencies, and her decision to show interest in wide-ranging leadership thinking. It is not likely that she will be motivated to develop this aspect of her potential. The company needs it, but she may resign her position before seeing the value of making the effort. In the end, she must develop this part of her mind for her own sake—because she wants to be this kind of person, and not because the company needs it.
3. Creativity and the unconscious: 9/4. In practice, she uses her unconscious in a rich and spontaneous creativity. But this art is neither understood nor developed. Like any other child prodigy, she is no longer precocious at her current age. It is now time for professionalism: deliberate and wise cultivation of her unconscious and creation of a life-style devoted to creativity.
4. Expanding and exploring inner or subjective space-time: 1. Like many other technologists in today's industry, she has not touched this area. Her ignorance of it results from disinterest, not from ill will or lack of ability. Exploration of this tactic

could be a high-leverage area for increased visionary thinking.

   Strategy—Reality: 5. She is a realist because
she is a scientist and a businesswoman. But she is *not*
a realist in that she has not had to deal with the
genuinely tough management and marketing crises
of the real world.
   Formula statement—Have no illusions: 5. She
still lives too much in the indulgent world of the
pampered scientist, which is nice but not adequately realistic for an effective business leader.

1.   Meticulous attention to practical details, attending to the precise needs of your immediate and
end customers: 9. She is a devoted team player and
a loyal company person. To the best of her current
ability, she does what the company needs. But she
fails her organization by not meeting its need for a
larger leadership perspective. This is a vision deficit. She has been promoted to a position of leadership because of her talent, but her willing obe-
dience in carrying out the requisite technical
details is not sufficient to bring to completion the
critical project for which she is now responsible.
2.   Extensive information and objectivity: 4. She is
a quick reader and has access to much information,
but it is only technical. That is important, but she
misses the economic and human issues that are
now the fulcrum of her accountability. She is not
well enough organized to find time to keep herself
updated.
3.   Survival—relentless results orientation and
market orientation: 9/5. She is keenly aware of her
external and internal markets, and she can be
counted on to act accordingly. That follows from
her devotion to the team and her loyalty to the
company. Nevertheless, she was not educated on

the streets but in expensive schools, and her raw survival instincts are blunted. That will diminish her effectiveness as a leader of men and women.

4. Direct contact and embodiment: with yourself, with other selves, and with how others perceive you (definition of mental health): 7/3. She is a healthy person, in touch with the world, from her body to her family to nature. But she is less good than she could be at seeing herself objectively, not because of any lack of intelligence but because of childlike underdevelopment of her reality skills. Her intelligence has given her so much success that she does not need other survival tactics. She is therefore not mature enough to see herself through the eyes of another, especially if that other person is more experienced and worldly than she is.

Strategy—Ethics: 5. She is a good and very likable person but not yet a moral giant, because she has not been required to be one.

Formula statement—Be of service: 7. She is devoted in her service orientation.

1. Teamwork, loyalty to task forces: 9. Exceptionally high in this area.

2. Meaning: 5/3. She is happy with her life and finds meaning in it, but not with passion. Meaning comes naturally to her; she does not give it much thought. She could not handle a collapse of meaning in her life. So far, her meanings have not been seriously endangered, mostly because of a benign environment. But to use meaning and meaningful work as key management tools is quite foreign to her. It would not occur to her to emphasize meaning in designing work or in addressing her customers, subordinates, or peers.

3. Communication, caring, love: 8. Very high. She is a lovable person and wants to ensure that every-

one in her environment loves everyone else. Her behavior indicates that friendliness, sensitivity, and closeness are more pronounced than compassion.

4.   Integrity, morality, and principle: ?. Surely very high, but it has not been called in question or tested and is not likely to be. She has been protected from the vicissitudes of tough leadership confrontations, aggravating frustrations, and painful choices.

Strategy—Courage: 4. Uneven. Sometimes good, at other times unimpressive.

Formula statement—Act with sustained initiative: 4. She is learning willingly how to act with more initiative, but her efforts so far are not adequately sustained.

1.   Aggressive education and management of markets, product advocacy: 7. She knows what is right for the product. But her new "product" is people, and she finds it difficult to fight for them. Even the concept that this is a key element is new to her.

2.   Aloneness, autonomy, and independence of thought: 3. Independence of thought is inevitable for such a bright mind, but she is frightened of the isolation of leadership. She avoids thinking about it. Immaturity in this tactic limits her usefulness and promotability.

3.   Anxiety: 3. Anxiety is not a part of her life. Up to a point, that is good; but, in the sense of helping her company's competitive posture by steering her project to a successful conclusion, she can make only a modest contribution. Her job is in fact pure anxiety; avoiding anxiety is therefore avoiding her job. Her talented life has not prepared her for the anxiety of leadership.

4.   Free will, energy, centeredness, and power: 4. Her thinking is superb, her loyalty unimpeachable.

She delights others with her frequent spurts of freshly creative ideas, but she lacks the presence of will, the power of freedom made visible. She lacks the strength of initiative and the vigor of independent action that identify leaders in difficult times. Her youth makes it difficult for her to be centered.

Not undertaken in this analysis (as was also true of the earlier example) is an exhaustive examination of psychodynamic (internal, personal) and systemic (organizational, cultural) resistances. That would require more detail than can be managed here.

What should this executive do with this evaluation?

At present, she is not suited to the job to which she has been promoted. She is only half prepared. She must decide whether she is willing to make the profound personality changes required to meet the needs of her company. These character transformations should not be attempted solely for the sake of the company. She is happy as she is; there is no moral reason for change. She may decide, however, that her personal development, in health and in her career, requires leadership growth — that she wants to awaken dormant areas of her personality. In that case, a program of deep growth is appropriate. The stakes are high, for her and for her company.

The leverage points are clear: greatness; systemic and strategic thinking; expanding and exploring inner or subjective space-time; extensive information and objectivity; aloneness, autonomy, and independence of thought; anxiety; free will, centeredness, and power. Work in these areas is not easy, and it is deep. It means renewed commitment to her possibilities. It means being stronger and being willing to risk the anxiety of taking more initiative. It means using the powers of her mind in new areas. She is intellectually brilliant but emotionally young. Life has not yet toughened her sufficiently. Her next leadership step requires growth in the direction of making tough choices. With that, her future will know no limits. Even modest attention to her weaknesses, or leverage points, is likely to bring quick and visible results. This person is ready for and receptive to systematic leadership learning and committed leadership coaching.

Using the Leadership Diamond model for executive growth means learning to apply it. The first application is self-diagnosis. Through it, two values are achieved: the usefulness of the model becomes clearer, and you gain insights on how to work "smarter" rather than harder. In overcoming your weaknesses, you develop the lost parts of your personality. That increases your effectiveness and, rather than adding to your burdens, lightens them. The model can be used to diagnose not only individuals but also organizations. Greatness is a function of the person, but it can also be a trait of organizations. To that endeavor we now turn.

11

Expanding Organizational Skills

As we have seen, the essence of the Leadership Diamond model is the leadership mind, or leadership intelligence, which is different in kind from the so-called ordinary mind. Shifting gears into that new consciousness is the secret of power and control. This transformation can be described by observing leaders and by detecting the hidden leadership potential within oneself. And leadership begins by being a leader in one's own life.

In passing, think of this: it is useful to conceptualize oneself as a company, a business, or an organization—even as a state. Each of us, then, needs a marketing department, a finance department, and a planning department. If we are a state, we need a defense department, a legislative body, a judiciary, and so forth. But this is basically an individualistic view. There is even more power in transferring this attitude to organizations. Effective accomplishments occur, not when we think of individuals as the units of explanation, but only when these units become organizations. How does one achieve in the real world? By raw will power? Not usually. Accomplishments result because we think *in organizational terms*. It is therefore of the greatest importance that we move the perceptual and conceptual mindsets that we call the Leadership Diamond from individual leaders over to teams and organizations.

If we wish to achieve significant objectives, we must utilize the power of organizations—a truth that holds as much under socialism as under capitalism. Even the isolated artist needs the support of the society that he or she may condemn. Plato, in his

Republic, understood that the state is one large person. In significant respects, the organization is one large individual, and all the Diamond points and all the insights concerning leadership intelligence must now be projected onto the organization, the organization that we have chosen as the vehicle through which we cope with the problem of existence.

The Leadership Diamond is like the benzene ring, the fundamental molecule for synthetic chemistry. It is a molecule that comes naturally with human existence; vision, reality, ethics, and courage are basic human needs. When organizations are challenged to adhere to the requirements of the Leadership Diamond, they are simply confronted with the basic fact that their own fulfillment is of the same order as that of individuals.

Is it important that all leadership traits be exhibited in one person? Or should there be a division of labor, so that one executive is the visionary, another is the realist, a third concerns himself or herself with human relations, and a fourth is the agent, the doer? The proper response to this frequent question is that both positions are correct. Each individual executive must exhibit all four traits. That is the essence of Leadership Diamond theory. In addition, however, the organization or partnership works best if specific tasks are assigned to different people. Thus, a good partnership is one in which one person works on the strategy, another knows how to establish close and trusting human connections, a third sees to it that results actually occur, that actions are in fact taken and real decisions made, and so forth. Such a team would work well together.

For such teamwork to actually take place, however, each individual member must exhibit all four strategies, for the thinker or strategist must possess enough realism, personal-relations skills, and courage to establish a workable division-of-labor partnership in the first place, and that would be true even if his or her function in the partnership were to work primarily on strategy. The reflective and scholarly strategist is action-oriented if he or she enters into an effective partnership with a doer—a partnership in which he or she nevertheless remains the strategist.

We saw before that practice in applying the Leadership

Diamond model requires diagnosis. We now address ourselves to this endeavor. The following diagnoses were developed by executives of various organizations, attempting to describe business leadership situations with which they were struggling. Their efforts may be of help to you.

A Sample Company Diagnosis

How does one diagnose specific companies or organizations? In the following analyses, the external consultant who provided this service concentrates on the dominant leadership strategies alone, omitting the detailed tactical examinations of individual diagnoses.

Company A is a remarkable financial-services company of two thousand employees. It is over one hundred years old and is deeply entrenched in its community. How does the company rate on the Leadership Diamond? Is it a leadership company? How does the corporate culture rate in supporting that company? (A company that lacks support from its culture will have top management just spinning its wheels.) What about top management? How does it rate in terms of the desiderata of the Leadership Diamond?

Let us start with vision. The vision of this company is maintained by the CEO virtually alone, singlehanded. In vision, he personally is rated "very strong," and he is to be admired and commended for it. The company's executive committee, on the other hand, is rated "relatively weak" in vision. Committee members try to understand and they try to follow; they even try to imitate, but they lack the initiative for great visions that distinguishes their CEO. Specifically, the company's leaders are engaged in good strategic thinking, which makes their visionary ranking "high," but the vision is not distant enough, nor is it viewed as a high enough priority or coupled with adequate commitment, seriousness, and courage. The total ranking for vision therefore remains "modest."

On reality, both the CEO and the executive committee are rated "strong." In fact, the CEO may be just a bit of a dreamer, so that he needs the common sense of the executive committee to

keep his nose to the ground. Reality ratings include also competence, and here this company generally rates "high." This is an
added reason for rating the company "strong" in its reality
strategy.

The company's rating on ethics is "very strong." Both the
CEO and his executive committee have a deep commitment to
ethics. This point may well be what the company primarily rests
on; its strength, reputation, and credibility are based heavily on
that factor.

On courage, the CEO rates "very strong," the executive
committee "modest." The committee members are carried along
by the CEO's power of personality. Therefore, the company, as an
organization demonstrating courage, can be rated only
"modest."

How is company A's corporate culture to be diagnosed?
Here, we distinguish the total culture from its top leaders. It is
rated "weak" on vision and courage, "acceptable" on reality, and
"strong" on ethics. On technical competence, it is rated "high,"
but "lower than necessary" on marketing aggressiveness, so that
its composite profile in the reality strategy would still be "on the
weak side" or, at best, "modest." On vision, it is "confused," partly
because of numerous recent acquisitions. The cumulative effect
of all this has been to weaken the market orientation of the
company, thereby seriously endangering the viability of the
bottom line.

What is to be done? How can the company be strengthened? First of all, a thoughtful, determined, and persistent campaign to instill reality into the culture is essential. For too long,
employees have been protected from the mercilessness of market forces; they must now feel those forces directly. They must be
challenged to make a commitment to meet the financial needs
of the company. And that cultural commitment must come not
only from additional incentives, which may be mechanical, but
also from a dramatization of the truth that reality is key to all
human life, and that a heightened reality consciousness testifies
to a person's general maturity. To be in touch with reality is good
for the soul. It will also be healthful for the company. Employees'

pride must be aroused: they can be on a winning team of their own making.

Efforts must also be undertaken to give the company a single direction — marketing. This is a matter not only of realism but also of vision. After all the acquisitions, it is now one unified company, although employees' loyalties are still disparate. Here, structuring (that is, utilizing "people architecture" principles, which means reorganization) can be helpful. Rotate people where possible. Bring them together in significant work teams; socializing, as a tactic, is incidental, but working together unites people. Give them interactive assignments, tasks that are inherently important, and make it clear that success belongs to the team. People will feel close if they are joined by a single task. The more teams are created from different branches, the greater the opportunities for building cohesion. But team members must also remain in touch with one another after completion of their assignments. Management can see to that by the way follow-up work is structured. These techniques must be applied on a large enough scale to create a critical mass that makes a difference.

Ethics, in this company, needs validation and reinforcement. It is the company's and its culture's first source of strength, and everyone should be proud of it. It is the employees' obligation as human beings, far more than as businessmen and businesswomen, to maintain this deservedly high ethical profile.

Courage is, of course, a tough issue in any company and in its supporting culture. In many instances, courage is not even manifested at the very top. In this company, however, it clearly is. But too many people choose lethargy and alienation over courage, and the others choose security. The most difficult thing in the world is to instill a kind of corporate patriotism in a company. In the case of this company, the solution is to insist that the executive committee clearly model courage, even if that means transfers of executives. Modeling courage is not a business decision but an existential human one. The executive committee is the Achilles' heel of this company. It needs all the support and stimulation it can get.

A mentoring campaign to instill vision and, especially,

courage in the executive committee (based on members' self-interest) will have the greatest leverage for this company as a whole. Moreover, since the company's morale is not particularly high, the purposes and commitments of this company should be raised to much nobler levels of significance, so that employees can realistically be expected to be loyal to worthy ideals while they devote themselves to the company. The higher the purposes that employees, including the executive committee, can fulfill in working for Company A, the more effective the total organization will be. This company must redouble its efforts to become a visionary business, not so much in the narrow sense of strategy as in the grander sense of mission, and its mission must have a very high moral content, for that is the strength of Company A in the first place.

To make these principles work in a school, for instance, significantly raise standards and program offerings. Teachers will be loyal to a true center of learning and to an exciting national center of research. Reputation, learning, and ethics go hand in hand, and they motivate to courage. Raising standards of behavior, commitment, and performance—in short, raising expectations—can have similar consequences for our Company A.

The Leadership Diamond in Organizations

The following diagnoses, developed by many different types of executives, serve as models for thinking in Leadership Diamond terms. They are classified into several loose categories. You should develop your own set of diagnoses, to ensure that you will in effect have taken the "oath of leadership," that is, made a commitment to view your leadership concerns in the Leadership Diamond format. The least you can expect is to double your leadership effectiveness on any measures you choose.

Diagnoses of Business in General. In a typical company, one executive argued, the planning department represents the vision strategy and a good portion of the reality strategy. Operations concerns itself principally with realism. Human relations

Figure 11.1. One View of a Typical Company.

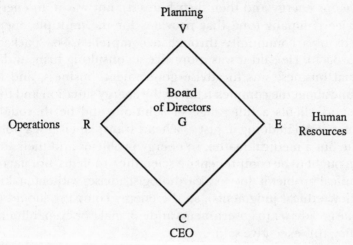

works with ethics. Courage is the responsibility of those who spend the money and make the decisions, and that task falls principally to the CEO or to the management committee. Finally, to oversee greatness is preeminently the task of the CEO and the company's board of directors (see Figure 11.1).

Another executive directed his attention to the search for root causes. He believed that often the wrong problem is addressed. The analysis or the solution system is either too narrow or too broad, too superficial or unnecessarily deep. An energy company (his example) requires public and political support to maintain its nuclear capability, which is threatened by popular antagonism to nuclear power. What should be the company's strategy for dealing with conflicting values and contradictory claims on the loyalty of its scientists and technicians? Should it be to cultivate influential political figures? To advertise? To seek favorable press? To lobby for favorable legislation? To become political and join the antinuclear or the pronuclear forces? To maintain a low profile—that is, to discuss the issues as little as possible? The debates at high levels of management are endless. The root cause of this company's confusion, however, may not be where its people are searching for solutions.

This executive argued that the company was no longer an

energy company (that is, a company that mines, purchases, or develops energy and then distributes it), nor was it an energy-service company (one that provides for the multiple energy needs of a community through a comprehensive, "package" approach). He said it was more like a consulting firm, and its actual business was to advise government, business, and the public about the complex truth of the energy situation and then offer its clients a full range of solutions and be thoroughly professional in doing it. Just as a heart transplant is not a policy issue but a medical matter, so energy problems and their solution ought to be comprehensive scientific problems, not narrow political problems. Just as a cardiologist advises without making policy (ethical judgments), so the energy company should become an adviser to governments and not make or even influence policy, this executive said.

The redefinition of the energy company as a consulting firm of the highest ethical probity would, he thought, be the first step toward solving its problems, for that redefinition would address the root issue, the issue that, once resolved, would meet the demands of the company's problems. In his opinion, a mind trained in the Leadership Diamond model would be able to move from unsolvable to solvable problems. He then used the Leadership Diamond grid to stimulate the uncovering of root causes.

What, he asked, should be the company's visionary strategy in response to popular doubt and antagonism? The leaders must ask the following questions: Does the problem, as stated, reach the right level? Is its formulation too general, or is it too detailed and specific? What is real? Does the formulation of the problem take account of all realities, of all constraints? Or does it see only the immediate constraints (governments and public opinion do change)? (The true long-term constraints may in fact be the danger of extinction of the human race.) What is ethical? Has the team approach been properly explored? (Remember, the belief that you are not free to be a genius can be a constraint in itself.) What about courage? Is the organization afraid to change its narrow procedures, its customary ways of thinking and behaving? Is the company's lack of clear ethics with regard

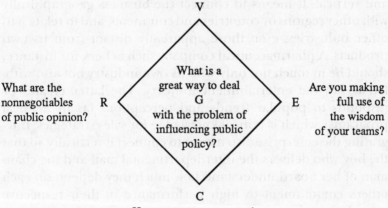

Figure 11.2. The Search for Root Causes.

to nuclear energy mere inertia? (It always takes courage to reach and confront root causes.) Does the organization ignore the fact that it is one of the agents creating a future for us all? That it must act, and not just react? What about greatness? Are senior managers looking for a breakthrough and challenging their minds to genius-level performance? Or are they satisfied (which in itself is, of course, acceptable) with incremental improvements alone?

The central question, this executive said, was "What is a *great* way to deal with the nuclear-power issue?" Specifically, are you being visionary? What are the dimensions of realism to consider? What is the spectrum of ethical issues, questions of sensitivity and service, of morality? Finally, what acts of courage must you and others perform to deal authentically with the nuclear-energy controversy? If the company, not satisfied with incremental answers, were to seek breakthroughs, then, he felt, there would be the best chance of its making the kind of leadership progress required by today's complex business climate (see Figure 11.2).

Another executive asked, "What are a company's focal

concerns? What are some of its major strategic themes, as gener-
ated by the Leadership Diamond?" Figure 11.3 is her diagram.
Integrating the enterprise, she maintained, is both horizontal
and vertical. It means to connect the business geographically
with other regions or countries and continents, and to relate it to
other industries, even those apparently distant from its own
products. A pharmaceutical company such as hers, for instance,
should be in touch not only with its own industry but also with,
let us say, the entertainment industry. The latter creates or
responds to popular trends and perceptions (as in medical
programs), which is critical knowledge for sales strategies. Integrating the enterprise also means to connect it vertically, so that
the boy who delivers the interdepartmental mail and the chairman of her board understand how much they depend on each
other's commitment to high performance in their respective
roles. Integration, she felt, requires great courage. It means one
must make decisions about major investments in money and
people, and it often may mean reorienting the direction of the
entire company. You meet the competition with innovation, she
said, and you promote quality because you believe in people and
service—and because you take pride in how you live your life.

Figure 11.3. Focal Concerns.

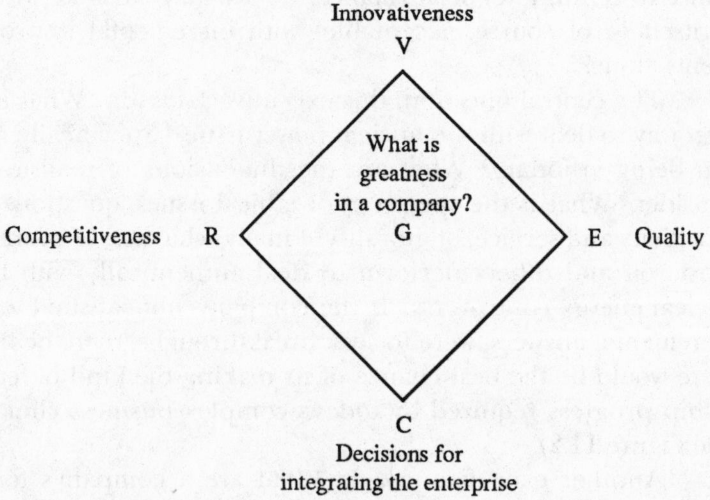

Innovativeness
V

What is
greatness
in a company?
Competitiveness   R   G   E   Quality

C
Decisions for
integrating the enterprise

Figure 11.4. Corporate Culture.

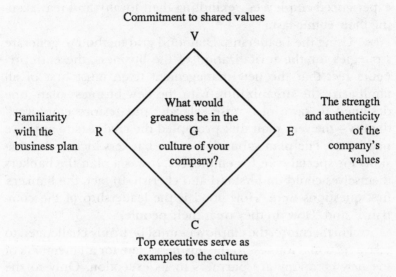

Commitment to shared values

V

Familiarity
with the   R
business plan

What would
greatness be in the
G
culture of your
company?

E

The strength
and authenticity
of the
company's
values

C

Top executives serve as
examples to the culture

Everyone, she said, knows that these things need to be done, but few have the will and the courage to act and make a real difference. The successful executive is willing to make these difficult choices.

Let us now study an example that directs the Leadership Diamond toward corporate cultures. Corporate cultures, in the opinion of another executive from an insurance company, can be assessed according to the criteria shown in Figure 11.4. The four dominant leadership strategies represent one answer to the question proposed by greatness.

Let us consider another executive's specific example along the same lines. Suppose that two entrepreneurs, the executive and his partner, buy an ailing company with five hundred employees. Its founder-owner has stayed on too long, and the company's creditors feared for their investments. The commitment of the new, youthful, energetic owners is to reclaim the old glory of this once distinguished corporation. In addition to providing innovation in marketing and realism in financing, they must pay attention to the culture they have just purchased. The sale of a company can be traumatic to its employees, and the value of the company is preserved and enhanced by retaining its experienced employees, rekindling their loyalty, and reawakening their enthusiasm.

Using the Leadership Diamond grid method to generate strategies for the revitalization of the business, the entrepreneurs feel that the new management team must first of all familiarize the organization with the new business plan, one designed to save jobs, raise salaries, and restore employees' dignity—the very plan that prompted the creditors to approve new loans. The plan submitted to the bankers included provisions for special care for employees. It was a plan the bankers themselves could understand and cherish. In fact, the bankers' first questions were "How good is the leadership of the company?" and "How do they treat their people?"

Furthermore, the employees must be firmly challenged to take a personal interest in the business plan, for all members of the new company are partners in its execution. Only to the extent that employees are in realistic contact with the operation of the total company and its larger economic context, understand the rationale for the business plan, and, above all, feel close to the final and actual customers can the new management count on a dependable and mature work force.

The shared values must be a merger of the old ones (which the new management team needs to respect) with the new ones that the new management team brings to the organization. If the new team's values are not yet clear, even to the teams themselves, then now is the time and here is the opportunity to make them clear and real. Finally, the two sets of values, the old and the new, must be integrated into one partnership of shared ideals. Only to the extent that these values are indeed authentic human virtues—not greed or selfishness, but service and caring; not self-serving arrogance, but exemplary statesmanship—can the corporate culture make a significant commitment to its new directorate.

The new top executives know that they must serve as an example, partly by their serious engagement in the ethics program of their new company. One proof of their commitment to serve the company will be the devotion of the new management to hard work, very hard work, to demonstrate dedication to solving the innumerable and taxing problems that have now descended upon them: creating and installing a marketing plan that works, satisfying creditors, risking their own future, understanding the needs of employees, making decisions that require significant courage, even risking their own lives. It is with their own lack of sleep—their own sweat, blood, and tears, as it were— that this new management will show its devotion to the old employees.

Another executive, this one in the wholesale food business, chose leadership effectiveness as his topic for diagnosis. Below is his description of it suggested by the Diamond. Leadership effectiveness requires skill, of course, and executives without it could never last in positions of managerial responsibility. Skill means that they understand the basic techniques and practices of effective leadership: setting up management systems, concerning themselves with morale, getting the job done, balancing sternness with human cordiality, setting up incentives, being conscious of the importance of discipline, supervising, and motivating.

Effectiveness in leadership also requires knowledge and experience; that is, leaders must know their business, their industry, their profession like experts. They must be well trained in what it takes to do what they expect their subordinates to do. Engineering managers must know engineering, deans must know the professors' subject matter, dentists and physicians must know their science exceptionally well, lawyers must know the law, and so forth. Such knowledge requires experience. We all know the homilies that experience is the best teacher and that there is no substitute for experience, but we must also bring these hackneyed maxims thoroughly to life.

Effectiveness also requires personal maturity. Leaders must be grown up, or they cannot earn the respect of their subordinates. Leaders are people who place the needs of the organization above their own. They do not say, "I want to become president of this company, and I want to benefit," but rather "I will support what this company needs for its success, for then everyone benefits." Maturity means service, not selfishness. Mature people are easy to get along with. They are not neurotic, jealous, petty, or irrational.

Finally, effectiveness requires philosophic wisdom. That means depth—understanding the human condition, seeing things in perspective. To have such wisdom is to find the deeper meanings, to understand human frailties, to know that colleagues and customers are concerned with death and freedom, guilt and love, and not just with profits, advancement, and greed. Summarizing his position, this executive said that, in this context, the definition of *greatness* is *effectiveness*. Skill is the meaning of realism. Wisdom is found in ethics. Maturity implies taking risks: it means courage. Knowing the business becomes, from a very pragmatic point of view, the vision (Figure 11.5).

We cannot forget to also diagnose vision in companies, for that is a central aspect of their general structure. In conclusion, let us therefore look at a large chemical company, whose executive committee organized their vision statement by establishing three categories: profits (the success of the business), people (employees, suppliers, and customers—in short, stakeholders), and the earth (ecology, protection and restoration of the environment).

Figure 11.5. Greatness as Effectiveness.

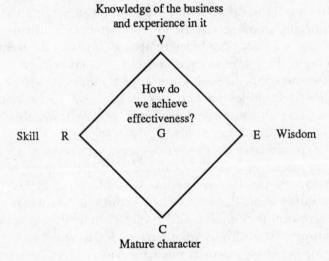

Knowledge of the business
and experience in it

V

How do
we achieve
effectiveness?
G

Skill   R   E   Wisdom

C
Mature character

Figure 11.6. Mission.

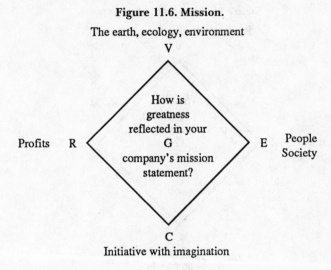

The earth, ecology, environment
V

How is
greatness
reflected in your
Profits R G E People
company's mission Society
statement?

C
Initiative with imagination

In this company, all decisions must be measured against these three socioeconomically significant criteria. What is more, there is an independent audit for each one. Not only do accounting firms monitor their profit-and-loss statements, the stock market will eventually demand it. There are also independent auditors for the company's people and social consciousness, as well as for achievements in this area. The consciousness of ecology and environmental sensitivity are likewise monitored by an appropriately established independent agency. Carrying out the demands of the vision statement requires initiative with imagination. This company's Leadership Diamond looks like Figure 11.6.

Diagnoses of Functions. Organizations, divisions, or functions within companies were diagnosed by a set of executives with the Leadership Diamond grid method. They were program managers of the product-development department of a large manufacturing company. Their complaint was that managers did not keep commitments and forgot promises. They did not show concern for the problems they caused people down the line and elsewhere in the organization by not having satisfactorily completed their own tasks.

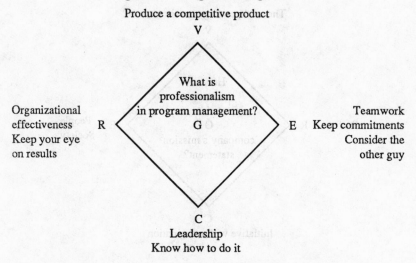

Figure 11.7. Program Management.

Produce a competitive product
V

What is
professionalism
in program management?

Organizational   Teamwork
effectiveness   R   G   E   Keep commitments
Keep your eye   Consider the
on results   other guy

C
Leadership
Know how to do it

A total picture would look like Figure 11.7.

This example shows how the fundamental needs of program managers, the desiderata listed above, can be fitted around the four corners of the Leadership Diamond.

Another set of executives took a diagnostic look at the human resources function in corporations (at least, one group's opinion about the current situation). These executives believed that the vision of the ideal human resources function can be limitless. Human resources deals with the prime ingredient of business: people. How we manage people should be the highest priority of any organization. Employees need to find meaning in work. They need to grow toward their fulfillment. They need to become self-realized at work. In short, they need to know that their organization's business objectives coincide with their own deep needs as human beings. These needs are four: creativity, an immortality project or a legacy, integrity and character, and validation. The workplace must express that. It is the joint responsibility of employees and management to set up a workplace that imaginatively meets these criteria. Not only will business prosper as a result, there is also, in the end, no other way for business to prosper, for where people grow, profits grow.

This group felt that its human resources function might well be on the way to obsolescence. The realities of business have changed from the days when human resources was instituted. The problem is systemic, not personal. In most organizations, human resources executives are among the best trained and most devoted members. Their role, however, is, in their opinion, becoming self-contradictory, creating problems for the personnel department as well as for those it serves.

These executives' core issue was their feeling that leadership could not be delegated. Besides labor relations, training, and benefits, the central obligation of human resources is to assist line and operations managers in leading. Not infrequently, line managers would just as readily delegate that onerous task than discharge it themselves; they claim that they have work to do. When is there time for leadership? There are, of course, sterling exceptions, but whenever leadership is delegated to human resources personnel, the effect can be disastrous.

The ethical issues concern human resources professionals as much as the people they serve. Much noble effort is spent by the human resources function to find ways of improving its professionalism and increasing its effectiveness in managing people issues. This seems to be developing today into the ethical dimension. These professionals need and deserve everyone's appreciation and cooperation. Courage, they concluded, is always the same: do something. Act. Take the initiative. Get results. (See Figure 11.8.)

Diagnoses of Training. One set of executives utilized the Leadership Diamond grid to design a seminar for the management group of a large engineering and manufacturing facility. The participants have two functions: they are both project and line managers. Their need is to become more effective as an organization and to greatly increase productivity. Their productivity requirements are measured by three criteria: on-time deliveries to their internal and external customers; reduced costs in development, but especially in manufacturing; and quality engineering solutions, so that, through styling and design, they can lower

Figure 11.8. The Human Resources Function.

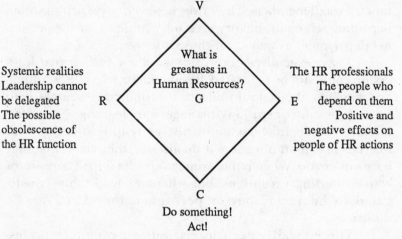

What could be (potentials)
Leadership required for survival
The human core and its increasing
importance in successful business

V

What is
greatness in
Human Resources?

Systemic realities   G   The HR professionals
Leadership cannot   The people who
be delegated   R   ◇   E   depend on them
The possible   Positive and
obsolescence of   negative effects on
the HR function   people of HR actions

C
Do something!
Act!

manufacturing costs and, more important, be competitive on the market.

This group's diagnostic model is shown in Figure 11.9.

In the order of their presentation in the seminar, the following are the points the group wants to cover. Each one will be amplified with appropriate exercises.

1. The *vision* of such a seminar is understanding the theory—in this case, the Leadership Diamond model. Without adequate theoretical preparation, leadership work is in danger of being amateurish instead of professional. Even though executives are impatient to act, which is good, they must nevertheless take time for theory so as to remain competitive. No one hires an engineer who is not trained in theory.

2. The *ethics* of such a seminar is to enhance teamwork. Teamwork is part of every other aspect of such a seminar. For instance, the discussion of theory consists, first, of small-group work and only later of general discussion. Right at the outset, participants practice teamwork. More intensive teamwork can

Figure 11.9. Leadership Diamond Used for a Seminar.

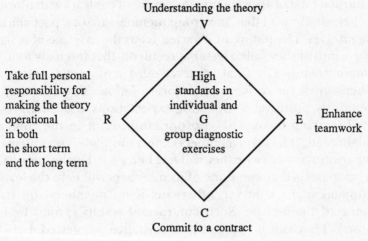

Understanding the theory
V

Take full personal
responsibility for
making the theory
operational   R
in both
the short term
and the long term

High
standards in
individual and
G
group diagnostic
exercises

E   Enhance
teamwork

C
Commit to a contract

be stimulated later, after the seminar cycle is complete, by sharing personal leadership diagnoses. In practice, this means that I diagnose myself, and you diagnose me, and then we compare notes. This process is then reversed, so that you diagnose yourself, and I diagnose you, and then we compare notes.

3. *Reality*, in this seminar, is perhaps the pivot. It is to challenge each individual, and then the full group, to take full personal responsibility for making the theory operational, in both the short and the long term. Each person is asked to give a few examples of precisely what he or she can do, the day after the seminar, to make the Leadership Diamond principles live in that part of the organization for which he or she is immediately responsible. Then, more examples are requested for long-range planning. To make the theory come to life may mean one small incremental improvement in process, or it may mean the courage to install a breakthrough innovation.

4. The sense of *greatness* in leadership is touched by two critical exercises, one in personal leadership diagnosis and the other in organizational diagnosis. The first enhances individual responsibility; the second, teamwork. Both individualism and teamwork require the spark of greatness in the modern organization.

5. *Courage* means to challenge the group to draw up a contract. First of all, each member makes a contract with himself or herself. Beyond that, the group members make a pact among themselves. The nature of it varies, from the extreme of resigning jointly if they fail to lesser agreements that intensify mutual commitments. The final contract must have teeth, sanctions. There must be consequences for violation. The currency is emotions: approval for meeting expectations and disapproval for betraying them. The appropriate phrases in the contract might read, "The team members expect the leader to implement the contract; otherwise they will feel betrayed. Furthermore, the team expects that every one of its members will help the leader implement the contract; otherwise, team members will have betrayed themselves." Such contractual results cannot be imposed. They can be guided into existence, suggested, but the force that realizes them must always evolve from within—from the desire to succeed, from the quest for greatness in people's work.

From time to time, organizations need to check how well they are meeting the leadership challenge. One way is to devise, as one organization did, a *quarterly greatness review*. This organization uses the Leadership Diamond grid to measure its performance. One review is directed to team performance, another to individual performance.

Greatness can be found in how well the group supports its leader, and, conversely, in how well the leader is supportive of the group—internally, such as by coordinating group work, and externally, such as by representing the group to other divisions of the organization, to upper management, and to unions, as well as to customers, the government, lawyers, stockholders, suppliers, and so on.

Vision can be tested with one simple question: Are we losing sight of the larger perspective?

Reality means project review. Whatever the group's task is, whatever is needed to satisfy the customer, internal or external—that is the project. It may be to devise a process, create a product, or provide a service. How are we doing with the prod-

Figure 11.10. Quarterly Greatness Review.

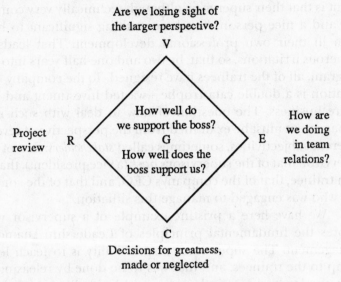

Are we losing sight of
the larger perspective?

V

Project
review   R

How well do
we support the boss?
G
How well does the
boss support us?

E

How are
we doing
in team
relations?

C

Decisions for greatness,
made or neglected

uct we must deliver? That question, asked daily, must nevertheless be repeated during the greatness review.

Ethics means checking on conflict resolution, feelings of emotional support, the status of team spirit, and the quality of personal relations among the members of the team. The team also discusses whether every member of the team displays personal ownership of the team tasks, takes personal responsibility for making significant contributions to the team, and feels accountable for the success of the team.

Courage means sharing with each other decisions for greatness that, over the past three months, were made or neglected, have been accomplished, or are now overdue. This organization developed a general model for the quarterly greatness review, shown in Figure 11.10.

Here is a final training example, which demonstrates how damaging the lack of leadership development can be to a company. A company hires four promising graduates of a business school as trainees. A supervisor is placed in charge of them. The company invests much money and time in developing them.

After a while, the trainees are dissatisfied. Their primary complaint is that their supervisor, although technically very competent and a nice person, has done nothing significant to help them in their own professional development. That leads to numerous irritations, so that, by two and one-half years into the program, all of the trainees have resigned. To the company, this situation is a double catastrophe — wasted investment and lost future business. The question of how to deal with such mismanagement must be examined from the perspective of several different subjectivities, sometimes called *stakeholders*: that of the supervisor, that of the supervisor's boss (a vice-president), that of each trainee, that of the company's CEO, and that of the consultant who was engaged to manage this situation.

We have here a pristine example of a supervisor who ignores the fundamental principles of Leadership Diamond management. The supervisor's responsibility is to teach leadership to the trainees, and that was to be done by releasing in them the leadership mind, or leadership intelligence. It is to empower them to think and act the way leaders do. It is precisely those employees who were interested in leadership intelligence who have left. Those who stayed may not be similarly motivated to think and act as leaders do. The company, however, needs nonleaders to go and leaders to stay.

The supervisor should have raised, with all trainees, the issue of whether their professional lives were developing as expected. For example, he should have explored vision (What are your visions of yourselves, your future? Is your work connected to them?), ethics (Do you feel that I am listening to your visions, that the company hears your visions and cares enough to try to respond to them? Do we care enough about you to train you? To give you opportunities for growth?), and reality (Are we, in this department, truly professional? Is the company? Are you learning the business while working here?).

Some small companies cannot compete with larger organizations in the professional experience they offer to their employees. To aspire to offer precisely that, however, is a company's or a department's best possible stimulus to excel. That is one solution. Not to hire trainees who are overqualified is another. Still a third would be to have a moral agreement regarding how much trainees should contribute overall to the organization that trains them and makes them more marketable.

The dimension, or strategy, of courage means, principally, having the good sense to pursue leadership intelligence development vigorously (in addition, of course, to carrying out daily business routines). Is everyone (that is, every concerned subjectivity, every stakeholder) taking full personal responsibility for organizational success?

The trainees' responsibility, if they are properly mentored in leadership intelligence, is to succeed against all odds: assume autonomous responsibility to define their own jobs, seek interesting assignments, support their colleagues, make their supervisors successful, help the company, and be loyal. Looking out for themselves alone would represent the same kind of narrowness of which the trainees accused their company. In short, trainees are as responsible for applying Leadership Diamond principles to their own behavior, with respect to the company, as the company is for applying those principles to employees.

The CEO must see to it that his company is thoroughly professional and, although small, capable of competing with the biggest when it comes to the sophisticated and advanced services it offers customers. To remedy the structural defects that were the trainees' reasons for leaving—that is, to provide more opportunities for learning, self-development, and advancement and, above all, better examples of leadership greatness in management—also constitutes an answer to the fundamental profitability problems of the organization itself. Thus, to meet the trainees' demands for themselves is also to improve the company's overall performance.

What now? The problem has cost the company $1 million. Let the learning that the company derives from this experience be worth $2 million, so that the whole episode turns out to be a good return on investment. In fact, the company can choose to get new trainees, fire the supervisor, and double its expectations of new hires. The consultant's diagnostic diagram is shown in Figure 11.11.

Figure 11.11. Solutions to Lack of Leadership.

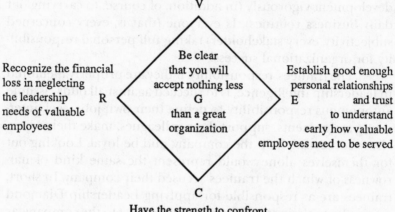

Understand the importance of leadership
development in retaining good people
Create imaginative solutions to the problem of
how to compete as a small company with bigger ones
in what is offered to promising employees

V

Recognize the financial
loss in neglecting
the leadership
needs of valuable
employees

R

Be clear
that you will
accept nothing less

G

than a great
organization

Establish good enough
personal relationships
and trust
to understand
early how valuable
employees need to be served

E

C

Have the strength to confront
the mismanagement weaknesses
in the present organization

Diagnoses of Values in Business. Continuing with this loose classi-
fication of diagnoses of business situations, we now take a look at
values and what happens to them when seen in Leadership
Diamond format. Let us first consider an example of the arts in
business. A museum curator and part-time business consultant
comes up with the following practice diagnosis of the arts.

The arts enhance the meaning of greatness in leadership,
with power unequaled by any other medium. Vision is the
hallmark of the arts. The artist creates the symbols for tomorrow.
Art—poetry, painting, music, sculpture, architecture, drama—
thrives on innovation. Art is dedicated to new modes of perception, to breaking through the barriers of old habits. When
visiting a museum, one can move from a room of Flemish
paintings, with their gray and dark colors and their depressed-
looking figures, people suffering poverty and oppression, to the
next room, one of expressionist paintings, full of vigor and color

and craziness. Art helps us burst out from tradition and welcome the revolutionary newness of the visionary spirit of human beings.

Accurate perception of reality is also one of the roles of art. Art, for example, puts us in touch with political realities (Goya's *The Disasters of War*; Picasso's *Guernica*). It connects us with the realities of nature, as does El Greco's *Storm over Toledo*. Picasso held that the artist is a socially conscious being, a "political being, constantly alive to heartrending, fiery and joyful events" (Piper, 1986, p. 666). Edvard Munch's famous *The Scream* connects us with emotional reality. Naturalism, Impressionism, Pointillism, Cubism, Expressionism — all these are schools of art that dramatize the reality of the perceptions that our interpretations distort. Do you want to know the truth? Do not view the world with common eyes; use your sensitive artistic eyes instead. Then you are in touch with what is real.

Ethics also means love and integrity. An operatic aria from Puccini's *La Bohème* or Mozart's *Don Giovanni* perfectly illustrates the tenderness of love. Some symphonies, like Beethoven's Third and Fifth, are memorable statements of ethical integrity.

Courage is powerfully illustrated in Delacroix's *Liberty Leading the People* and David's *The Oath of the Horatii*.

To underscore the significance of each Leadership Diamond point, what can serve us better than using the arts for what they were meant to signify in the first place — namely, greatness? (See Figure 11.12.) In the year of his assassination, President John F. Kennedy wrote, "The life of the arts, far from being an interruption, a distraction, in the life of a nation, is very close to the center of a nation's purpose — and is a test of the quality of a nation's civilization."

Now let us consider team spirit. One consultant uses mythology to promote team building. Team spirit, she contends, can be enhanced by an understanding of the language of the mythology that expresses its anthropological origins. The need to be a team is more than purely pragmatic; it is the residue of our tribal instincts. To the extent that an organization can respond, even marginally, to the unconscious memories of our tribal ancestry, it will receive our loyalty. Leaders need to explore how their teams can approximate satisfying the central human needs common throughout the history of mythology.

Humanity began when humanoids became aware of death. Here was the first step from consciousness to self-consciousness. It occurred 1,800,000 years ago, when these creatures set up mounds and buried artifacts to remember their dead. They evidently began to reflect on the fact that there is death, and they responded to this first insight. They thought about death and commemorated it. This marks the beginning of self-consciousness, in the form of mythology as early philosophy. Campbell (1984) suggests five universal mythological (and therefore philosophical) themes: to have an answer to death; to participate in something greater than we are and that existed before us and will exist after us; to be the chosen people, to be special; to give meaning to existence by explaining life, including the mystery of creation; and to value and support one's independent individual identity, as in the hero myths. These ancient themes are also corners of the Leadership Diamond. The need to face death is a confrontation with reality. Death is

Figure 11.12. Art and Greatness.

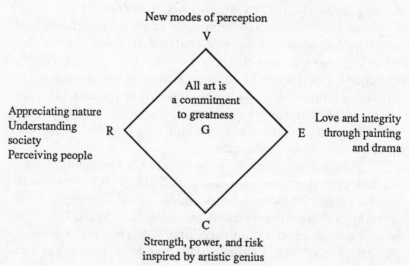

New modes of perception

V

All art is
a commitment
to greatness
G

Appreciating nature
Understanding   R
society
Perceiving people

E   Love and integrity
through painting
and drama

C

Strength, power, and risk
inspired by artistic genius

Figure 11.13. Mythology and Greatness.

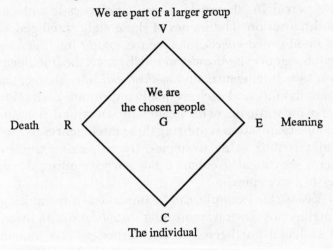

the clearest example of the finality of what is real, the impenetrability of our limits. To participate in something greater than we are, something that endures and that was here long before we were, is a form of vision. Vision is expansive, and visionary thinking moves both forward and backward into the realms of infinity and eternity. The need to be special, to belong to the chosen people, is the meaning of greatness. You are chosen by how you face the reality of death, chosen by the stature of the group to which you belong, and so forth. The meaning of life—the discovery of your reason for being, your destiny in this world, the explanation of your moral code, your need for wisdom—concerns the ethical strategies of the leadership mind. Finally, to be an individual is the ultimate act of courage, for didn't the first man and the first woman defy God in the Garden of Eden and thereby affirm their own separate existence? Expelled from Paradise, didn't Adam and Eve have to face the final act of courage in how they made a lonely life for themselves? (See Figure 11.13.)

Finally, let us consider the phenomenon of multiple intelligences. A further example of practicing Leadership Diamond technology is to take the theory of multiple intelligences (Koestenbaum, 1987) and translate it into the Leadership Diamond model. There are eight ways of being intelligent, eight ways of perceiving the world. This is a democratic and a mind-expanding notion. The names of these eight intelligences are *logical* intelligence, *esthetic* intelligence, *somatic* intelligence, *marketing* intelligence, *transcendental* intelligence, the intelligence of *wisdom*, *team* intelligence, and *motivational* intelligence. Each is different in kind, and each is equally important. Each is also an aspect of the strategies of the Leadership Diamond. Ask yourself how your organization is utilizing these intelligences to increase the effectiveness of its strategies. By enhancing these intelligences, we can also enhance the corresponding dominant leadership strategies.

Vision, for example, can be improved by promoting logical intelligence (abstract reasoning, visualization, analysis) and transcendental intelligence (consciousness as fact, nonattachment, exploration of inner space-time). Reality can be improved by practicing somatic intelligence (the language of sensuality, muscular dexterity and strength, kinetic orientation, physical and nutritional health) and marketing intelligence (survival, systems, wonder, flexibility, adaptability). Ethics can be strengthened by further developing the intelligence of wisdom (experience, communication skills, philosophy of life) and team intelligence (identity through community, service, working through and with others). Courage is mostly motivational intelligence (the preeminence of action, self-energization, will, greatness). The ideal of greatness itself, underlying the full theory of the Leadership Diamond, can be enriched through esthetic intelligence (verbal, musical, pictorial), for metaphor empowers whatever it touches (Figure 11.14).

The Third World. A worthy conclusion of these illustrative analyses comes from a business and political gathering, held in Latin America, where the fate of the Third World was discussed.

A Third World industrialist needs global consciousness. Even more than industrialized nations, Third World countries must be fully aware of what occurs in the rest of the world. What happens there deeply affects events in the Third World. One example is the price of petroleum. The disposition of the Third

Figure 11.14. Multiple Intelligences.

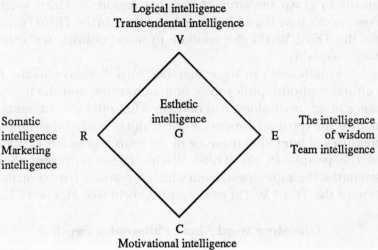

Logical intelligence
Transcendental intelligence

V

Somatic intelligence
Marketing intelligence

R

Esthetic intelligence
G

E

The intelligence of wisdom
Team intelligence

C

Motivational intelligence

World debt, which depends on decisions made by First World governments and banks, also affects how the fate of the Third World is sealed. It is therefore a critical need of Third World business executives to manage their relations well with the industrialized world. These are all matters of vision.

Realism, in the Third World, means to size up economic problems in terms of the idiosyncrasies of the local culture. It means to face up to the work ethic, bureaucracy, and corruption. (It has been theorized that the absence of a viable work ethic in parts of Latin America stems from the three sources of the population: the Spanish *conquistadores*, who had no interest in work, for they were lords and plunderers; the black slaves imported from Africa, for whom work was punishment; and the Indians, the natives, who were nomads and hunters, and to whom the discipline of work made no sense.)

The ethical dimension is customer focus. What matters is that the customer's needs are met, not adherence to bureaucratic rules; and this the Third World business culture must learn and promote.

Courage in the Third World means determination and perseverance. It means never to get discouraged. It also means idealism and patriotism, national and ethnic pride. Courage means to grasp the strengths of that region. A Third World country can have the ambition to be a leader in the Third World, for the Third World can mediate in world politics; few other nations qualify.

Finally, one can argue that the Third World is sensitive to culture, tradition, philosophy, human warmth, and the importance of art, mythology, and religion. The softer side of human nature, the spiritual dimension, the realm of inwardness — those treasures of humanity resonate in the souls and hearts of many of the people in the Third World. These represent their strengths, their greatness, from which can arise a true contribution of the Third World to the entire world (see Figure 11.15).

One More Word About Philosophic Depth

Among management approaches, the Leadership Diamond model is positioned as the mindset (that is, the attitude — the way of thinking, perceiving, and experiencing; the philosophy of life, belief system, world design, or metaphysics) that underlies, is necessary to, is the critical success factor for, and is the

Figure 11.15. The Third World.

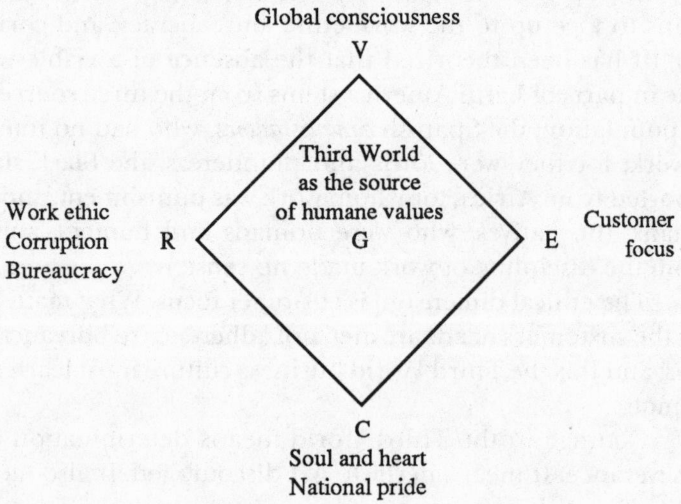

Global consciousness

V

Third World
as the source
of humane values

Work ethic
Corruption   R   G   E   Customer
Bureaucracy   focus

C
Soul and heart
National pride

Figure 11.16. Leadership Diamond Flow Chart.

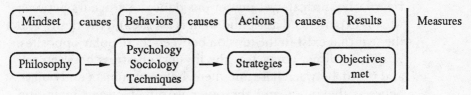

necessary condition for understanding and, above all, implementing, bringing about, the behaviors (visible, describable, teachable, and measurable) that are recognized as managerial skills and that lead to certain actions, which are strategies, tactics, plans, and programs conducive to consequences, or results, which in turn accomplish the organizational objectives. Furthermore, to reinforce motivation, and for the sake of professional precision, measures must be introduced. This complex chain can be represented in a flow chart (Figure 11.16).

What is philosophy? Philosophy deals with the purely human, with the eternal questions, and, in the language of the German philosopher Immanuel Kant, with immortality, love, justice, that is, with God, meaning, and consciousness.

Philosophy represents the in-depth mindset required for leadership. At the level of behavior, we resort to the techniques developed by the behavioral sciences, among which are psychology and sociology. But to understand them, we must return to the regions of depth explored in philosophy. The actions recommended or taken by this process are strategies and practices. These, we hope, will lead to results, which should be the business objectives of the organization. To make sure that we know what we are talking about, we require measures; we must monitor results. Thus, the philosophic roots of the Leadership Diamond strategies are seen most clearly in the philosophic-level tactics, or resources.

The philosophic roots of an executive's capacity for visioning we find in the structure of pure consciousness, a field that requires both conceptual and experiential training in philosophy for its exploration.

The philosophic roots of the reality strategy lie in the

connection between the ultimate subject and object of all experience, the intricate yet mysterious dance that occurs between what is experienced as *me* and what is *not me*, and the desire and the fear that exist in the tension between these polar opposites. Reality, as direct contact, is the mysterious stress between self and world, between here and there, between subject and object, between the inner and the outer worlds, between male and female, young and old, between (in the immortal words of Martin Buber) the *I-Thou* and the *I-It* (Buber, 1970).

The philosophic roots of ethics lie in what Kant ([1781] 1969) so aptly expressed when he wrote, in the conclusion to his *Critique of Pure Reason*, "Two things fill the mind with ever-increasing wonder and awe, the more often and the more intensely the mind of thought is drawn to them: the starry heavens above me and *the moral law within me*" (italics added).

Finally, the philosophic roots of courage lie in the full understanding of freedom as the ultimate structure of our being. Freedom explains the world, but the world cannot explain freedom.

The fundamental rule of health is that problems are created at the philosophic level of depth, and it is there that they are resolved. Significant change, therefore, can occur only to the degree that the mind returns to its philosophic source. In Leadership Diamond language, the best results come from activating the philosophic tactic of each dominant leadership strategy. Philosophy can reveal to us our most powerful resources.

12

Leadership for the Next Decade and Beyond

The larger perspective in terms of which business must be understood is the statesmanship dimension. It is the largest vision possible—not the quarterly reports or the annual profit-and-loss statements, nor the decades in terms of which competent leaders think. Here, not even the century is sufficient. Leaders must think in terms of the millennium. James Freeman Clarke, the nineteenth-century American Unitarian clergyman and writer, said it well: "The difference between a politician and a statesman is: a politician thinks of the next election and a statesman thinks of the next generation."

Strategic Issues for the Next Generation

There are five issues leaders need to face to achieve the transformation to the Third Millennium: technology, globalization, the acceleration of change, cooperation, and freedom.

The first statesmanship issue today is *technology*—automation. Automation means, specifically, information and communications technology, space exploration, nuclear energy, robotics, computer-assisted functions, such as CAD, CAM, and CAE, biotechnology (such as antibody engineering), and so forth. Resistance to technology is based on the presumed loss of jobs, ignorance about what technology really is and what it can do, blind prejudice against change, the dangers of dehumaniza-

305

tion, and the fear that it will neglect human depth and feelings. Technology often is used where it is not needed, as in war, oppression, and bureaucracy. Just as often, it is not used where it is needed, as in Third World self-improvement projects, in the elimination of hunger and illiteracy, in the strengthening of world justice, and in increasing the efficiency of everyday living.

Technology both amplifies and compresses. In amplifying, it makes evil worse (as in terrorism and organized crime, drug trafficking, and homelessness for the unskilled and unemployable). In compression, it makes the globe into a single economic, political, cultural, and social weather system in that a low-pressure area in one place (lax tax laws, cheap labor, high indebtedness) produces winds in another place (strict law enforcement, expensive union labor, substantial surpluses). Capital flows across nations as does the jet stream and the Gulf Stream. It leaves severe turbulence in its wake. The Vietnam and Gulf Wars were fought in the living rooms of the United States of America; these are the all-time dramatic examples of social compression through communications technology.

Machines can do virtually everything but be leaders, and the responsibility of leaders is to act as leaders, not as machines. The future will divide the world into leaders and nonleaders, with the former having to assume responsibility for the latter.

The second issue for statesmen, in politics and business as well as in science, the arts, and the professions, is *globalization*. That is, of course, a spillover from technology. Globalization means increasing interdependence of political, social, economic (labor, capital, energy, management) and intellectual (world views, religion, mythology, political theory) currents. It is no longer possible to say, for instance, in which country an automobile is built. It is no longer possible to set fiscal policy in one nation alone. It is no longer possible to set energy policy and ecological standards in one nation without considering the others. It is now more difficult than it used to be to fight a war, for today's collaborating industries must first disengage themselves from one another before one nation can build missiles, tanks, and airplanes to crush another.

The new leader must always think globally—that is as

much a mindset and a series of expectations for how problems are to be conceptualized as it is information and experience. Leadership in global markets requires integrating the enterprise. The corporate leader, in a model recently developed for one corporation's leadership forum, must consider such varied phenomena as global competition; shifting markets; organizational transformation, culture, people, and skills; enabling technologies; and international relations, and all that from the plethora of perspectives represented by government, business, academia, and information technology.

In less than one century there will be no more nations. Europe, through the Common Market and the openings to the East, will soon supersede economically the United States of America and Japan. Soon we will have the United States of Europe. Not much later, there will be the United States of the Pacific Rim. Among the resistances to global thinking and acting we will find nationalism and protectionism, as well as the hardening of the mind—an atavism that fixes thought at a much earlier state of historical evolution.

The third task with which the transition to the next millennium must cope is the *acceleration of change*. Change alone is difficult enough, but its acceleration is even more threatening. Organizations today are fast-paced; to reflect, regroup, and consolidate often means to be left behind.

What does change mean? What are some of the trends? The specific issues change; not all are equally timely. But the general outlines remain the same. The biggest change is the threat to the environment, but there are many others, including the stock market's volatility, currency fluctuations, developments in European politics and Middle Eastern politics, the increasing debts of the United States, the emergence of newly industrialized economies, the continuing breakup of the nuclear family, the erosion of the values of commitment and hard work, and drug addiction as evidence that large numbers of people cannot cope with life.

Environmental problems are also intensifying:

- The destruction of the rain forests (much of it by man-set fires) in the tropics, most perniciously in Brazil, where fifty million years of evolution have been going up in flames daily, the fires having by now irreversibly destroyed close to 20 percent of the jungle

- The resulting greenhouse effect, which heats up the planet, extends the summers, dries up the land, and fosters forest fires
- The fast extinction of species, diminishing the critical biological diversity required for the sustenance of life itself on the planet
- The ozone hole
- The fact that cities like Mexico City, Cairo, Tokyo, New York, Los Angeles, and Calcutta are becoming unlivable (given crime, pollution, poverty, AIDS, disaffection and alienation, and congestion, although the danger exists that people will try to adjust to such inhuman conditions)
- Famines, massacres, and floods in various parts of the world

All these problems and changes are accelerating, and high technology is involved in all of them. High technology accelerates change, for there is a technology of change, a technology for changing the technology (such as computer-generated computer programs).

Beyond change and the acceleration of change, there is the *direction* of change, and that is uncertain. Life and work are a series of capricious frustrations and arbitrary surprises. One cannot be adequately prepared for the unexpected, which nevertheless is certain to occur. Change is what is normal; stability is the aberration. The desired future state is no longer the successful transition from change to stability but rather the ability to thrive on the acceleration of change itself.

It is always interesting to assess the world situation in terms of the changes that are occurring. It is also interesting to select trends, directions that may give us some indication of where we may find ourselves in the future. Nevertheless, anyone who has lived at least half a century must reach at least one inevitable conclusion: life is unpredictable; events just cannot be foreseen. Who would have thought that the Berlin Wall would come down, and as quickly as it did? Who would have thought that Germany would be reunited, and as speedily as it has been? Who would have thought the Soviet Union would be accommodating—with Germany, with NATO, with the United States? Who would have foreseen the United Nations alliance against Iraq? Who could have predicted the gradual disintegration of the Russian empire or the declarations of independence of many of the Soviet republics? Who could have predicted the mushrooming of market economies? The list could go on and on. It is precisely this uncertainty that requires us to make our plans accordingly. Here is where our creativity and imagination, our capacity for strategic thinking, our leadership competency, are tested to their limits. How do these changes appear in your life and in your work? How do they affect you? How do you react? What changes do you need to make to be more competent in managing change itself?

Such chaos demands *cooperation*, the fourth task. Cooperation means overcoming alienation, learning to work and live together, taking the initiative to support one another. Cooperation is the task of creating dialogues among people and taking a strong position on eliminating violence. It means to work through people and with people. It means to manage the tribal, gregarious, and territorial instincts (which, on the one hand, lead to intense loyalty and team spirit but, on the other, can also result in barbaric bloodshed). Corporations and nations must overcome their bitter rivalries and restore ethics and love to business and politics. Teamwork is needed, and not only in business and the professions; it is also required among nations.

Power today resides heavily in world business. Leadership means to make an unconditional commitment to use that power wisely; with power comes responsibility. The creation of a cooperative, moral world order may belong more to business than to any other institution of society, since today's world seems to be governed more by economic than by military alliances.

Cooperation today must take a new turn. In the past, conflict among ideologies created wars; today, struggles are more likely to form along ethnic and religious lines. Therefore, it is a matter of the highest urgency to build cooperation on the common principles of humanity that bond us all. It is equally important to find ideas and feelings in the world religions that all human beings can share. We must discover those beliefs that connect us, emphasize them, teach them, and promulgate them, so that we can be more tolerant in areas where we disagree.

The greatest danger in this world is unthinking people — people who feel passionately but do not think, people who have no education, people who have nothing to lose. Universally, lack of education is the result of poverty, just as poverty is the result of the absence of education. This loop, which turns into a downward spiral, must be reversed. A virtuous circle must be established to replace the nefarious results of the vicious circle that prevails today. This is the ultimate meaning of cooperation.

The fifth task for the forthcoming millennium is to increase *freedom* in the world — to enhance our understanding of it and to mount a crash program to protect it. (The same, of course, applies to all other basic human values — most of which, however, grow straight out of the soil of freedom.) Freedom centrally entails responsibility — that is, autonomy, the ability and willingness to take care of oneself, to assume stewardship over one's own life and over the destiny of one's people. The development and preservation of the individual, in a depersonalizing world of increasing population and ever more powerful corporations, international conglomerates, and national alliances, becomes the humane task for the Third Millennium.

Freedom expresses itself politically, economically, and spiritually. The state must protect the freedom of conscience of all its residents. The economy must be permitted to express the free actions of free men and women. People must be encouraged to experience the natural success of their ethical business commitments and skills. The obstacles to freedom are an understandable but unhealthy obsession with security, the myopia of the bureaucratic mind, and oppression by those whose own limitations are exposed in the burgeoning freedom of others.

Developing freedom is the direction of history; it is the evolution of the spirit. It is the source of energy for the political, religious, and philosophic issues of our day. Freedom movements proliferate, from *glasnost* to the *intifada*. Nevertheless, the danger to freedom increases daily. The need to nurture it has never been greater.

Out of these five issues confronting a world in transition to the next millennium grows the requirement for a new conception, impetus, thrust, robustness, and depth of leadership. Take a look at your organization. How close is it to the ideal? What will be the consequences for the future, if you and your organization continue with business as usual? What are the alternatives? What is a preferred future? What needs to be done? Ask yourself how these five issues — coping with technology, globalization, the acceleration of change, cooperation, and the question of freedom — manifest themselves in your life and in your organization or company. What are your leadership choices? What acts of courage does life demand of you, and how are you managing them?

To be a leader is to know that only part of your career time can be devoted to management and maintenance. The rest must be given to the development of leadership intelligence. For example, middle management should devote one-third of its work time to leadership, and two-thirds to maintenance and managing. For upper management, these figures rise to 50 percent. An organization demands leadership of its bosses but gets mostly management. An organization also severely interferes with the efforts of its executives to be leaders. Real leaders succeed against all odds.

A Moral World Order

Webber (1987, p. 115) states the issues well:

> Global competition. Technological change. The renewed value of human capital. Demographic changes that presage market shifts. The changing role and responsibility of governments. Corporate values. These crosscurrents challenge old assumptions and old practices. Not that everything tried and true should be abandoned; sometimes back to basics is the wave of the future. But the company

that isn't actively re-examining its thinking is probably already dead from the neck up, and look out
below! Companies on the move recognize that
change begins as soon as you begin to think about
how you think about what you do. Habits of mind
govern habits of behavior. And a manager's mind is
a terrible thing to waste.

Why develop the leadership mind? Why pursue leadership intelligence? The ancient Greeks, in their philosophy,
valued intelligence and character most of all. The former meant
brilliance; the latter, morality. The final good, for Aristotle, is the
image of God appreciating himself—that is, God deriving satisfaction from understanding the sharpness of his intelligence
and the nobility of his character. We find ourselves hard pressed
to recover the feeling of this ancient age. What mattered then
was not companies or wealth, power least of all; not even security
was a final value. What mattered was who you were, how developed your mind was and how mature your character. These were
ends in themselves. Possessing them, exhibiting them, demonstrating them, was inherently valuable. The virtues of intelligence and character did not serve any ulterior purpose; they
were intrinsically beautiful. They are still fulfilling, satisfying,
and pleasurable simply as they are, alone and by themselves.
The values, of course, are demonstrated and manifested by,
made visible in, your behavior, your actions, your creations. The
good life is not static. Like growth, intrinsic values are not things
but processes, and you do not own a process; you live it. To
understand these values, to have experienced the peace and
security they make available—that is maturity.

Are you made for the company, or is the company made
for you? Should you develop your intelligence and your character for the sake of the company, because the company needs it?
Or is the company your instrument, your vehicle, your tool to
develop your mind, to sharpen your intelligence, and to give you
practice for your character? Companies expect individuals to fit
into the needs of the business. The deeper truth in the history of
Western civilization is that worldly goods exist for the develop-

ment of the soul. That is the philosophic way to leadership. Certainly, as you grow, the company grows. If you put your own true and authentic development first, then the company wins. If you put the company's materialistic needs first, and if you subject yourself to the unfeeling and indifferent bottom-line needs of the business, then the company loses. The only way the company can win is if you have your values straight: the company is your training ground for intellectual clarity and strength of character. In the end, that is the sole path to authentic leadership. To the average executive, these thoughts may be too idealistic or visionary, but from the perspective of philosophy, they represent the last truth about human reality and personal values.

Why play chess? For the sake of the game? For the sake of winning? No: because it improves the mind. Is there a point of termination, a conclusion, when you no longer learn but only play? No. Unless the mind continues to improve, the joy is gone. Why play tennis? To win? Winning is a sign of accomplishment. But without the thrill of continuous improvement, there is no joy. Joy means growth. Growth for its own sake is what fulfills, gives meaning to life. Your interest holds only so long as you grow, and the growth that counts is growth of intellect and character, for they are the core values of our civilization. That is what leadership is all about. Business is one arena where one can practice the art of leadership.

In the end, philosophy in business is the commitment to establish, through the power of commerce, a moral world order, in the best and most realistic sense of history and politics. Philosophy in business is a matter of destiny—personal and corporate, social and international, secular and religious. It is the desire to make a contribution, to honor the fact of your existence, and to be a credit to the greatest of all gifts: the consciousness with which you are endowed and graced. Society and the world have a right to expect no less from you. Such is statesmanship, the highest level of leadership.

A New Vision

Quality in business depends on high-quality persons. What is a high-quality person? A high-quality person is, of course, a skilled professional; but that point is only half the story and is not the purpose of this book. A high-quality person is also grounded in two sets of experience: personal and vicarious, direct and indirect. Personal experience comes from a rich and varied life, an open life dedicated to growth, wonder, and accomplishment. Vicarious experience is learning, for education is the collected experience of mankind. Education, specifically in the humanities, sums up for us the total wisdom of the human race. Education is, therefore, accelerated experience, and the kind of education required for human authenticity is found by combining four areas of human endeavor: theology, religion, and mythology; psychology, psychiatry, and in-depth psychotherapy; literature, the other arts, and history; and philosophy, including ethics, logic, and cosmology.

What is the best model for a company? An army? A family? A state? A brain? An organism? Is it a symphony orchestra? What about the university as a model for business, a university where the sciences, professional skills, attention to the body, and the humanities are well blended? We must not develop people for the sake of work; work exists to develop people. Not only is that morally right, it is also commercially savvy. Much teaching goes on in business anyway. Why not view business as a university where character and leadership are taught, not in military fashion but through an elegant integration of business realism and belletristic sensibility? Only in this way can we train the leaders of the future.

This leads us to a new vision: all organizations will exhibit a thorough understanding of the inevitable connection between results and heart, where heart also includes spirit. They will show the merger of results and heart in their internal behavior (their management systems and production processes). They will demonstrate the marriage of results and heart in their external behavior (their products and services). Organizations know that there is a necessary tie between effective operations and how people think. Installing this results-heart loop (Figure 12.1) will be the key to the new way of doing business, worldwide. In sum, results require heart. Organizational cooperation and efficiency require a new way to think. Power requires wisdom;

Figure 12.1. Results-Heart Loop.

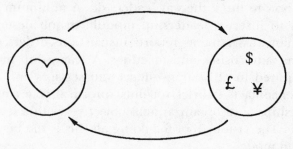

that was Plato's message. Organizational effectiveness requires love, caring, and compassion. The competitive advantage requires human depth and understanding. Productivity requires meaningful work and personal fulfillment. Consistent profitability requires human authenticity—that is, self-disclosure, being true to yourself and to others. High-quality products and services require high-quality people and high-quality human interactions. The same professional attention given to high-quality production and delivery of services must be devoted to the development of high-quality people and high-quality human relations. A surgeon cannot fake it in an operation. An engineer cannot fake it in an aircraft. A manager cannot fake it in developing a human being. People cannot fake it in how they treat each other. And a leader cannot fake leading.

The vision's methodology is to inform all people (in human relations, management systems, processes, and products) with leadership consciousness. That is the challenge to leadership. One must implement an organization's number one business objective by training managers to teach leadership, to themselves and to all stakeholders. One should administer periodic "shots" of leadership challenge to the organization. People must be continually challenged to reassess their leadership performance. People must be challenged to reassess the quality of their leadership minds. Are they thinking as leaders do? Are you? Is the organization? One must insist that perceptions and thoughts, at all times, exhibit greatness in leadership.

Leadership begins with a different way of thinking. Exec-

utives need to be trained to teach their organizations and customers how to think the way leaders do. A minimum requirement is to insert a leadership module in job descriptions,
performance assessments, reports, instructions, orders, communications, advertising, and meetings. A leadership module is
also required in all your products and services and all your
customer contacts. In brief, you must inform all your employees,
relationships, and organizational objectives with a leadership
message. The vision's tool for doing all this is the Leadership
Diamond model.

The Promise

Here is the leadership promise that has been made to you: if you
open your mind to the following leadership challenge, then
measurable success of your performance as a leader, on any
criterion or criteria you choose, should *at least double*.

1.   How committed are you to the premise that organizational
success is directly proportional to how intensively its members
think and act as leaders, are challenged to be leaders, and are
supported in their leadership? How much of that commitment is
shown in your behavior?
2.   A leader is defined as a person who is truly effective in
achieving worthy results, in any field, and no matter what the
obstacles, with unfailing regard for human beings. Do you know
what results you want to achieve? Are they worthy? In these
respects, what do people say about you? Do they define you as a
leader? The fields for results include the five intersecting "Olympic rings" of life: work, family, self, social responsibility, and
financial stability. Since balance may be impossible, you must
strive for integration. Unless you feel powerful in at least three
areas, your leadership potential is limited. The precise challenge
is that to lead is to manage by teaching leadership, by empowering. In leadership, to teach means to challenge, to provoke people
into actualizing their leadership potential. Socrates said that
teaching is not giving ideas to people but helping ideas be born.
3.   You must therefore train people to teach greatness in

leadership. Develop them, empower them to do so. You teach by personal example, by working together, and through the usual educational methods. You help individuals and teams learn how they can release the power of their creativity.

4.   Expect people to behave as great leaders do. Be clear that you behave in this fashion. Expectations motivate. Managers drain energy away from organizations; leaders infuse them with energy. The secret lies in what you expect.

5.   Expect people also to be great in learning leadership. A great teacher expects students to be great learners, even from bad teachers. Leadership, like character, you develop for your own sake. In this respect, expenses for leadership training should be shared equally by employer and employee.

6.   Support individuals and teams in their quest for leadership greatness. The leader with greatness serves others by releasing their power and stimulating their creativity, by sensitively understanding their mistakes. It is in supporting people in their failures that true leadership quality is shown. Do your people say that you care for them?

7.   Make clear to people that the leadership mind thinks differently from the nonleadership mind. Greatness in leadership simply means that you see things differently, that you use a different intelligence from that of the ordinary mind. Even continuous process improvement can be carried out in a breakthrough manner. The leadership mind is full of surprises. Because it is creative, it does the unexpected. Do you think differently?

8.   Challenge people to translate the consciousness of their leadership greatness into task-specific, visible behaviors. *Action, results, accountability,* and *implementation* are sacred, nonnegotiable words for the executive with a leadership mind. Do you get results?

9.   Understand that the principal instrument of policy implementation is teaching leadership. Strategy is translated into effective action only through the heartfelt support of the full organization. Therefore, organizations are to be measured by the initiative their executives take to teach leadership. How do

you rate the initiative of the organization, no matter how large or small, for which you are responsible?

10.   Present yourself to people, and be in contact with them, as you truly are. Do not manipulate. Do not pretend. You have nothing to fear, if you are a leadership mind. This is your formula for leading the effective organization of tomorrow.

11.   In leadership, *greatness* matters. There are four ways to express greatness. The authentic leader is committed to greatness in all of them. A visionary leader always sees the larger perspective, for *vision* means to think big and new. A realistic leader always responds to the facts, for *realism* means to have no illusions. An ethical leader always is sensitive to people, for *ethics* means to be of service. A courageous leader always claims the power to initiate, act, and risk, for *courage* means to act with sustained initiative.

12.   Organizations need employees and executives who know exactly what to do and then do it, with patience and perseverance. They understand that resistances are high and rewards are low. Nevertheless, they act in the best interests of the organization. This truth holds for all levels of management — from mail clerk to CEO, from soldier to general, from student to dean, from humble citizen to president, and from piano mover to conductor. Are you perceived as one of them?

The Leadership Diamond model can help people honor the inner side of greatness. The tools of Leadership Diamond theory, by virtue of their roots in philosophic depth, are designed to make traditional leadership technologies operational, not to replace them.

Take all this to heart — that managing is teaching, teaching is empowering, and what you teach is the Leadership Diamond model. Then monitor your persistence and measure results on your own terms. Successful leaders measure their achievements by the following three criteria: financial and bottom-line factors; morale and culture, the quality of the experience of working with the organization (sometimes called *quality of work life*); and the pride, reputation, respect, credibility, and status of the organization (How often is it quoted? Is it a desirable employer in the community? Are headhunters interested? How important is its contribution to society? To history?). How do you measure greatness in your organization?

You have now covered much ground in search of leadership — theory, practice, and applications. Let us hope that the Leadership Diamond model has become your helper and friend in your quest for personal significance.

Let us also hope that, by your training your mind to think along the lines of greatness, your journey through life makes this world, because of you, a better one.

Remember, it is not that we have so much to do that we cannot find time to think and act as leaders; on the contrary, it is because we do not think and act as leaders that we have so much to do.

Now is the time to cut and polish your very own Leadership Diamond — designed uniquely *by* and *for* you.

Resource

Tips for Achieving and Sustaining Inner Greatness

This Resource contains reinforcement practices. Their purpose is to give you practice in using the Leadership Diamond model and in applying Leadership Diamond technology directly to your most pressing leadership concerns. These activities have been tested and work well in actual business situations.

Affirmations: Toward Genius-Level Leadership Intelligence

Instructions. Your performance in all the Leadership Diamond strategies can be raised by your simply making a personal, firm, irrevocable decision to organize and control your mind — that is, to direct your leadership intelligence toward its genius potential. How can you reinforce that decision? You start with the right ideas, with the proper understanding of what the mind is: how the mind works, what kind of mindset you wish to achieve. Then you are resolute about doing it.

Right now, make a major commitment to a new mindset or a new level of leadership intelligence for yourself. *Imagine, through the device of thought experiments, how it would be to possess separately each dimension as affirmed in the following statements.* Then act on making real, in the spaciousness of your mind, each one of these demanding images — first for short periods of time, and then longer. First review them mentally, but then make changes in your real-world leadership. At all times, you must keep alive the freshness of your interest, for it is true that a motivated student and a devoted and competent mentor can together conquer the world, and we all are both students and teachers all the days of our lives. From now on, everything you do should demonstrate this type of awareness. You are, in effect, taking an oath of leadership, of excellence, of greatness.

Leaders — people with a developed leadership intelligence — are alert and awake. In the affirmations that follow, you will find descriptions of what it means for a leadership intelligence to be awake. In familiarizing yourself with models of genius in all-around leadership, you can promise yourself that you will experience increased personal success as you reach for these goals. Make your choice right now. This is meant to challenge you ultimately to be the kind of mind or leadership intelligence that embodies these affirmations. Follow these instructions as you read the affirmations:

1. Be in a state of alert relaxation.
2. Visualize each affirmation sharply, and with as many senses as possible. Think of examples.
3. Affirm, will, own, and appropriate each affirmation.
4. Practice them frequently and consistently.
5. Meditate on them before you embark on any important task, project, or job.
6. Monitor the quality of your visualization.
7. Monitor the effectiveness of the affirmations for your leadership work.
8. Create your own list of affirmations, tested affirmations that you know work for you.
9. With each affirmation, evaluate your achievements with this checklist: my interest __ my performance __ my potential __ my plan for improvement __.

People occasionally say that it is impossible to live up to these affirmations. Of course it is impossible, but that is not the point. The point is to think them, to fantasize them as real, to shift your mind into genius gear. You may not be able to play blindfolded fifteen games of chess simultaneously — and then win most of them! Few people can. Nevertheless, you can fantasize what it would be like to have the kind of mind that could do it, and affirm that you have or that you are this kind of mind. The effect on what you do next can be miraculous.

The final result of utilizing these affirmations should be that you talk to your unconscious. Your unconscious is actually listening and is consequently making the appropriate in-depth perceptual and character changes. In this way, you become more true to yourself. You become the person you are, for there is nothing artificial or contrived here. You wake up your unconscious to help you become the natural leader you were meant to be.

Vision

- I am an extraordinarily clear mind and lucid consciousness.
- There is pervasive clarity and distinctness in all my thinking.
- I am gifted with a superb memory.
- I have quick recall.
- I have comprehensive recall.
- I am skilled with tricks that stimulate my memory.
- I readily distinguish between what is important to remember and mere trivia that clogs the mind.
- I enjoy practicing the art of sharply focused attention.
- I treasure the skill of recalling virtually anything I need to remember.
- I have the mind of a chess champion.
- Since my early youth, I have been a mathematical wizard.
- Mathematics is so easy for me that I can do it in my sleep.
- Science is so easy for me that I can do it in my sleep.
- I have strong powers of concentration.
- I think precisely what I choose to think.
- I have complete control over admitting and excluding external and internal stimuli.
- I exert total control over my mind, how it works, and what it concentrates on.
- I am accustomed to making very fast logical connections.

- I understand quickly, whether receiving instructions, reading a passage, seizing the heart of a problem, discovering a solution, giving or getting directions, or performing a calculation.
- In complex conversations, I get the point immediately and can respond instantaneously.
- I can see solutions to even the most obdurate problems.
- I learn very quickly.
- I demonstrate speed in mathematics, reading, reasoning, acquiring skills, learning new words, and familiarizing myself with foreign languages.
- I am able to complete complex assignments in a very short time.
- I have an excellent vocabulary.
- My vocabulary expands with my voracious reading.
- I possess extraordinary facility with language.
- I possess extraordinary facility with mathematics, calculations, and proofs.
- I never suffer from information overload.
- I can get a very quick and highly accurate overview of any complex, chaotic, or confusing situation.
- I have unquenchable faith in the continuous sharpening of my mental abilities.
- I have an expanded breadth and depth of interest, information, and knowledge.
- I have an excellent grasp of detail.
- I have an excellent view of perspective.
- I have consummate control over both the intensity and the relaxation of my mind. My control over my mind is like flexing muscles and relaxing them.
- My mind leaps over centuries of history.
- I see clearly with my mind's eye the world of a thousand years ago.
- I see clearly how dramatically the world has changed and how that change accelerates.
- My mind is always ahead of itself. I see today the distant future — the year 3000 A.D.

- I always look ahead, whether driving my car, planning for the day, thinking about life, or making strategic choices.
- My mind is as clear as empty space.
- My mind is as clear as empty time.
- My mind is as vast as the universe it embraces in thought.
- My mind is a pair of powerful binoculars to inner space.
- My consciousness is an infinite field of space-time.
- Inside my mind there is an inner eye I know exists but that I can never see. The existence of that "I" is nevertheless more obvious to me than any other aspect of being.
- My innermost eye is invisible to itself.
- I always think big.

In sum, the key structures of visioning, illustrated by the above affirmations, fall into several partially overlapping categories. Among them are these traits of a fully developed consciousness:

1. Visibility (clarity, distinctness, sharpness)
2. Recall (memory)
3. Control (priorities, concentration, control over the mind, getting to the point)
4. Flexibility (the intensity-relaxation alternation)
5. Discoveries (the equivalence of consciousness and space-time, the invisibility of the ego)

Reality

- There always is freshness in my appreciation of reality.
- It is natural and easy for me to see beauty.
- I readily understand sorrow.
- I have an absolute respect for facts.
- I never lie to myself about the truth.
- I have a keen eye for what is normal and healthy.
- I know exactly how to adapt myself to any situation.
- My common sense is highly developed.

- I possess an uncanny sense for what is real, factual, objectively true, and clear to the dispassionate observer.
- I behave intelligently in the areas of fundamental health, such as nutrition, rest and recreation, education, career, finances, law, and social responsibility.
- I feel exceptionally well informed about public affairs, politics, scientific advances and technology, developments in literature and the other arts, economy and finance, sports, core world problems, and expectations for the future.
- I always have the fortitude to move forward, and do so with confidence, from the most frustrating and confusing situations.
- I have an excellent understanding of how others perceive me.
- I feel fully in touch with everyone I meet.
- I have full access to my unconscious.
- I always get results.
- I can look at all situations with perfect objectivity.
- I love a challenge.
- I love competition.
- There is only one world, and that is the real world.
- I am in touch with the real world, and I am not interested in anything else.
- "When the going gets tough, the tough get going." I live every day by this principle.
- I have no illusions.
- I know that specific unpredictable events will occur and have impacts.
- I know also that life proceeds in cycles and that the nature of the cycles themselves is unpredictable.
- I know that my leadership mind, which is a product of evolution, can cope well with these realities.
- I know that the world is made for the leadership mind.
- I can translate this mindset into continuous action.
- I know that as I act on these principles, the world responds and becomes familiar and congenial.
- I feel a mystical bond between my leadership intelligence and the power of the cosmos.

Ethics

- I feel myself to be a very wise and experienced person.
- People consult me about their deepest problems.
- I am confidently familiar with the most profound regions of the human soul.
- I understand the human mind as well a taxi driver knows the city and an umpire knows the rules of the game.
- I achieve great success in bonding.
- My people relationships are excellent.
- People trust me, without reservations.
- I have some exceptionally close friends.
- I like people, and they like me.
- I know well how to connect with people.
- I am an excellent communicator.
- I am a very genuine person.
- In my life I have a great love, a rich and abiding passion.
- I have supremely fulfilling relationships with my family.
- My professional and business contacts are deeply satisfying.
- I feel very secure.
- I have abiding peace of mind.
- I live confidently on a bedrock of solid core values.
- I clearly and effortlessly distinguish between right and wrong, without dogmatism or fanaticism.
- I am supremely comfortable with my values.
- I am daily realizing my fundamental values in life.
- I live exactly the way I want to live.
- I lead a very rich life.
- I live with a gratifying sense of fulfillment.
- I feel the deepest compassion and empathy for all human beings and for all sentient beings.
- I have unbounded capacity to understand and to forgive.
- I am exceptionally trustworthy and fair.
- Everyone fully trusts me.
- My life is a noble sense of justice made visible.
- I willingly sacrifice myself for others if they are not treated fairly.
- I always speak out for human dignity.

- People always compete to have me on their team.
- I have an excellent record of making teams successful.
- I am a very good person — kind, considerate, generous, understanding, helpful.
- I am a very happy person.
- Life for me is complete.
- I am an extremely fortunate person.
- I treasure wisdom.
- I am rich in wisdom.
- Humility, compassion, devotion, and wisdom are the most desirable of all human traits.
- I am a compassionate person.
- I am always sensitive to people.

Courage

- I possess extraordinary independence of thought.
- I totally live my own life. I live in my own life-style.
- I freely exert my own judgment.
- I have my own considered opinion on most issues.
- I have personally developed my own belief system.
- I am never bizarre. My courage is always rational.
- I am able and willing to make decisions of hair-raising difficulty.
- I always make my decisions at the right time. I know the importance of timing.
- I am very good at making decisions instantaneously or with imperturbable patience, as circumstances warrant.
- I have boundless energy.
- I possess undying enthusiasm.
- I have the strength to manage my anxiety.
- I always make constructive use of my negative feelings, such as guilt and anger.
- I am a person of substantial credibility.
- I am a very dignified person.
- I am a person of inexhaustible self-confidence tempered by the wisdom of experience.
- I am always highly motivated.

- I am indefatigably persistent, and I will always be rewarded for my persistence.
- I possess unflappable singleness of purpose.
- I always live with the ambition to be the best I can be.
- I remain very calm under grave provocation and intense stress.
- I know I will grow continuously as long as I live.
- I have exceptional tolerance for severe physical pain.
- I am not afraid. Nothing can scare me.
- I am very centered and secure.
- I have exceptional tolerance for severe emotional pain—fear, guilt, and anxiety.
- I am an excellent example of how a person tolerates moral pain—ethical conflicts, betrayal, and confrontations with injustice.
- I am fully willing to face death. I am not afraid to die.
- Others count on me in an emergency.
- I willingly face evil. I can be trusted always to stand up to evil.
- I am a very strong person.
- I am always in touch with my inner freedom.
- Only I can change the world I have created.
- There is no danger in change.
- To get what I really want, I must change.
- I have the power to change.
- I am a free person in an unfree world.
- I always act with initiative.

Daily Tips

The following ideas are collected from seminar participants and other sources on how to insert leadership teaching into the life of your daily operations. They illustrate, in a modest manner, how to teach leadership, how to empower:

- Be a student. Take the responsibility to initiate teaching leadership to yourself—through modeling, study, and personal reflection.

- Be an educator. Develop your own leadership teaching materials, and use them.
- Be a teacher. Teach your own brief course or seminar to your people about your leadership ideas and style.
- Be a dean. Know how to teach leadership in four directions: inward to self, down to subordinates, laterally to peers, and up to superiors. Each requires unique leadership skills.
- Be a facilitator. Encourage honest discussion of your leadership style and how it affects others. How are you perceived as a leader? People act on their perceptions of you. Do you understand these perceptions? Do you know their causes? How willing are people to be open with you in discussing your and their leadership styles?
- Be an acknowledger. Acknowledge people's efforts to accomplish greatness in leadership by sending out attractive VIP (Values-In-Practice) cards. People value them; some end up posted on bulletin boards, others are collected in drawers and referred to with pride. If you find someone exhibiting greatness in vision, realism, ethics, courage, or several of the tactics, let that person know by sending the individual a VIP card. You can design your own VIP cards.
- Be a thinker. Develop your own leadership philosophy, and base it on a careful summary and analysis of your own experience.
- Be a scholar. Familiarize yourself with literary and business writings on leadership.
- Be a secretary. Keep a log of what you are learning about leadership and about teaching leadership.
- Be a trainee. Improve daily in leadership competence.
- Be a therapist. Learn how to listen. (People say they listen, but they often do not.)
- Be an inventor. Be open to new ideas. (People say they are open, but they often are not.)
- Be a genius. Always be sure that, whatever you do, you do it as a leader.
- Be an advocate. Begin and end your meetings, telephone calls, letters, reports, and memos with leadership awareness.

Be sensitive and subtle but adamant and sincere. (This is called "framing business and professional activity with leadership philosophy.")

- Be a chief of staff. Devise a plan. What is your own thoughtful, personal definition of leadership? Give examples. What are your principal projects at this time? To whom do you need to teach leadership? How do you plan to teach leadership? Develop detailed scenarios and strategies.
- Be a coach. Apply the Leadership Diamond grid technique to your personal leadership style, to your work life, to your home life, to your inner personal or spiritual development, to your boss's leadership style, to your colleagues' leadership styles, to your subordinates' leadership styles, to your principal project, to any individual task.
- Be conscious. Develop a monitoring system to ensure that you continuously maintain leadership awareness.
- Be an observer. Whenever you discuss a business or technical issue, divide yourself in two: leader and observer of your leadership. As observer, ask yourself, continuously, "Am I acting in a leadership fashion? Do I, at this moment, fulfill the criteria of the Leadership Diamond?"
- Ask others to continually feed back to you information on how well you are doing as a leader.
- Prepare calendars, appointment books, and other accessories that refer to the basics of your leadership philosophy.
- State the essentials of your leadership philosophy on your business cards and stationery.
- A complete program of personal and organizational development in Leadership Diamond terms requires four steps. Understand the theory. Diagnose your own leadership authenticity and that of your organization. Create a master plan for leadership development, both for yourself and for your organization. Keep a daily journal in which you plan and record the appropriate tactics for the day.
- Craft a leadership mind for yourself. Spend several minutes early in the morning to organize your leadership day.

A Multiphasic Effectiveness Program

The focus on productivity results means attention to a single topic: quality, high-quality products and services, high-quality organizations and high-quality people to support them. Quality requires action plans. What do you need to make action plans work? You need a multiphasic effectiveness program for the area where company and individuals overlap.

Ideas. You must have the ideas. Understand them, see them as tools, apply them, practice them, and improve on them. You must read, write, and use images as clarifying and mnemonic devices. You must appreciate the wisdom of the deeper, the philosophic side of life. Ideas can be taken home. They are gifts that can be passed on. Their value increases with use and generosity, and their magic is contagious.

People. Everyone requires a support group. You cannot do it alone. You need people who understand you, care about you, and are willing to help you faithfully through difficult times. Furthermore, you need people for whom you can do the same. You will grow as a person to the degree that you give support to others. Do not be afraid or ashamed. Actively seek out people who will really help you succeed, who want to help you and have your interests at heart. The world is large, and no matter how isolated you feel, there are friends to support you. Even if you do not feel the need for a support group, you probably do need one and have little idea of how helpful other people can be. You need a network. You need inspiration and stimulation. You need bonds and loyalty, friendship and camaraderie. Since, for executives, distances are great and times are short, it is essential that the modern leader understand and use the latest in communications technology and contribute to its continued development.

Commitment. This is the area of will power, self-discipline, and determination. You need to make up your mind and know in your heart that success is mostly a function of personal decision, resoluteness, and acceptance of your existential aloneness. You must be fully prepared to exist as an independent and autonomous person, have your own visions, and always think for yourself. You must continuously maintain the big picture, although you must also always be prepared to revise it according to current feelings and realities. To think for yourself is to always exist in two worlds: the realm of distant and overarching goals, and the earthy soil of the fully engaged here-and-now. There is no substitute for will power, determination, and persistence. Executives with leadership responsibilities are often much weaker in this area than they think they are.

Setting Priorities for Productivity. The successful use of time is a function of enthusiasm, energy, joy, hope, authenticity, health, and love of work. It also is related to self-acceptance, to the faith one has in oneself. Can lack of self-confidence be remedied? Yes. Find ways to do those things with which you have had success.

Mentoring. Mentoring is to identify potential leaders and teach them the leadership mind, on the job. The prerequisite is respect for learning. Mentoring, developing subordinates, is a crucial responsibility of leadership and is also good for the mentor. An old Chassidic saying assures us that in teaching the teacher learns five times as much as the student.

     Remember, you are of service not when you are dependent and servile (for then you are of no use) but when you are independent and autonomous. Then you can focus on the consciousness and needs of others. Do not think of yourself. Think of others. This is what the market (reality) wants, and it will respond.

Multiple Intelligences. You must know your intelligences. The eight intelligences, discussed earlier, correspond to the Leadership Diamond points. Vision is enhanced through the practice of logical and transcendental intelligence. Reality is reinforced through training in somatic and marketing intelligence. Ethics can be developed through team intelligence and the intelligence of wisdom. Courage is an outgrowth of motivational intelligence. Esthetic intelligence, which thrives on metaphor and imagery, generally enhances the spirit of greatness.

Control. Leadership means control over the mind. The authentic leader does not accept the mind as he or she finds it but chooses either to construct or to wake up to the specific leadership mind: an inner space, unified, with room enough for conflict, paradox, and contradiction, committed to greatness in vision, realism, ethics, and courage. Athletic achievements and sports training usually provide us with good examples.

Knowing Your Tools. You have two kinds of tools. Use them. One set is ideas. Science and other forms of conceptual systems help us cope successfully with our environment and with life as a whole. This skill certainly has been a key to what it means to exist as a human being in the world.

   The other set of tools is feelings, emotions. In human-core matters, feelings are tools in leading people—above all, the feelings that you arouse in them as boss or subordinate, authority or supporter. Feelings are what people remember and respond to. In boss-subordinate relationships, feelings and deep-seated agendas may be mobilized. In managing these feelings, both supervisor and subordinate grow as persons and authenticate their relationship. To use these feelings as a management tool may become manipulative and unethical; but to talk about them, reflect on them, and share them can be magnificently growth-producing, for it elevates the boss-subordinate relationship to a higher level of human connection and communication. The process of reflection moves the relationship from consciousness to self-consciousness, from having feelings to reflecting on these feelings. Two people may be angry with each other. That is a normal or ordinary human feeling. But they may step up to a higher contact and jointly reflect on their anger. What does it mean? Where does it come from? What is its value? What is its price? What are the consequences? As they uplift their communication, they reach an energy-releasing rather than an energy-draining level of human interaction. Such a radical shift of awareness produces personal growth; perhaps no real growth occurs without it. But the act of reflection, of stepping up from consciousness to self-consciousness, is usually accompanied by significant anxiety. The presence of anxiety is how it feels to grow. Anxiety is the growth process itself. To learn the ethical use of ideas and feelings is one more step in applying the Leadership Diamond model.

Proposals. The Leadership Diamond leads to the following strategic proposals and structural recommendations:

1. One-third of organizational resources (money, attention, emphasis, energy, time) should be devoted to leadership—not to production, administration, maintenance, or management. How? By, for example, framing meetings with leadership (the way a religious school frames science and mathematics classes with devotionals); training everyone in leadership; managing by walking around and discussing leadership with employees; providing incentives for spending leadership time and effort and, in general, promoting, as the highest priority, the spirit of leadership throughout the organization. Specifically, assign a different person at each meeting to make a brief presentation on the challenge to greatness in leadership. This assignment affords each team member an opportunity for imagination, creativity, research, and wisdom. Assign another to end the meeting with a greatness-in-leadership audit. This person is in charge of evaluating the team's performance in the meeting: How well did we conform to the desiderata of the Leadership Diamond? Citing examples, both positive and negative, will be of great help.

2. Colleges and universities should offer a degree in leadership and require of all their graduates a minor in the field, where leadership training emphasizes its reliance on the humanities.

3. Leadership training in business and the professions must be viewed as remedial work in the humanities. Students today graduate often with technical skills but not with human skills. At the beginning of a business or professional career, deficiency in the humanities may mean little, but as promotions are achieved and responsibilities shift from things to persons, the need for the humanities multiplies. Ten years into a job, the

executive with a background of skills and no humanities will suffer from the lack.

4. Healing is probably no more than 50 percent medicine and surgery. Easily the other 50 percent, often the critical difference, is personal attention, care, dialogue, and intelligent and compassionate understanding of the subjective needs of patients. With love, it is possible to take the anxiety out of medical procedures and thereby accelerate healing. Thus, leadership philosophy is as important in a hospital as it is in a factory.

5. There must be continuous integration of leadership philosophy and depth into the daily work experience.

6. One has a right to expect slow but consistent improvement.

How can philosophic depth in leadership become operational? Consider the following philosophy-in-business model seminar: Starting at the top, work down and help line managers become leadership teachers. (Leadership, whether in your private life or in your organization, cannot be delegated.)

Set up three-and-a-half-day off-site seminars to teach the tools for individual functions. These seminars have several special features. Nights are needed for incubation (decompression and integration). The function's boss (the leader of the intact team) starts the seminar by setting the tone. Best is to use a "requests-commitment-obstacles" framework. The boss, carefully and with emotional honesty (that is, from the heart), states what he or she wants from people, what he or she is committed to give, and what are the obstacles to accomplishments. Specifically, here is advice to the leader addressing his or her people:

- Speak from the heart. Only in this way will you be heard.
- Tell the group members what you need and want from them for your own success.
- Tell them what you plan to do for them, what you will give them for their success. Address individual needs as well as group concerns.
- Discuss the obstacles that stand in the way of achieving your goals. Explain why what you hope for may never happen.
- Give proof that what you say is not just words but will occur.

- Explain your personal leadership philosophy. Avoid clichés.
- Expect the team to monitor how well you adhere to your philosophy.

This exercise can be repeated by all participants. It is useful to videotape it and play it back at the end. It is always an emotional experience to see yourself reflected talking about your own depth, about the things that matter most to you.

Clients join for half a day. A bank may invite some of its major customers. First they hear, from the bankers, the bank's philosophy. Then they tell the bankers what they as customers need from them. An automobile company invites a group of satisfied customers from a competitor. This module generates a lot of energy.

One day is devoted to action planning and, above all, to acting. Take a step, a stand. Make a commitment, irreversibly. These things must be allowed to happen spontaneously. They must never be forced.

The following incident illustrates the "requests-commitment-obstacles" framework:

A highly qualified Saudi Arabian scientist was running the engineering-research division of a large high-technology company in West Germany. Anti-Arab feelings were strong in Germany because of a series of Libyan-inspired terrorist activities. The scientist's group of direct subordinates conducted a team-building seminar. Speaking frankly, the scientist started with this purpose statement: "I am an Arab, in West Germany. Arabs have had bad press. We are a good and proud people. It is unfair to condemn a whole people for the actions of a few. We all regret terrorist actions, profoundly. I need to be successful, for the sake of my people. I need to show that an Arab is a civilized contributor, and especially to a Western country. I am doing my very best to be a good engineer and a good leader. I need to be successful for the sake of *all* people, for if one person is judged unfairly, then society itself is unfair. If democracy is denied to one, then it does not exist for anyone. Our vision is greater than this business. Only you can make me successful. I know that, and you know that, for it is your efforts and your loyalty that make all of us meet our objectives. What do I want from you? I want you to help me be successful, and I want you to know that without your devoted help I can never be successful." Then he cried, for the first time before his people. He did not lose credibility. On the contrary, he earned it. After that, his own boss, a senior vice-president, was overheard to say, "The engineering-research organization has become the star of our company. I wonder why."

Participants choose projects, individual or collective, that are key to their jobs. Every participant chooses one (or participates in a group endeavor). These projects are then carried out, with supervision, in terms of the principles of the Leadership Diamond model.

Periodic review sessions of tools and projects are established. These sessions can be short but must be ongoing. Success measures are developed and agreed to by participants. Here, it is useful to distinguish between micromeasures (such as morale and continuous improvement) and macromeasures (such as profits and stock values). Individual CEO mentoring, executive support, leadership coaching—that is, personalized instruction in philosophy—is necessary and should be provided. Do not conduct an off-site seminar if it feels like taking time off from work. Do it only if that is where some of the organization's real leadership work is being done. The common error is to do too little, too late.

Leadership Strategy Exercise: How to Get Promoted

Instructions. Following is a typical checklist, a kind of worksheet, of how mentoring for middle management, in the context of

Leadership Diamond theory, can be accomplished. Mentoring is the task of the leader. Leadership is to develop people, to empower them. Carefully perform the tasks suggested in the following assignments.

Range

In your life, there are five interlocking "Olympic circles" of concern: work, family, self, social responsibility, and financial stability. In this exercise, you emphasize work, but you are nevertheless conscious of and sensitive to how work spills over to home and self, as well as to the other regions—and how, conversely, the latter affect work.

Goals and Contract

List your goals, dates and all. Indicate that, by a specific date, your performance-appraisal rating will be (for example) "exceeds job requirements" and your potential will be rated confidentially (for example) as "director," "general manager," or "vice-president." Commit yourself to the following contract: "I know that these goals can be realized, and I am determined to make that happen. But unless my heart is in my contract, it will not work."

History

Write a brief record of your performance and evaluation histories, consisting of both positive and negative comments, of actions you have taken and not taken, and of results or consequences they have brought. Correlate these evaluations with other events in your life. (How, for example, are events in your childhood related to your job performance?) Assess the fairness of these evaluations. As is true of a medical anamnesis, history gives us clues about what needs work, to ensure our future health and success. Our work biography gives us clues to trends. Are we slipping? Are character defects showing that have been hidden until now? Are there pockets of success that are new to us?

Feedback

Continuous and accurate (that is, honest and courageous) feedback is critical to career success. Who are the people whose feedback is important to you? What can you do to elicit frequent and reliable feedback from them? Who are the people who really understand the workings of the organization? What are your resistances to asking for feedback? To accepting feedback? What are the resistances of your supervisors to providing you with meaningful feedback? What should you be told that you are not being told? Why not? What can you do about it? What has been the cost to you of not sufficiently emphasizing feedback? If you get accurate and continuous feedback from a responsible supervisor, committed subordinates, and concerned peers for one year, then you give yourself the best possible chance for success. Do you make it easy or even possible for your supervisor to provide you with useful feedback? Are you sensitive to your supervisor's own career needs and personal difficulties? The serious request for meaningful feedback not only provides you with information on how others perceive you but also develops good personal relationships with people critical to your career success. You must create a sense of alliance with them. Write a careful analysis of your feedback requirements, spelled out in detail. Use the preceding questions as a guide.

Reciprocity

Evaluations in the feedback contract should be reciprocal: the boss evaluates the subordinate, and the subordinate evaluates the boss. Perhaps the presence of a third party can help the evaluation be intellectually profound, behaviorally accurate, and emotionally safe. People can also help each other learn what kinds of evaluation make sense. A subordinate can inform the boss about how he or she responds to evaluations, how evaluations can be carried out more effectively, and vice versa. All these forms of human relationship are delicate. Many people just do not have the skills to ensure that they will produce growth rather than resentment, but all human contacts, in business and the professions as well, are opportunities for personal development. To be an effective leader is to stimulate growth in all management contacts. An appropriate action step here is to suggest to your superior how the performance-assessment process could be improved (that is, made more productive).

Results and Effectiveness

Are you effective? Do you achieve results? Can you operate independently and alone? What, in your case, are results? You may follow superiors' orders, suggestions, and guidelines but still not achieve results, and it is by results that you are measured. Results are up to you. They go beyond what your supervisor advises. You will be measured not by how well you follow instructions but by the results you bring. What do you need to do in order to be effective? Whose help do you need? Who is your customer? What is your schedule for results? To what degree do your supervisors and colleagues support your effectiveness, and to what extent do they interfere with it? What are your strategies for dealing with sensitive boss-employee relationships? How aware are you? How realistic are you? How perceptive? How smart? In your career, feedback and results are everything. Write an assessment of your effectiveness and strategies for improving it.

Study

Create an outline of a leadership-study program. (This program may include university classes; individual coaching; reading; developing a bibliography of critical readings; seminars; discussions with leaders you admire; subscriptions to newspapers, magazines, and other publications that you should consult regularly; friends and support groups; and so forth.) Then develop a detailed schedule of readings and assignments.

Diagnosis

Analyze the value of your own personal leadership style. Out of this analysis should come a useful diagnosis of your leadership style and an effective strategy for seeing exactly where your leverage is for progress and improvement.

Repeatedly diagnose your own style, and have your colleagues also diagnose your style. You can then learn by comparing notes, which will also enhance your relationship with your colleagues.

Obstacles

Write a thoughtful statement of the obstacles you find to be in the way of your achieving the goals set out in your personal leadership strategy. Never underestimate the importance of ferreting out unconscious resistances and suppressed assumptions by checking for obstacles. Examples are lack of training, lack of experience, transfers, resignations, poor coaching, blindness and ignorance on your part and on the part of supervisors, poor examples, a difficult corporate culture, reorganization, irrational behaviors, human insensitivities, turf conflicts, stresses at home, and so forth.

Future Scenarios

As a leader, you need to understand the possible future scenarios of your business and your organization, and you must have contingency plans for them. Describe in writing some of your alternative futures, with corresponding action plans.

Spillovers

How does your work situation affect your private life and your sense of self? Conversely, how do the latter two affect your work? Write down your thoughts.

Measures

How do you know that you are successful? Are you being recognized for good work? What can you do to get the credit you feel you deserve? Are you making progess fast enough? Do you lie to yourself? Identify the milestones by which you can monitor your progress, and write them down.

Teaching Leadership

Should you plan a seminar or an off-site session with your people? What should it look like? What is its design? What could you achieve? Are there other ways to reach the same goals? Are some objectives achieved by an off-site seminar that cannot be accomplished in any other way? Do you need a facilitator? Are there new ways in which you should conduct your meetings? Should you change your mode of participation in meetings? Consider making a leadership module a standard part of meetings, job descriptions, advertising, communications, memos, and so on. Write down your plans for extending leadership greatness to your work group, department, organization, and so on.

Project

What are your business priorities? List your principal job objectives, in the order of their importance. Select one of them to work on, using the Leadership Diamond grid technology as a guide to creating a diagnosis of your principal project. Note down your strategy for executing it with greatness. Be sure you deal with root causes, that you devote yourself to what will yield the results required for genuine leadership success in your present work. Here, it is easy to deceive yourself.

Reality Check

Remember that there are emotional and unconscious forces undermining many rational solutions. When you request feedback, always add these questions: "Are we discussing the right issues? Are we completely missing some key points? Are the real issues elsewhere?" People are emotionally dishonest with themselves and with others. Envy, fear, saving face, pride, and residues of childhood behavior patterns have no rightful place in one's current business and professional realities.

Seeing Yourself Objectively

See yourself as others see you. See yourself through the eyes of your boss. Imagine that you are being interviewed for a job. The interviewer is your present boss, and the job for which you apply is your present job. Pretend that a stranger, on whom you are depending for employment, asks you the kinds of trick questions that induce job applicants to reveal more of themselves than they want to: "Tell me about yourself." "What don't you do well?" "Describe your previous boss." "What would be an ideal job for you?" Reflect on your answers. What would you think of them if you were the prospective employer? Can you see yourself objectively? In answering these questions yourself, can you put yourself in the shoes of your interviewer? That person is not interested in you (as your mother might be) but in finding a suitable employee.

Miscellany

List any important items for your leadership strategy not previously covered.

Character Strength

One basic point not covered so far is the strength of personality required to make certain that your contract is not mere words but also is translated into real and meaningful action. People often do not know why their plans do not materialize. There exist character defects, as well as lack of self-knowledge and outright self-deception, that people absolutely refuse to see. The soul needs to protect itself against the truth, for it chooses not to tolerate the anxiety mobilized by the ensuing conflicts.

Making your contract work requires clarifying your own values. Who are you? What do you live for? What is important to you? Are there things more important to you than life itself?

Under what conditions would you resign? Too many business-growth programs begin with the statement "Give me your goals, and we will show you how to get there." These goals can be goals for life, regarding values, or they can be business, professional, and financial goals. But for many deep people and deep organizations, the problem is not how to reach goals but how to find the goals in the first place. We may have the technology to reach goals, but we lack the wisdom to know what they are. The modern surge in technology has taken us not one inch closer to answering the most ancient question of all, that of the meaning of life.

It is also necessary to manage the self in an impersonal organization. Organizations often try hard not to be impersonal, but the system often makes that impossible. One aspect of the systemic need of an organization is to be prepared to sacrifice the individual — even though, presumably, the organization exists for the welfare of individuals. But the decision test always is plural, not singular; it is *individuals*, not *the individual*. That is not because organizations are malicious; it is an inherent contradiction in the very concept of an organization, and individuals must learn how to protect themselves. Subjectively, that dilemma appears as a series of painful issues: how to live ethically in an unethical world, how to find justice in an unjust world, how to find freedom in an unfree world, how to find love in an unloving world, how to find understanding and compassion in an indifferent and cruel world.

This conflict leads to the last character requirement needed to breathe life into the contract. It is to realize that what happens in your world is the result of your own actions, of your access to your own free will, your center, your inward power. In other words, if you are not *acting with sustained initiative*, then your contract is null and void. An organization may have its own life. An organization may be impersonal. An organization may be a collection of isolated individuals. But it is also a collection of dialogues, of reactions and interactions, of responses, of requests and commitments. And there are dialogues with other dialogues, dialogues within dialogues. Think of all the hearts that are now beating, and of how they interplay with their environments. In many of these dialogues within other dialogues, you play a role, perhaps the central role. And you become part of the dialogue of the whole.

Organizing Your Leadership Day

Instructions. This is an exercise to be done daily. It takes about fifty-five minutes. Its purpose is to ensure that your life will follow the requirements of the Leadership Diamond and will therefore increase your chances to double your leadership effectiveness. If you think you cannot afford the time, you can adjust this exercise to do it once a week (preferably on Sunday evening, if you work on a regular five-day-week schedule).

Secure the Leadership Mindset (5 minutes)

An airline crew uses a preflight checklist. Among the many items on it is the requirement for the aircraft's wing flaps and slats to be in the proper position for takeoff. Just as there is danger in not readying an aircraft before takeoff, so there is a problem with not having a properly tuned mind before embarking on a day of leadership responsibilities. You need to organize your leadership mind in the morning. Make certain that you have completed your inner checklist, which is the Leadership Diamond model. When all systems are confirmed, then take off.

Start your day in total solitude. Ensure yourself a moment of integrity, a zone of absolute and total health. Give yourself a greatness moment. Guarantee yourself time with just you, time about you and for you. Start the day reclaiming your life, so that you will be yourself, and not someone else, so that your day consists of the leadership mind that you in fact choose to create. Feel the center.

Choose to be a leader in all aspects of your own life. Go over the Toolbox (see Chapter Two) and make the effort to organize your mind in accordance with its principles. Create a clear image of what it means to do everything in keeping with the strategies, formula statements, and tactics of the model. Keep all of them in mind at the same time. Be certain that all the elements of your leadership mind are in place, and do not lose sight of them during the rest of the day.

Know your diagnosis. Have a plan to respond to it during your leadership day. For example, if your weakness is attention to detail, and if you understand the costs and have an insight into the resistances (what you do not wish to face), then, if that is what you choose to do, you can consciously correct this deficit during the day and watch the results pour in.

Monitor your achievements and, at a future time, record them in a journal. Remember, your goal is growth in leadership intelligence. Set yourself clear objectives, and seek small victories. What, in a larger sense, do you expect to be different as a consequence of turning on and locking in leadership intelligence? Develop a long-range system to keep track of results.

Get Information (5 minutes)

Know today's world, the world you are about to enter. Learn to glance over key publications. Train yourself to read quickly and scan instantaneously. In this fashion, cover at least one trade journal, one company report or publication, one local newspaper, and two international newspapers, one for general news (such as the *International Herald-Tribune*) and one for economic news (such as London's *Financial Times* or the *Wall Street Journal*). If you have the staff, ask for a professional briefing each morning. But it is not enough to read. You must also reflect on the importance and relevance of what you read. You must distinguish between hard and soft news, core facts and irrelevancies.

Set Priorities (5 minutes)

Have your priorities in order, so that whatever you do during your day, you experience it in the context of your fundamental values and priorities. You need three levels of priorities.

Level one is the meaning of life, for you. It is your answer to the question "What is your philosophy of life?" Whatever you can write down to at least show awareness that life needs a meaning, a goal, a legacy, will help you in your day. Goals may be as diverse as to find God, to live every day fully, to be a great father or mother to your children, to make a fortune, and to discover a cure for cancer.

On level two you find your distant or mediate goals. These also may be diverse, since they probably cover at least three areas of your field of existence: work, home, and self. These could be to build a vacation home, to provide for a college education, to become vice-president, to take a trip, to complete a complex business project on time, to be a candidate in the school-board election.

Level three comprises your daily or weekly tasks, your immediate obligations. This list must be complete. Make it as long as necessary, but you must revise it continuously during the day. The order is critical. Plan to do only the top three or four items. Whatever does not make it to the top does not get done. Keeping these three lists of priorities before you will organize your values and contribute to making you an effective leader.

Rehearse Your Day (5 minutes)

Be well organized the night before. Look at your schedule. Think ahead. Anticipate problems. Plan solutions. Get the big picture. Know what needs to be accomplished by the end of the day. Be prepared for obstacles and frustrations. Be ready for surprises, so that you may not have any. Produce your own mental psychodramas with the people and events you may meet, especially those that may cause you frustration and lead to anxiety and depression. Be flexible, adaptable, responsive, and alert.

Review Your Levels of Resistance, Self-Deception, Obstacles (5 minutes)

Watch for self-deception. Self-disclosure, self-revelation, self-knowledge, clarity about oneself—these are the results of overcoming self-deception. You can waste your life pursuing false gods. Don't do it.

Try to hear your inner voice. Consult it for what you believe are the things that matter most. This is the most difficult task each morning. Do not be afraid of conflict and pain, but do expect joy and exhilaration. Expect a new health. Do not revert to type. Be ready to enter into fresh dialogues with the range of people with whom you work.

The levels of resistance against the leadership success that you genuinely need and also deserve, the levels of self-deception with which most people live, fall into the following categories of increasing depth:

- Psychodynamic, individual—the biases you bring with you from childhood, assumptions that you do not know you are making. Try to understand them. Be open to them. Compare yourself with others. Touch on your possibilities.
- Systemic, cultural—the mass hypnosis resulting from the strength of the various cultures in which you exist. Again, these assumptions operate without your knowing. Herein lies their insidious power.
- Ethnic—your heritage, which, in addition to stemming from the cities of Athens and Jerusalem, for most Westerners, derives from your family's unique background and tradition. Here again, you may tend to simply swallow assumptions about what is right and wrong, good and bad, valuable and worthless, without awareness or examination. Do not be victimized. Instead, be in charge.
- Philosophical—the universal human condition: facing death, needing love, requiring justice, sensing guilt, being anxious, craving joy, aspiring to immortality or deathlessness, leaving a legacy, expecting warm and supportive human relationships, belonging, defining home and identity, and being a winner against the competition.

Resistances are at the same time the source of your insights, the seat of profound and satisfying values. In the existential crisis, anxiety leads to character, and the exploration of doubt can lead to certainty. In resistance, self-deception leads to answers. The obstacles may be sources of deceit, but they also can guide you to answer the eternal questions.

Review Your Promises (5 minutes)

During the day, you should keep a record of promises and commitments you have made and of outstanding requests and promises that others have made to you. You must note to whom you made the promises and when, of whom you made the requests and when, and the promises that you expect others to fulfill. Business and professional relations are mostly matters of making and requesting promises, keeping them, and expecting the same of others.

Promises are not merely explicit. People base their expectations on what you say and on what they *think* you say. Violations of expectations feel like betrayals, even such relatively insignificant matters as telephone disconnections, incorrect billings, erroneous shipping, conflicting information, delayed or canceled flights, lost luggage, lost mail, and so forth.

Keep your promises. Expect others to keep theirs. Renegotiate any changes. It is through keeping promises and expecting the same from others—in business, the professions, politics, or personal relationships—that you achieve credible leadership performance.

During these five minutes, you must review your list of promises and ensure that they are kept or at least acknowledged and perhaps renegotiated. You are not expected to be tied down, only to be consistent. If you need to change a promise or a request, then discuss it with the party concerned.

Assess Progress on Your Project (5 minutes)

Are you managing your principal project in a leadership way? Are you doing it with greatness?

You need a strategy for your projects and tasks, especially your most significant, critical project. This project may cover all aspects of your life, from changing careers to improving your marriage or your work, to setting up more effective and cost-conscious systems for quality control. Remember that you are the program manager for your project, whatever it is.

How are you doing on the project? Are you satisfied with your progress? Are you on course? Are you keeping or losing interest? Are you getting complacent and bored, or is the original surge of energy still there? Are you getting results? Are you, daily, keeping before your eyes your commitment to achieve greatness in this project? Are you revising and updating your strategies? What do you need to change to enhance your leadership effectiveness in your principal project and be assured of results?

Make Suggestions (5 minutes)

Make three specific and vigorous suggestions to yourself and three to your organization, in Leadership Diamond style, on what steps you can take to improve your leadership effectiveness. During the day, keep a record, evaluate the ideas, monitor your actions, and measure results. This simple rule will preserve your alertness, the key ingredient of the leadership mind.

Watch for Results (5 minutes)

Measure your progress. Keep a daily log. Reinforce your resolve. Reward yourself for progress. Feel the exhilaration of new hope.

References

"America's Toughest Bosses." *Fortune*, Feb. 27, 1989, pp. 40–50.

Block, P. *The Empowered Manager: Positive Political Skills at Work.* San Francisco: Jossey-Bass, 1987.

Buber, M. *I and Thou.* (W. Kaufman and S. G. Smith, trans.) New York: Scribner's, 1970.

Campbell, J. *Myths to Live By.* New York: Bantam, 1984.

Carlson, M. "Dukakis' Type of Place." *Time*, May 23, 1988, p. 19.

Castro, J. "Where Did the Gung-Ho Go?" *Time*, Sept. 11, 1989, pp. 52–56.

Cousins, N. *Anatomy of an Illness as Perceived by the Patient: Reflections on Healing and Regeneration.* New York: Norton, 1979.

"Daddies, Too, Have Needs That Companies Fail to Answer, Researchers Say." *Wall Street Journal*, Apr. 4, 1989, p. 1.

Eliot, T. S. *The Four Quartets.* San Diego: Harcourt Brace Jovanovich, 1968.

"Everyday Heroes." *Newsweek*, July 10, 1989, pp. 46–60.

Fanon, F. *The Wretched of the Earth.* (C. Farrington, trans.) New York: Grove Press, 1965.

Gibbs, N. "How America Has Run Out of Time." *Time*, Apr. 24, 1989, pp. 58–67.

Gibran, K. *The Prophet.* New York: Knopf, 1988. (Originally published 1923.)

Gruber, G. G. *Gruber's Complete Preparation for the SAT.* (4th ed.) New York: Barnes & Noble, 1990.

Jowett, B., and Allen, R. K. (eds., trans.). *The Dialogues of Plato.* New York: Bantam, 1986.

Kant, I. *Critique of Pure Reason*. (N. K. Smith, trans.) New York: St. Martin's, 1969. (Originally published 1781.)

Kanter, D. L., and Mirvis, P. H. *The Cynical Americans: Living and Working in an Age of Discontent and Disillusion*. San Francisco: Jossey-Bass, 1989.

Koestenbaum, P. *The Heart of Business: Ethics, Power, and Philosophy*. Dallas: Saybrook, 1987.

Lakoff, G. *Women, Fire, and Dangerous Things: What Categories Reveal About the Mind*. Chicago: University of Chicago Press, 1987.

McNeil, B. "Beyond Sports: Imaging in Daily Life. An Interview with Marilyn King." *Continuum Center Newsletter*, Fall/Winter 1987.

Malcolm, A. H. "Aged Inmates Pose Problem for Prisons." *New York Times*, Dec. 24, 1988, pp. 1, 6.

Meyer, J. R., and Gustafson, J. M. (eds.). *The U.S. Business Corporation: An Institution in Transition*. New York: Ballinger, 1988.

MIT Staff. *The Machine That Changed the World*. New York: Rawson Associates, 1990.

Nanus, B. *The Leader's Edge: The Seven Keys to Leadership in a Turbulent World*. Chicago: Contemporary Books, 1989.

"Nuclear War Plan by I.R.S." *New York Times*, Mar. 28, 1989, p. D16.

Otten, A. L. "People Patterns." *Wall Street Journal*, May 22, 1989, p. B1.

Piper, D. *The Illustrated Library of Art*. New York: Portland House, 1986.

Plato. *The Republic*. (F. M. Cornford, trans.) Cambridge: Cambridge University Press, 1945.

Plato. *Timaeus*. (H.D.P. Lee, trans.) New York: Penguin, 1965.

"Random Boeing Flaws Raise Safety Questions on Workhorse Planes." *Wall Street Journal*, Apr. 11, 1989, pp. 1, 5.

Samuelson, R. J. "Beyond the Budget Fuss." *Newsweek*, Nov. 28, 1988, p. 33.

Schumpeter, J. *The Theory of Economic Development: An Inquiry into Profits, Capital, Credit, Interest, and the Business Cycle*. Cambridge, Mass.: Harvard University Press, 1934.

Servan-Schreiber, J. L. *The Art of Time*. Reading, Mass.: Addison-Wesley, 1988.

Shakespeare, W. *Hamlet, Prince of Denmark.* In W. G. Clark and W. A. Wright (eds.), *The Complete Works of William Shakespeare.* Chicago: Belford, Clarke, 1886.

Shakespeare, W. *The Tempest.* In W. G. Clark and W. A. Wright (eds.), *The Complete Works of William Shakespeare.* Chicago: Belford, Clarke, 1886.

Shakespeare, W. *Twelfth Night, or What You Will.* In W. G. Clark and W. A. Wright (eds.), *The Complete Works of William Shakespeare.* Chicago: Belford, Clarke, 1886.

Shaw, G. B. *Man and Superman.* New York: Penguin, 1950.

Sperry, R. W. *Continuum Center Newsletter,* Fall/Winter 1987.

Stein, H. "Who's Number One? Who Cares?" *Wall Street Journal,* Mar. 1, 1990, p. A16.

Sternberg, R. J. *The Triarchic Mind: A New Theory of Human Intelligence.* New York: Viking, 1988.

Sveiby, K. E., and Lloyd, T. *Managing Knowhow: Add Value . . . by Valuing Creativity.* London: Bloomsbury, 1988.

"Technology and Tragedy: High-Tech Horror—How a $600-Million System Figured in a Ghastly Accident." *Time,* July 18, 1988, p. 4.

Tinbergen, J. *Schumpeter: Social Scientist.* Cambridge, Mass.: Harvard University Press, 1951.

"Top Quality Is Behind Comeback." *USA Today,* Mar. 28, 1989, pp. 1B–2B.

Wallace and others. *A United Methodology for Developing Systems.* New York: McGraw-Hill, 1987.

Webber, A. M. "Staying at the Top: the Life of a CEO." *Harvard Business Review,* 1987, *65,* 114–118.

"Where the Schools Aren't Doing the Homework." *Business Week,* Nov. 28, 1988, pp. 76–92.

"Why Do Japanese Bosses Share Blame While Americans Hang Tough?" *Wall Street Journal,* Apr. 4, 1989, p. 1.

Yalom, I. D. *Existential Psychotherapy.* New York: Basic Books, 1980.

Index